PRAISE FOR *MY YEAR OF LIVING SPIRITUALLY*

"Anne Bokma's book serves first as a moving personal story, that essential mechanism by which we all seek and find meaning in this thing we call life. It is a reassuring balm for those of us who have been scarred by the obstinate structures and people in our lives, and reminds us that we can be stronger because of the struggle. Anne also shows us that we are not alone, and that how we connect with what's important in our own lives cannot be separated from what we cherish in the lives of others. Above all, this book is an honest attempt to identify what it means to be a part of something bigger than ourselves; a brave work that points to life's inherent value, and our calling to connect with ourselves, each other, and the world around us."

— Brent van Staalduinen, author of *Boy* and *Saints, Unexpected*

"What begins as a light-hearted quest becomes a tenderly beautiful and insightful search for connection in a fractured world. Anne is fun-loving, adventurous and sensitive—just the sort of person you want to follow around as she seeks answers to the questions many of us have. What does it mean to live a spiritual life in a secular world? When what we know and care for is pulled from us, who does that make us and how do we make ourselves? And, most importantly of all, how do we live a meaningful life?"

— Alison Wearing, author of *Honeymoon in Purdah*
and *Confessions of a Fairy's Daughter*

"Anne Bokma's tour through the garden of spiritual delights is earthy and entertaining, grounded and informative....It's all about the journey, and it's all good."

— John Terpstra, poet and author of *Skin Boat:
Acts of Faith and Other Navigations*

"In one experimental, life-changing year, Anne Bokma sets out on a series of spiritual adventures that range from taking magic mushrooms and hanging out with witches to hosting a death dinner. In the process she discovers new truths about herself, her childhood, and her complicated relationship with her mother. Her writing is fearless and honest, never settling for easy answers. Bokma gives us a model for how to seek a more authentic and grounded spiritual life with curiosity, openness, and passion. Read *My Year of Living Spiritually* for inspiration and tips on how you can take a walk on the wild side in your own spiritual life."
—Lori Erickson, author of *Near the Exit: Travels with the Not-So-Grim Reaper*

"*My Year of Living Spiritually* explores a cornucopia of all things spiritual and new age. But what elevates this tale from the trivial, is the memoir Bokma so deftly weaves throughout—the story of her painful break from the rigid religion of her childhood, and subsequent search to find a spirituality of her own. Along the way Bokma wins our hearts. This memoir is more wonderful than woo woo, and you won't want to put it down. A moving and inspiring read!"
—Kelly Watt, author of *Camino Meditations*

"If you liked *Eat, Pray, Love*, you will go wild for *My Year of Living Spiritually*. Bokma's adventures, from the carnal to the sacred, from the divine to the outrageous, will take you to the centre of yourself and the outreaches of your imagination, leaving you enriched, enlightened and invigorated!"
—Tracey Erin Smith, founder of SOULO Theatre

"Reading this book is a spiritual journey in itself...full of knowing laughs, tears, 'aha' moments, and a non-dogmatic invitation to a life more truly and deeply lived."
—Kimberly Carroll, coach for Changemakers

MY YEAR OF LIVING SPIRITUALLY

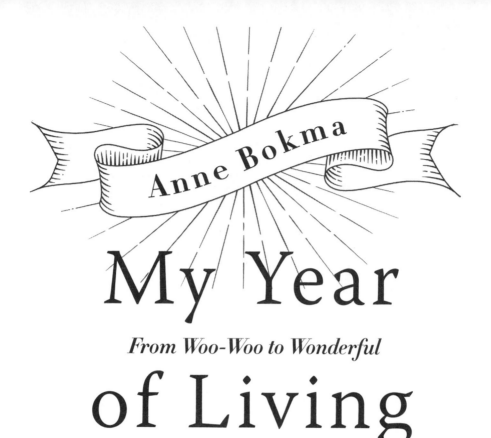

Anne Bokma

My Year

From Woo-Woo to Wonderful

# of Living

One Woman's Secular Quest for a More Soulful Life

Spiritually

Douglas & McIntyre

Douglas and McIntyre (2013) Ltd.
P.O. Box 219, Madeira Park, BC, V0N 2H0
www.douglas-mcintyre.com

All photos courtesy of the author
Edited by Barbara Pulling
Cover design by Anna Comfort O'Keeffe and Carleton Wilson
Text design by Brianna Cerkiewicz
Printed and bound in Canada

Douglas and McIntyre (2013) Ltd. acknowledges the support of the Canada Council for the Arts, which last year invested $153 million to bring the arts to Canadians throughout the country.

Nous remercions le Conseil des arts du Canada de son soutien. L'an dernier, le Conseil a investi 153 millions de dollars pour mettre de l'art dans la vie des Canadiennes et des Canadiens de tout le pays.

We also gratefully acknowledge financial support from the Government of Canada and from the Province of British Columbia through the BC Arts Council and the Book Publishing Tax Credit.

Library and Archives Canada Cataloguing in Publication

Title: My year of living spiritually : from woo-woo to wonderful--one woman's secular quest for a more soulful life / Anne Bokma.
Names: Bokma, Anne, 1962- author.
Description: Includes bibliographical references.
Identifiers: Canadiana (print) 20190157887 | Canadiana (ebook) 20190157925 | ISBN 9781771622332 (softcover) | ISBN 9781771622349 (HTML)
Subjects: LCSH: Bokma, Anne, 1962- | LCSH: Bokma, Anne, 1962-—Religion. | LCSH: Spiritual biography—Canada. | LCSH: Spirituality. | LCSH: Self-realization.
Classification: LCC BL73 .B65 2019 | DDC 204.092—dc23

To my daughters, Ruby and Lucy—precious gems

And my women friends—pure gold

"And the world cannot be discovered by a journey of miles, no matter how long, but only by a spiritual journey, a journey of one inch, very arduous and humbling and joyful, by which we arrive at the ground at our own feet, and learn to be at home."
—*Wendell Berry*

Contents

Note to readers: For narrative reasons, the timeline of some events has been slightly rearranged or compressed.

Introduction

WHEN I WAS NINE YEARS OLD, CHML RADIO IN HAMILTON, ONTARIO, aired a show asking kids to call in with their ideas about what heaven looked like. My mother encouraged me to dial the station and proudly stood by as I spoke to the host about the celestial kingdom I was certain awaited me. I was raised to believe I was one of God's chosen people. Religion was the core of my life—church twice on Sunday, private Christian schools, weekly catechism classes, prayer before meals and Bible readings after. Simply being baptized as an infant in the *one true church*, specifically the Dutch Calvinist Canadian Reformed Church, which numbers about ten thousand people in a few dozen mostly rural communities across the country, meant I'd won the religious sweepstakes. At the end of my life I'd reap my reward: eternal life in heaven.

I had a very specific, albeit limited, idea of heaven. I told the host that it had streets of gold, of course. And angels, trumpets, harps and halos. There was lots of praise music and hymn singing. And God lived there, along with a very select group of people that would eventually include me and everyone who went to my church. I couldn't think of much else to say. It might be the end goal, but this longed-for promised land didn't have a very detailed property listing.

The personality of God was more complex. He loved you if you were good and believed in him. But he might fling you to Satan and the pit of fire if you lied to your mother or touched yourself *down there*. He was all-powerful but still let bad things happen, like earthquakes and acne. He listened if you prayed to him, but might not give you what you really wanted, which in my case was for Danny Linde in Grade 4 to like me. God was invisible, but ever present. Loving, but angry. A bipolar deity. Still, I believed in that invisible man with my whole heart.

Until one day I just didn't anymore.

From the time I was little I had been instructed by the authority figures in my life to "have faith like a child." It was the simple answer to any religious question. If God could stop it, why did he let children die of starvation and cancer? "Have faith like a child." Did Moses really part the Red Sea, and did Noah really get all those animals onto the ark? "Have faith like a child." Wasn't it mean of God to send billions of people to hell save for the few thousand people who belonged to our obscure denomination? "Have faith like a child." Infantile acceptance trumped intellectual rigour. True believers did not ask questions.

Even though I was one of God's chosen, I hadn't done anything to earn this birthright. It was generously granted thanks to Unconditional Election, the theological principle of the sixteenth-century theologian John Calvin, who said certain people—the "elect"—were randomly predestined by God to receive salvation while others were left to continue in their sins and wind up in hell. Calvin also promoted the principle of Total Depravity—the idea that, because of original sin, all human beings are fallen people, intrinsically unworthy and inclined to evil. Basically, wretches.

My doubt in these sorts of ideas as a young woman created a problem. Loss of faith meant risking the connection to everything I held dear—a mother I was very close to, three younger siblings, my extended family, my childhood friends and my Dutch culture. Church life was the centre of our existence. I'd lose everything if I left the church, but even at that age I knew I'd lose myself if I stayed. My mother and stepfather perceived their reality through the lens of religion—that was their way of making sense of the world. But it no longer made sense to me. I left the Canadian Reformed Church when I was twenty, and things would never again be the same with my family. They could not forgive me.

The word *religion* comes from the Latin word *ligare*, meaning "to bind." In my case, religion had the opposite effect. Leaving the church was the right thing to do, but hurting my family was hard.

Dr. Marlene Winell, a trailblazing San Francisco psychologist, has coined the term "religious trauma syndrome" to describe the impact of breaking away from repressive religions. Winell isn't anti-religion so much as anti-dogma. The religious communities that cause trauma, she says, are those that prevent people from thinking for themselves. Mind control and emotional abuse may be most closely associated with cults, she writes in her book *Leaving the Fold*, but "fear-based apocalyptic thinking" is a tactic that's also employed by strict religions where conformity is demanded. Devout and often well-intentioned parents in these communities feel justified in their use of power tactics to brainwash their children into belief. Leaving such a religion can be devastating, says Winell. "It's like the rug gets pulled out from under you in every way, because religion defines everything—it defines who you are, your relationships, your purpose in life, your view of the world, your view of the future, your view of the afterlife. The whole house comes down."

I certainly felt my own foundation crumble when I left the church, especially in regards to my mother, whom I had idolized as a child. Our closeness was forged in part because my biological father left our family when I was three and she raised me and my younger brother as a single mother until she remarried six years later. During that time we lived on welfare and any extra cash my mother earned picking fruit in the summer and cleaning houses. I never noticed any lack. She was a loving mother, and I always wanted to please her. But when I left the church I became the biggest disappointment and shame of her life. It got easier to avoid her than to endure the look of gloom on her face when we were together. She considered me hopelessly lost. We would not share eternal life in heaven. Looking back, I believe that her concern for me, however misguided, stemmed from love. But control played a role, too. I had stopped having faith like a child. I had stepped out of line. There were times I so longed to be back in her favour, I was tempted to return to the church. But once you see the light, you can't go back to living in the dark.

Over the years, guilt about disappointing my family lingered. Our infrequent visits felt forced. I tried to steer clear of controversy, but I'd become a liberal pro-choice feminist who believed in evolution, gay marriage, climate change, the right to die and the New Democratic Party, all things my parents viewed as abominations. Keeping quiet was the trade-off if I wanted to attend Christmas dinner, if I wanted any sense of familial belonging. It was inevitable that our relationship would suffer.

AS HARD AS IT IS TO LEAVE REPRESSIVE FUNDAMENTALIST RELIGIONS, many people do get out, fleeing denominations that wield their authority in destructive ways. But it's mainline churches that are seeing the biggest drop in membership. Some people leave because church doctrine isn't relevant to their lives. Others question the very idea of organized religion in a contemporary world. Some would simply rather sleep in on the Sabbath, then go to a yoga class or take the kids to soccer practice. The majority of millennials, for their part, refuse to even set foot in a house of worship. Almost three million Americans join the ranks of the religiously unaffiliated every year, and four thousand churches close annually, according to the US Census Bureau. In Canada, almost ten thousand older churches—a third of all faith-owned buildings—are expected to close in the next decade, according to the National Trust. All this means traditional religion in the West is gasping for breath as elderly faithful churchgoers die off.

But while millions abandon religion, many still want a spiritual life. There are so many of us, we have acquired our own designation—"spiritual but not religious," or SBNR for short. Almost eighty million North Americans (39 percent of Canadians, according to Angus Reid, and 27 percent of Americans, according to Pew Research) identify as SBNR, making us the fastest-growing "faith" group in the Western world. The SBNR are sometimes referred to as "nones" (because they typically check the box for "none" on surveys about religious affiliation) and "dones" (because they're done with religion). In 2019, these "nones" became statistically tied with those who identify as Catholic and evangelical in the US. "Spirituality will be the religion of the new millennium," says Siobhan Chandler, one of Canada's leading scholars on this growing demographic.

The SBNR may shun formal religious worship, yet the majority believe in God and feel a deep connection with nature and the earth. Most say they still pray, at least occasionally. They value autonomy over groupthink and don't follow a prescribed set of beliefs, other than maybe the Golden Rule. Some critics have accused the SBNR of taking a cafeteria-style approach to belief, picking and choosing from various spiritual practices rather than digging deeply into a single religion. "Burger King spirituality" is one derisive term applied to this supposed "have it your way" approach to tending to spiritual life. But I wonder—what's wrong with sampling a wide variety of practices from the spiritual smorgasbord if it leads to a richer life?

For the past four years I've reported on the SBNR demographic as the Spiritual but Secular columnist for the *United Church Observer* (now renamed *Broadview*), the national magazine of Canada's largest liberal Protestant denomination. Increasingly, my research on SBNR practices made me want to experience them first-hand, especially as I felt my spiritual self was flagging. After some deliberation and a bit of financial planning, I decided I'd immerse myself for a full year in spiritual living. I'd engage in a holy host of practices—New Age, pagan, mystical, transcendental, supernatural, soulful and just plain woo-woo. I would devote myself to being more devotional.

I was inspired in part by journalist A.J. Jacobs and his year-long quest to follow all seven hundred rules in the Bible as closely as possible, chronicled in his book *My Year of Living Biblically*. His commitment included following the Ten Commandments and tithing 10 percent of his salary, but also observing many arcane and obscure laws, such as not shaving his beard or wearing clothes of mixed fibres and being willing to stone adulterers. (To live up to this last admonition, he half-heartedly tossed a pebble at a man who had admitted to cheating on his wife.)

I was interested in following Jacobs' lead, but not in following Biblical rules. I'd had enough of that. I didn't aspire to anything as ambitious as enrolling in theology school, trekking the Camino Trail or dancing like a wild woman at Burning Man. Rather, I made a list of simple, easily doable and ideally enlightening experiences I was eager to try. I wanted to see what I was missing out on. I had been raised in a closed-minded religion, but I was determined to bring a seeker's eagerness, combined with a reporter's skepticism, to my experimental year. When it came to the spiritual smorgasbord, I was ready for the big buffet.

Photo on next page: Frolicking with my
fuzzy friend Henry at goat yoga.

January

Waking Up

"How we spend our days is, of course, how we spend our lives."
—*Annie Dillard*

RELIGIOUS PILGRIMS TRAVEL TO THE HOLY LAND, LOURDES, THE
Ganges or Mecca. Secular seekers might choose Stonehenge, Sedona,
Machu Picchu or even Graceland. Sometimes when we discover new
places we discover new things about ourselves. But we don't need to
travel far to find enlightenment. We can live more deeply right where
we're planted. Henry David Thoreau, who moved to a tiny cabin where
he lived for two years in solitude and contemplation, proved you can be

a pilgrim in your own backyard. The same would be true for me. Most of my spiritual experiments would happen close to home.

THINGS BEGIN PROMISINGLY ENOUGH ON JANUARY 1 WHEN I OPEN my eyes to the realization that I don't have a hangover. It's been years since I faced a New Year's Day so clearheaded. I'd stayed up late the night before at a neighbourhood party, toasted friends with a solitary glass of champagne, and stopped there. This was so out of character, some people noticed. Several friends asked why I wasn't drinking. You'd think I'd renounced a citizenship of some kind.

Alcohol has always figured prominently in my idea of what constitutes a good time, and New Year's Eve is the booziest of holidays. But I don't want this year of soulful living to begin with a throbbing headache.

One driving reason for embarking on this spiritual experiment is a conventional one. At fifty-five, I am exactly middle-aged (if I live to be 110) and what I experience too often seems predictable, from the grey hairs on my head to the plantar fasciitis in my feet. In the past year I've attended four funerals. There are now more days behind me than ahead. I want these days to count. I am among legions of baby boomers, almost one hundred million North Americans, who are in this particular stage of life.

My kids Ruby, twenty, and Lucy, seventeen, are almost launched and ready to let loose on life. The house will be quiet without them. I'm married to Jeff, a fellow journalist, and after more than thirty years, it seems like some sort of miracle we're still together, given our different temperaments and the challenges of living with any one person, day in and day out, for decades. I still struggle from time to time with the estrangement from my family. The sadness has eased as the years have passed, but there are still moments when a spiritual emptiness creeps in and I haven't been sure how to fill it.

The psychotherapist and former monk Thomas Moore, perhaps the best-known spiritual writer of our time, believes that the great problem of our time is the loss of soul. There's evidence of this misery of the spirit all around us. At least one in four American women takes a psychiatric medication. In 1980, 20 percent of Americans reported feeling lonely; today it's 40 percent—and 35 percent of people over forty-five say they are chronically lonely. Clearly our souls are starved for something. We are spiritually bereft, living insular lives in houses that seem to get bigger and bigger while our sense of community becomes smaller.

I begin the new year the way I always have, with a bunch of earnest resolutions. For decades they've been pretty much the same: get in better shape, save more money, get organized. It's the trinity of trials we feel we must endure. But these goals are superficial. This year I'm trying something new. I've got a long spiritual to-do list, but first up is changing my morning routine. There's got to be a better way to begin the day than spending the first half-hour repeatedly hitting the snooze button or scrolling through Facebook on my phone. "Each morning we are born again. What we do today matters most," said the Buddha. I don't think he was talking about scanning other people's carefully cropped, flatteringly filtered vacation photos on Instagram.

I've never been a morning person. That hasn't stopped me from wondering what it would feel like to be one of those people who bounces out of bed, bends gracefully into sun salutations, writes morning pages, whips up a green smoothie fortified with ground flaxseed, and meditates for half an hour—all before the sun comes up. I imagine such a person would be in tune with the synchronicities of the universe and exceedingly efficient, a cross between spiritual guru Marianne Williamson and happiness expert Gretchen Rubin.

Caught up in the giddy enthusiasm that predictably accompanies New Year's resolutions, I craft a new approach to my weekday mornings, committing to a few new habits: stretching for five minutes, meditating for ten and journalling for fifteen. I'm going to avoid my phone when I wake up, find other ways to reduce screen time and also work some yoga into my days. All this, I'm convinced, will ensure my days begin with more peace and presence, less speed and scrambling.

My secret wish is to become more like my much-loved mother-in-law, Clarice, a woman I long admired and tried, mostly without success, to emulate. To her last breath, when she died at ninety-four with all six of her children at the edge of her hospital bed, Clarice was perpetually positive. She rose at 5:30 a.m. for her form of meditation: the cryptic crossword puzzle in that day's *Montreal Gazette*. Clarice lived in the moment. To my knowledge she never once cracked open a self-help book or watched an instructive TED Talk. I never heard her fret about the past or stew about the future. She always sang out the same cheery words when she woke in the morning: "It's another beautiful day!" She faced difficulties in life to be sure. A son, Keith, died at nine months from pneumonia, and she watched her beloved husband, Gerry, fade into the fog of Parkinson's over a ten-year period. But Clarice was stoic, and, most of all, *happy*, effortlessly so by the looks of it. My husband has some of her qualities. Whenever a conversation gets too serious or I'm drawn into introspective gloominess, he's apt to say something like, "Thinking too much always gets you into trouble," and go back to his Sudoku puzzle.

JANUARY 1 IS MY DAY TO GET STARTED. I SET MY ALARM FOR 6:30 A.M., an hour earlier than usual, and fling my sober self out of bed with the determination of the newly resolute. I throw on yoga pants and a T-shirt and head downstairs to the living room. As I light a scented candle, my fingers twitch, anticipating the usual reach for my giant-sized mug of medium roast coffee. This morning I knock back a glass of warm water with lemon slices instead. This will not only rehydrate my body, but apparently also flush my digestive system, which practically sounds like a religious rite in itself. I embark on a series of eight simple yoga stretches—including an upper back release, seated spinal twist and standing forward bend—that I found online. I keep a printout of the stretches in front of me, because these days I can't remember any list with more than three things on it.

When I finally reach for my phone, it's to log on to Headspace, a popular meditation app that's been downloaded more than thirty million times and promises to teach me how to meditate in just ten minutes a day. The app with the orange dot has turned its founder, Andy Puddicombe, a former Buddhist monk with a degree in circus arts, into the modern voice of digital meditation—and an immensely rich man. The *New York Times* credited Puddicombe with doing for meditation "what Jamie Oliver has done for food." I've dabbled in meditation before. Once, I even signed up for an all-day silent meditation retreat that had me counting down the minutes until I could be released.

Meditation ranks as one of the most popular habits of the SBNR, offering a few minutes of stillness in a noisy and frenetic world. Meditation has been proven to decrease anxiety, improve sleep, enhance relationships, reduce aging, make you smarter and boost empathy and concentration. And apparently all it requires is a few minutes a day with Andy, about the same amount of time as it takes to blow-dry my hair.

But as much as I try to concentrate on the steady in-and-out rise-and-fall of my breath, my mind keeps drifting. I attempt to follow Andy's gentle suggestion, communicated in his plummy British accent, to observe distracting thoughts as if they are mere bubbles that can be gently pricked so they'll disappear. I've always been an overthinker, though, and clearly it's going to take some practice to stop the errant ping-pong ball currently ricocheting around my brain.

Meditation is meant to guide us out of our heads and into the here and now. "How we pay attention to the present moment largely determines the character of our experience and, therefore, the quality of our lives," writes Sam Harris in *Waking Up: A Guide to Spirituality*

Without Religion. Journalling serves the same purpose, helping to quell our incessant mental chatter. I've kept a diary twice before, once as an angsty teen and then, in my mid-thirties, as an anxious new mom. I eventually ripped them both up because I didn't want anyone to find them after I died and see what a negative bore I could be. This year, however, I'm determined to give it another shot.

I set the timer on my phone and write for fifteen minutes without pausing my pen or thinking too much about the words that tumble out. I've never had trouble accessing my interior life, but when I actually pay attention to what's crowding my mind, the volume is overwhelming: nagging worries, repetitive musings, unresolved conflicts, ideas for creative projects, my damned never-ending to-do list, and all my up-and-down moods. In my work as a journalist, digging out the right words sometimes requires painful excavation; with journalling the words are right there, like loose gravel on the surface. It's a relief to tame the tornado of my thoughts, and when I set them down in deep blue ink on lined paper they become orderly, evidence of where my head and heart are really at.

As I make journalling a daily practice, I find my mother sometimes comes up when I write. We haven't spoken in years, ever since a Christmas gathering at my brother's home. We avoided each other for most of the evening, but as I was about to leave my mother walked over. We stood facing each other, at a loss for what to say. This was the woman I adored so much as a child that I would race home to make sure she wasn't hurt if I accidentally stepped on a sidewalk crack; the woman I would call from the payphone in my high school cafeteria if we'd had an argument that morning, because I couldn't get on with my day if I thought she was upset. The two of us are only eighteen years apart— when I was a teenager people would say we looked like sisters. We'd do sisterly things, too, like shop at the mall, smoke Du Maurier cigarettes at the dining-room table, and watch *The Young and the Restless* when I came home from school. But a chill had set in after I left the church.

It looked as if it might thaw that Christmas, until my mother broke the silence: "I pray for you every day," she said. A wave of shame passed over me, my face heating up. My adult self wanted to tell her I didn't need her prayers and I didn't need saving by a god I didn't believe in. My younger self, the one who felt like a bad girl who had stepped on a crack, won out and I kept quiet.

Getting the words out of my head and onto the page through journalling is an exorcism of sorts. It helps quiet the constant push-pull, back-and-forth arguments I have with myself over whether I should risk reaching out to my mother again. No clear answer arises, but I do feel less burdened.

My daily five minutes of yoga are another story. I want to like yoga, I really do. In fact, I want to love yoga. I want to love it as much as my friend Monica does. She gets up at 5:30 every weekday to do a ninety-minute ashtanga yoga class, during which she runs through a strenuous sequence of vinyasa poses. Monica says the practice has been "life-changing" since she began it three years ago. She says she's less judgemental, calmer about conflict and more open-hearted. She doesn't feel the need to read self-help books anymore—"because, ultimately, the answer comes from within."

Monica can also stand on her head.

I've been to a few yoga classes in the past. I found it was a lot like married sex: you may still feel the glow afterwards, but you just don't feel compelled to do it very often. Along with meditation, however, yoga is among the most popular practices of spiritual agnostics like me. Its benefits include cultivating awareness, quieting the mind and building fetching glutes. In the Bhagavad-Gita, Krishna says this about the ancient bendy practice: "Free from anger and selfish desire, unified in mind, those who follow the path of yoga and realize the Self are established forever in that supreme state."

I'd like to have what he's having. Maybe I just haven't tried hard enough.

A couple of weeks into the new year, I tag along with Monica to her ashtanga class. I begin with a respectful sun salutation, assert myself in warrior pose, flail at the extended hand-to-big-toe pose and surrender in a passive heap in child's pose. I can't keep up with the advanced practitioners who huff through their nostrils as they seamlessly move through jump-throughs, back bends, the plank, the splits, and headstands. I spend much of the class anticipating the sweet relief of the corpse pose, where all I have to do is lie down and play dead. When I roll up my mat at the end of the class, I think about the pain I'll probably be in the next day. Monica, meanwhile, is positively glowing.

Sure enough, the next morning I hobble out of bed.

I decide to investigate other types of yoga that might be less fierce and more fun. I pass on naked yoga (don't care to expose myself during downward dog) and pot yoga (don't smoke the stuff) but give aerial yoga a whirl. My first class is a bust. I scarf down an egg salad sandwich minutes before climbing into the anti-gravity hammock made of stretchy silk fabric and suspended from the ceiling. As it begins to sway, so do the contents of my stomach, and I realize that I'm about to toss my lunch. I make it to the bathroom just in time and hope that the other participants can't hear my hurls on the other side of the wall. I spend the rest of the class as motionless as a caterpillar while wrapped in my silk cocoon.

My return visit goes better. I manage the Superman-style swoosh— my body parallel to the floor, supported by a band of fabric across my hips, and my arms outstretched. And I'm giddy with a sense of accomplishment when I actually flip upside down, my hair grazing the floor and my feet moving up in the air while wrapped around the fabric. Despite several attempts, I can't quite manage the backward cape flip, the skirted star or the swan dive. Aerial yoga inversions are said to boost circulation and ease joint pain, and some believe that their spine-lengthening benefits can temporarily increase body height by over two centimetres. I'm not quite ready for the big top, but I do leave the class walking a little taller.

Later in the year, when the weather warms up, I give goat yoga a try. I head out to Brantford's Holly Hill Hobby Farm on a Saturday morning and unfurl my mat on an expansive green pasture, along with a couple dozen other folks. I meet Henry, the smallest of seven miniature goats, who prances over my mat, tries to nibble at my straw bag and lets out an adorable "meeeh" in place of the usual yoga "ooom." Goats are remarkably social creatures. They wag their tails like puppies and might mistake your raised backside for a mountain ridge, clattering up and over you. They might also poop a small mound of pebbles onto your mat, which is what happens to the man next to me. He just laughs, shakes out the mat and resumes his sun salutation.

I'm too distracted by the sheer cuteness of the goats to focus on my poses. At one point, I wander off to give Henry a handful of corn and stroke the soft felt of his fuzzy white ears, which feels incredibly calming. A bunch of small children also tear around the property, squealing after the goats, who seem delighted by the frisky chase. Kids, both the human and the animal variety, spread a joy that's contagious. Goat yoga doesn't provide me with much of a physical workout, but there's no beating the inner lift I get.

UNINSPIRING MORNINGS HAVEN'T BEEN THE ONLY THING HOLDING me back from living a more spiritual life. There is another problem: my addiction to busyness.

The truth is, if I'm not engaged in work, filling up my social calendar, relentlessly tidying my home, doing errands and generally keeping on top of everything, I'm not sure what to do with myself. It's as if my life only has meaning if I'm occupied every minute of the day. I have zilch in common with Marie Curie, the Nobel Prize–winning physicist and chemist, but I know exactly what she meant when she said, "One never notices what has been done; one can only see what remains to be done." For Curie, what needed doing was isolating radioactive isotopes and discovering polonium and radium; for me, it's meeting writing deadlines and getting dinner on the table. Still, the work never seems finished.

Busyness has always been a badge of honour for me. My version of the Ten Commandments is my to-do list, and I follow it faithfully. I tell myself I will get to all the things I really want to do—read more, spend more time with friends, volunteer, write poetry, take a cooking class, nap on the couch—when I complete my list. Of course, this never happens, because I keep adding things to my list. In a perverse way, this list is a comfort; it makes me feel good, the way addictions usually do. At least in the moment, when I experience the mood boost of crossing off another item; maybe not so much at night as I fall into bed exhausted and wonder why there weren't more moments of grace or simplicity or wonder in my day. Being busy makes me think I'm living life large, at full tilt. This, I know, is a problem.

My Calvinist upbringing is likely partly to blame. In 1904 Max Weber, one of the founders of modern sociology, advanced the idea of the Protestant work ethic, inspired in part by John Calvin, who argued that hard work was a calling from God and success a sign of salvation. This much-vaunted work ethic, which helped propel the development of capitalism, is especially vital to believers—a study of 150,000 people conducted by Groningen University in the Netherlands reveals that unemployed Protestants are far less happy than their secular counterparts who don't have a job.

My Dutch immigrant parents planted the seed that busyness is next to godliness by encouraging hard work at an early age. I landed my first job when I was eleven, picking Bing cherries during the summer at Pratten's Farm a few kilometres from home. I rode my bike there in the early morning, gathered cherries in six-quart baskets in the midsummer heat and gorged on so much of the candy-like fruit that my lips were stained purple and I got the runs. (I stopped when I realized repeat trips to the outhouse were affecting my productivity.) Two summers later, I was promoted to the cherry belt. I donned a hairnet over my feathered bangs and worked the 3:00–11:00 night shift alongside women three times my age, picking out the rotten cherries that chugged by on a loud conveyor belt. At fifteen, I got my teen dream job, working every day after school and on Saturdays at the Green Lantern, the sole variety store and restaurant in my small hometown of Fenwick in the Niagara Region in southern Ontario. I stacked magazines and displayed greeting cards, scooped ice cream, washed floors, worked the cash and saved enough money to put myself through journalism school after giving my parents half my earnings for room and board. With each new job my parents heaped on the praise.

Self-sacrifice often goes hand in hand with overwork. Women in particular are raised on the notion that good people take care of others first. We wait until everyone else has a full plate, and then we take the leftovers. It's challenging to tend to our spiritual selves when our lives are full of multitasking, duties and obligations. We can put ourselves on the back burner and become people who simply do things instead of people who experience them. And when we do put ourselves first, we often feel guilty. "Women are their own worst enemies," says the writer Erica Jong. "And guilt is our main weapon of self-torture. Show me a woman who doesn't feel guilty and I'll show you a man."

The trouble with believing your life has value only if you're productive is that you can never sit still. My husband can spend an entire Saturday afternoon on the couch, napping, playing guitar and doing puzzles. I admire this ability of his. I do. But I have to admit sometimes it makes me angry. Doesn't he see everything that needs to get *done*?

What my daughters have witnessed is a mother in constant motion. What kind of example have I set for them? Will they grow into women who do too much? Women who take care of everyone else and neglect themselves? Will they think their lives don't have meaning unless they are accomplishing some task or another? I didn't pass religion on to my kids, but I exemplify a go-go gospel. There's a very good chance they've inherited the Calvinist notion of salvation through productivity.

There are a lot of people like me who complain about how busy they are. The idea of adding spiritual practices to already jam-packed days can seem oppressive. Who's got time to meditate or read, join a singing group or go for a midday walk in the woods, no matter how enriching it might be? Yet the average woman spends five years of her life shopping and thirty hours a week doing housework. Maybe we owe ourselves a break. Maybe we need to lower our standards. Better yet, we can insist our partners and kids do their fair share. Until recently I did all the laundry for everyone in our house. Washing, drying, folding, sorting and hauling were pretty much a daily occurrence. No one made me do it. I'd just taken it on. Then one frustrating day while trying to sort socks whose matches seemed to have been swallowed up by the dryer, I did some calculations and figured out I had spent almost a year of my adult life preoccupied with this stuff. Then and there I stopped doing everyone else's laundry. There was barely a squawk of protest from anyone in my family; they stepped up and did their own. What had taken me so long?

Now I'm looking for more ways to claim back precious hours. By far the biggest time drain for North Americans is how we entertain ourselves. On average, we spend eight and a half hours, the majority of our waking time, "consuming" media on our tablets, smartphones, personal computers, video games, DVRs and TVs. Do the math, and you'll see where all our free time is going. More than 70 percent of Americans sleep with or next to their phones.

I've been as guilty as anyone. My phone had become my Bible, the thing I clasped in my hands as if it held all the wisdom of the universe. Similarly, Netflix had become my church; I regularly worshipped from the comfortable pew of my couch. I easily gave in to the lure of a new TV series, a cliffhanger podcast, the perennial ping of text notifications. I didn't daydream anymore, not in the waiting room at the doctor's office or standing in line at the grocery store. I wasn't leaving any openings for spacious boredom.

All this digital consumption, I'd come to see, put me in danger of never being fully present in my life. It also put me at risk of losing one of life's greatest pleasures: reading books. That formerly steadfast attachment had been replaced by more superficial attractions. Books could no longer compete with the slender and alluring piece of technology I cupped in my hand as tenderly as a lover's face.

It takes a truckload of willpower to release our grip on our phones. Ditto for our addiction to apps, which promise to make our lives easier in all sorts of ways, from calling a cab to creating a budget, streaming music, organizing photos, finding a parking space and even predicting the best time to rush out to the bathroom without missing a key plot point at the movies (Run and Pee).

I toy at first with the idea of turning my cell phone into a more soulful piece of technology. Apple's App Store is extraordinarily ecumenical, with six thousand religious and spiritual apps, including Confession, to help Catholics keep track of their sins; Virtual Hindu Worship, for praying to a variety of deities; myMasjid, to find prayer times at the nearest mosque; and KosherMe, to assist Jews in finding the perfect blessing. The Bible app has been downloaded 180 million times, which seems impressive until you learn the Angry Birds app has had more than two billion downloads.

Over the course of a week, I experiment with everything from Mindful Bite, which flashes a signal every thirty seconds to alert you to eat more slowly, to Prayer Beads, which rewards you with the ting of a bell after you tap your finger on a round of one hundred beads. It's an amusing exercise, but all these apps keep me even more tied to my phone. So I get rid of them all except the Spirit Junkie Alarm Clock, which wakes me at 6:30 a.m. with a gentle chime and a positive affirmation ("When I focus on what is joyful I bring more joy into my life"), and the Happy Tapper gratitude app, which I use to type out a quick list of several things I'm thankful for each day.

The screen time tracker I've downloaded indicates I spend about two hours a day on my phone. I resolve to cut this in half. I stop using Twitter, the Rolodex of mind-boggling news I can never keep up with. Ditto Instagram. "Comparison is the thief of joy," warned Theodore Roosevelt, more than one hundred years before anyone ever snapped a selfie. I'm reluctant to part ways with Facebook, because I truly enjoy most of the things my friends post and it alerts me to events in the community. Instead, I decide to reduce my Facebook fix to twenty-minute sessions twice a day. I also move my phone from my bedside table to a bookcase at the other end of our bedroom, take my work email off the device and silence the notifications. These simple acts soon mean I'm drifting off to sleep with my hands wrapped around a hardcover instead.

Netflix is next to go. Jeff and I have fallen into the habit of binge watching our favourite shows a couple of nights a week. Once we plunk ourselves in the den we tend to stay there for the night, often drinking several glasses of wine and staying up far later than we'd intended. This does not contribute to blissful mornings, and I want to stop wasting my time watching the lives of make-believe people unfold instead of living out mine.

Jennifer, one of my most culturally current friends, has never watched a single episode of *Seinfeld*, *Breaking Bad* or *Game of Thrones*. "I'll have lots of time to catch up when I'm in the nursing home," she says. "Until then, I want to live my life." I make that my new mantra. I'm in no hurry to get to the nursing home, but when I do, one consolation is that I'll be able to stream all six seasons of *Orange Is the New Black*. My husband misses our shared Netflix time. "Wanna watch something?" he suggests on a few occasions. But I've lost interest. Maybe this makes me a bad wife. There are other ways we can cultivate couple time, though, and watching TV together doesn't feel like a true connection.

BY THE END OF JANUARY, I'VE REDUCED MY SCREEN TIME SIGNIFI-
cantly, and it feels as if there's more breathing room in my life. I don't
miss Twitter or Instagram at all. Once I start scrolling on Facebook, I
sometimes lose track of time and go over my prescribed allotment, but
I make sure to clock in at under sixty minutes a day. Some days I don't
even open it, something that would have once seemed unthinkable. To
avoid the temptation of Netflix, I reserve lots of books at the library, so
there's always a stack on my bedside table.

My new morning routine is a different story. I don't like getting
up earlier. I desperately miss starting my day with coffee—the warm
lemon water tastes awful. Fifteen minutes of journalling feels like an
eternity, and my thoughts have begun to bore me. Even the few minutes of stretching seems tedious.

I'm disappointed by my lack of sticktoitiveness. We humans are
hardwired for failure, though, and it can take multiple attempts before
a new habit becomes a way of life. The good news is that we are also
hardwired to adapt. So that's what I do. I acknowledge to myself that I'll
never be a morning person. But for the forty-five minutes after waking
to the gentle chime of my alarm (now set for the more humane hour of
7:30 a.m.), I stay right where I am: in bed. First, I meditate to Headspace.
I know this is cheating and I should be sitting erect in a chair. I hope
Andy will forgive me. Morning after morning, in ten-minute segments,
he gently urges me to let go of thinking, to let my mind rest on the
breath. Cultivating greater awareness, he says, results in cultivating
more love. I truly believe Andy has my best interests at heart, so it
becomes easier to stick with him.

My husband puts on the coffee most mornings and carries two
cups upstairs as he gets ready for work. I bring the roasted brew to my
lips as if in hallowed communion. We talk about what we've got going
on that day, and then I open a book and read for half an hour. It's taken

me a lifetime to figure out that morning is the best time of day to read. There's no chance of dozing off, plus this is the time when the brain stores information with maximum efficiency, so there's a better chance of actually retaining what you've read.

In only a month, I've managed to make changes to how I kick-start the day. It's not a perfect start, but it's good enough. My mornings now glow a little more brightly. When I swing my feet to the floor and launch into action, I'm in a better frame of mind, ready for whatever comes. I channel Clarice, my mother-in-law. I really do believe it's going to be a beautiful day.

Photo on next page: Detail from the 1866 Dutch print The Broad and Narrow Way *that hung in my grandparents' home. Designed by Charlotte Reihlen and painted by Herr Schacher.*

February

Creating Sacred Space

"The soul needs a sense of home."
—*Thomas Moore*

THE MOST IMPORTANT RELIGIOUS ICON OF MY CHILDHOOD WAS A reproduction of an 1866 Dutch work entitled *De Brede Weg en de Smalle Weg* (or, in English, *The Broad and Narrow Way*). It hung in my Oma and Opa's dining room and was a vivid rendering of the contrast between worldly pleasures and virtuous living. I would stare at it for long periods of time, examining the two options. On one side there was a humble, uneven path dotted with a preacher's tent, pilgrims carrying parcels on their backs, poor widows and their children, a wooden cross and a healing fountain, all leading to a golden palace encircled by ten angels blowing trumpets. On the other was an expansive paved street lined with a theatre, dance hall, pawnshop and lottery table. Beautifully dressed women in floor-length skirts carried parasols, and glamorous couples danced in each other's arms. A group of men raised glasses of ale at an outdoor patio. There were clear signs of trouble on this carnal course—the almost hidden images of a man hanging by his neck outside the pawnshop, someone pulling a knife on an unsuspecting traveller, an angry man whipping his donkey. There was a battle scene in the distance and, beyond that, a city engulfed in fire with bodies falling into the flames. Black angels circled ominously above. At the top of the image a large eye encased in a triangle surveyed the scene. Just in front of the golden palace and the fiery pit were two bridges that connected these disparate worlds, offering a last chance to cross from one side to the other, thus avoiding the pitfall of Armageddon.

The picture encapsulated my theological education as I scanned, *Where's Waldo*–style, the dozens of figures in this moralizing tableau, all annotated with Bible verses in tiny type. I was raised to believe the narrow way, which glorified suffering and simplicity, was the only way to salvation. All other roads led to hell. But even as a kid I would hedge my bets, calculating that I could experience a bit of the worldly life, then take a quick right turn and, bingo, I'd be with the angels.

My early life was otherwise devoid of spiritual icons—no cross on the wall, no creche at Christmas and no portrait of a handsome, well-groomed, long-haired Jesus hanging over the living-room couch. Our church was similarly sombre. Catholics have their incense and candles, Hindus their dazzling gods, Muslims their colourful prayer rugs, Jews their crowned Torah scrolls and Sikhs their elaborate feathered plumes.

As far as spiritual bling, my church came up short. Even stained-glass windows were verboten because of the Second Commandment's warning against graven images.

There is nothing in the house I share with my husband and daughters to indicate my spiritual status. I attend the Unitarian Church in my neighbourhood a couple of Sundays a month (more on that later), but my home is bereft of Bibles and crucifixes, devoid of deities and devotionals. All I've got is a sad-sounding weathered wooden chime hanging on the porch. Now, though, I consider the idea of making a sacred space for myself and filling it with meaningful objects; it'll be a tangible way to bring the spiritual into the everyday. I've had altar envy ever since seeing the three displays my friend Marianne, a high school religious studies teacher, keeps in her home. One is a shelf with a braid of sweetgrass, a tiny butterfly, a medicine wheel, a prism and a jade Inukshuk. Another, created as a reminder of the positive aspects of religion, features a framed picture of Jesus, a gong, a menorah, four different Buddha statues, an image of Ganesha, a miniature totem pole and prayer beads. The third is a tabletop featuring a sculpture of five dancing women, a clay hand with a henna design and a rock emblazoned with the word *peace*. "They add meaning to my life," explains Marianne, who grew up in a Catholic home where a living-room end table did double duty as an altar, displaying a large white Bible, a statue of Mary with her hands clasped in prayer and a framed image of Jesus, his heart pierced by thorns. Similarly, my friend Doug, a fellow writer, carved out a corner of his condo as a "personal worship centre" after he returned from a spiritual retreat in Iona, Scotland, last year. "I don't read or use my phone there. Its exclusive use is mindfulness and reflection—my genre of praying," Doug tells me. He'll sit in the sturdy wooden armchair salvaged from the old train station in his hometown, surrounded by photos of beloved family members, a few travel photos and some hiking gear. "I love the outdoors, so the hiking boots and trekking poles are like my statues," he says. "They're my stained glass."

Creating a sacred space in your home for prayer, meditation, inspiration, reflection or simply to preserve family history is common in many cultures. Mexican Day of the Dead altars are festooned with gifts for the dearly departed while Hindu home altars are decorated with flowers and fruit laid at the feet of favourite gods and goddesses. Secular shrines are also popular among those who eschew church but want a bit of the holy in their homes. "In a post-church world, home is our sacred space. The windowsill is our shrine. The table is the new altar," writes Rachelle Mee-Chapman, author of *Relig-ish: Soulful Living in a Spiritual-But-Not-Religious World*. "Sacred objects and symbols mark your home as a place of sanctuary."

I have no intention of installing a golden calf in our den, but surely a Buddha head can't hurt? I want to fill a tabletop with pretty things, inspiring spiritual bric-a-brac that will prompt me to take a moment to ponder, meditate and appreciate. I want to make up for the divine decor deprivation of my past and spiritually spruce up my home—or at least a small corner of it. I give myself a $400 budget and call it research. It's about the same amount of money I spent when I splurged on a new TV a couple of years ago, and I have spent far too many hours worshipping in front of that particular fixture. I head out on a soul-shopping mission.

I don't have to go far. There are a bunch of stores selling metaphysical merchandise within an hour's drive of my home. *Retailing Insight*, the trade magazine for New Age retailers, reports that thousands of these spiritual stores have cropped up across North America and describes their customers as "spiritual hipsters," the type of folks who read *The Secret*, check their daily horoscope, stuff rose quartz crystals into their pillowcases to boost their love quotient and burn sage to banish negativity. Most of them are women, and they spend billions every year on products such as singing bowls, crystals, oracle and tarot cards, chakra-balancing kits, goddess jewellery, prayer flags, worry stones, yoga accessories, meditation cushions, statues, essential oils, dreamcatchers, incense and inspirational music and books.

My skepticism is as sharp as the point in John Calvin's beard when I enter Spiritual Emporium, a store that celebrates "all paths to the divine," and the first thing I see is a shelf lined with Charmed Floor Wash products in "magic" scents, such as Fast Luck Money Drawing ("for good luck and prosperity") and Dragon's Blood ("to cleanse negative energy"). The instructions indicate that the product should be poured into the warm scrub water while you concentrate on your desires. Nearby, something called Alleged Bat's Eye that comes in a purple satchel purports to ward off evil. There's a display case of a dozen or so large glass jars of exotic herbs, from mugwort to mistletoe, passion flower to patchouli, to help with menstrual issues, menopause symptoms, insomnia and depression, in that order. (Now I understand why there are so many mid-life women shopping here.) Ground sulphur, I learn, is an essential ingredient for exorcisms.

Store owner Maggie Costa tells me several of her clients have been "bamboozled and conned" by unscrupulous practitioners. "I know someone who spent thousands to remove evil spirits through an exorcism when they could have tried something as simple as a sage cleanse," she says. "It's important to have the integrity not to take advantage of someone who is in turmoil or desperate." I wonder how desperate someone would have to be to buy Alleged Bat's Eye.

I do find a few items that are appealing. There's a beautiful strand of rosewood and turquoise prayer beads with the requisite 108 mala beads used by religions around the world to encourage devotional chanting. It's been decades since I prayed out loud. Maybe these beads will offer a new approach to an ancient litany. A jewellery case features a row of rings made of hematite, a gemstone that's believed to repel negative energy. I recall my friend Emily telling me how her hematite ring suddenly shattered when she ran into her new husband's ex-wife. I guess the vibes weren't good. I don't have any exes to worry about, but I do have a habit of negative self-talk. It can't hurt to slip on one of these rings—maybe it'll be a reminder to go a little easier on myself. I also pick up a bundle of white sage and a large abalone shell smudge bowl with shimmering mother-of-pearl inlay. I'm keen to get fired up about smudging, a rite that involves the burning of herbs, often for spiritual healing and "energetic cleansing." My friend Rebecca recently smudged her marriage bed after a nasty divorce. Maybe burning some sage will help clear the air of the simmering resentment that can sometimes linger between my husband and me over some domestic grievance or another. Besides, science actually proves smudging works. Studies reported in the *Journal of Ethnopharmacology* found it not only has a calming effect, but can also reduce airborne bacteria by 94 percent. Sure beats Febreze. But as I place the sage and shell on the checkout counter, I feel a little uneasy. Smudging is a central ritual in many Indigenous cultures that's become a popular New Age practice. Is it appropriate for me as a white woman to bring it into my home? Am I co-opting another culture's sacred tradition for my own? I'm not sure. Costa purifies my purchases by bouncing a small mallet against the rim of a Tibetan singing bowl before ringing them through the till. The bill comes to $101.85.

With $300 still to spend, I head to Willow Den, where I navigate my way through the many aisles of karmic tchotchkes. I pass on the Attracts Money incense cones and the $2.75 Answer Feather, apparently based on an Indigenous tradition of holding on to a feather for twenty-four hours until you gain clarity on a burning question. (The instructions indicate the feather should be bathed in the moonlight before reuse.) I pick up a shaman's rattle and give it a shake. It's supposed to open up blocked energy. Seems like a steal for only $12, so I put it in my shopping basket. I bypass the lavender sleep stones and the Clouds of Unknowing perfume, a fragrance that promises to "steep the wearer in mystery." The kids' section includes a copy of *Babar's Yoga for Elephants* and a Crystal Growing Kit, the New Age equivalent of sea monkeys. I'm not impressed—so much of this merchandise seems garish and gimmicky, promoting false hope to the luckless and the lovelorn.

Then I spot an elegant $52 ceramic Buddha head and haul it over to the sales counter because, well, *Buddha*. It represents the exact "look" I'm going for—enviably eastern and indicative of a spiritual depth I don't possess but would like to. I know zilch about the Noble Eightfold Path, but I do know that the Buddha said lots of wise things, was a kind man and gained enlightenment after patiently meditating for forty-nine days under a banyan tree. I'd like to be wiser, kinder and more patient. Maybe having his head around will inspire me. Funny, Jesus was wise and kind too, but I wouldn't dream of putting a crucifix on the wall.

When I ask about the vast display of Himalayan salt lamps close to the checkout, a sales clerk explains that they clear indoor air of "electro-smog" from all the electronic devices we use. They're so popular the store can barely keep up with the demand. I drop $45 on a small desk lamp to suck up the negative electro energy my laptop emits. Even if there's no proof this actually works, the lamps do look pretty, casting a warm, orangey, coven-like glow. On my way out, I spot a hefty crystal ball on a marble stand. Originally used by the Celtic Druids to divine the future, today's purchasers use them as a "gazing focal point" in meditation, according to the sales clerk. Maybe if I put this orb at the foot of my bed it could enhance my morning meditation. I think of the ribbing I'd get from my husband if I came home with it—he'd ask why I didn't buy a turban while I was at it. But it *would* make a great conversation piece. I waffle until I look at the price tag. At almost $300 it's too dear for my budget. When I get home and do a little research, I'll discover Amazon sells crystal balls for as cheap as $19.99.

My next stop is Happy Soul, a metaphysical shop in Toronto that's one of many capitalizing on the crystal craze. These pretty stones are raking in a pretty penny in a billion-dollar industry that's gone mainstream thanks to an exploding demographic of buyers, including celebrities and CEOs, who believe these pop rocks have a positive effect on physical and emotional well-being. They're so popular that

Walmart sells them. With exotic-sounding names like bloodstone, celestite, nuummite, obsidian and tourmaline, they can be worn as jewellery, used as paperweights, placed on one of your seven chakras during a spa treatment or fondled if you're feeling stressed—you can even stick them up your yoni to boost sexual energy. One of the more questionable products that was sold on Gwyneth Paltrow's Goop lifestyle website was a $90 jade egg, supposedly fashioned after the kind used by royal concubines in China, which is inserted into the vagina to strengthen pelvic muscles for better sex. Me? I just like the idea of something pretty to wear around my neck.

People have been enamoured by the idea of the healing powers of precious stones for thousands of years. Egyptians buried their dead with quartz on the forehead to guide them into the afterlife. Cleopatra ground lapis lazuli, thought to enhance wisdom, to make her blue eyeshadow. The Bible has a number of references to gemstones. The book of Revelation describes the foundation of the New Jerusalem as being "adorned with every jewel," including sapphire, chrysolite, carnelian and jacinth.

"Basically, people come here to improve their lives," pronounces Joey, the sales clerk at Happy Soul, who tells me he keeps a $700 slab of citrine on his coffee table at home to help him maintain a positive mindset. "These stones are a gift from the earth. They are organically formed over millions of years and vibrate energy."

I pick a copy of the four-hundred-page *Crystal Bible* off the shelf, scan the index and see there's a crystal cure for almost every ailment: kunzite for depression, topaz for inspiration, amethyst for addiction. Their energetic properties are harnessed for technological uses—crystalline silicon powers computer processors and liquid crystal displays are used in cell phones—but can these fossilized resins bring inner peace or attract someone tall, dark and handsome into your life? There's absolutely no science to prove that crystals work. A widely cited 2001 study from the University of London revealed no real difference between what participants felt while holding genuine crystals and what they felt holding fake ones—any positive effect was simply the result of the power of suggestion. But the people who shop at stores like Happy Soul don't give a whit about studies like these. Ruby Warrington, who runs the popular "cosmic lifestyle platform" known as The Numinous, writes about the "Tinker Bell" effect of crystals, comparing them to the fairy dust that made Peter Pan believe he could fly. And who's to say these sparkly shards don't work on some level? The ancient Greeks believed diamonds were tears that fell from the eyes of the gods; the Romans thought they were splinters that fell from the stars. Today we imbue them with the power to convey love and commitment. Anyone who has ever gone gaga over a diamond slipped on the fourth finger of their left hand knows the power a simple stone can possess.

I think of the gemstones that are precious to me. My mother's simple gold wedding band from my father, Henk, had the date of their wedding—July 7, 1961—inscribed inside. After he deserted our family, she added three barely-there rubies to the ring to represent the July birthdays she and my brother and I share. She gave it to me decades ago and I wear it as a reminder of those early days when our little trio was a tight circle. The only other ring I wear is one I asked my husband to buy for my fortieth birthday, also with a ruby as well as an emerald, an alexandrite and a topaz, to represent the July, May, June and December birthdays of my husband, our children and me. Every time I stretch out my fingers I'm aware I hold the complex histories of two unique families right here on my hand.

It's easy to scoff at people who believe in crystals, but billions of people believe in things that can't be proven, including the existence of God. In an age of anxiety it makes sense that we want to hold on to something solid and elemental. Why not a nugget of amethyst? I carefully pick out a handful of candy-coloured gems and plop them into a velvet drawstring bag, considering who might benefit from their various properties: clear quartz for my daughter Ruby, who is coming up to exam mid-terms (helps improve focus); citrine for Lucy, who is working on a film for a school project (aids creativity); and rose quartz for a bunch of mid-life women friends who would love another chance at love (attracts romance). Since my Visa bill is overdue I throw in some shiny gold pyrite (known as the "abundance stone") for good measure.

As for a necklace, I'm overwhelmed by the selection. Joey tells me I don't need to pick the crystal, it will pick me. "How?" I ask. "You'll just know," he says. I worry that the wrong choice could have fateful consequences, but I finally settle on a $40 chunky pendant made of bright yellow and orange carnelian stone. When Joey tells me the stone is known for its ability to provide religious healing and spiritual awakening, I feel as though I've made the right choice. At the checkout I pull out my Visa and add an impulse purchase—a beautifully boxed Rumi oracle deck ($30) that promises "an invitation into the heart of the divine." As I stride out of Happy Soul, my shiny new pendant bounces off my chest like a ray of sunshine.

I'm down to $100, and I blow it all and then some at Saje Natural Wellness, a seventy-four-store North American chain specializing in essential oils. The oil business is booming ($9 billion in global sales in 2016) thanks to the chemical-free wellness trend that has people turning up their noses at fake air fresheners and opting instead for the relaxing properties of peppermint and patchouli. As with crystals, there seems to be a scent solution for every problem: tea tree oil for acne, bergamot for anxiety, eucalyptus for colds, jasmine for improved mood, juniper for concentration. Some companies even tout these elixirs as a cure for diseases such as Alzheimer's and cancer. In 2014, the us Food and Drug Administration censured Young Living and dōTerra, the multi-level marketing companies that have the biggest share of the oil market, for making false medical promises. Only a smattering of small studies indicate essential oils may be effective in helping with issues such as insomnia, anxiety and headaches.

The only new thing about essential oils is the vigorous marketing behind them. Egyptians anointed corpses with cedar oil as part of mummification, and pine oil was burned in the streets during the Bubonic Plague. More than a dozen botanical essences are mentioned in the Bible, including accounts of cedar wood treating leprosy and hyssop being used in the sponge that soaked up the sour wine given to Jesus on the cross. All four gospels tell the story of the woman who anoints Jesus' feet with a pound of costly spikenard oil from an alabaster jar. Today, Catholics use the sacramental oil of catechumens (olive oil mixed with balsam) for baptism. In 1953 the Queen was anointed with a blend of olive oil, jasmine and musk at her coronation.

I just want my home to smell good. With two cats, an occasionally incontinent old dog and a damp basement, the odour can get funky in my house, especially on a humid day. I also want to sleep better. Since the onset of menopause, a solid night of shut-eye has become elusive. The witching hour is usually between 4:00 and 5:00 a.m., when I lie awake and try to count sheep but more often than not count the seconds between my husband's loud snores. What I wouldn't give for a sleeping potion that will put me out for at least seven hours!

With its sepia-toned colour palette, oak millwork, bronze glass and pendant lights, Saje feels more like a temple than a chain store. A tall, elegant sales clerk dressed in black glides toward me like a high priestess. She waves her hand at the dozens of delicate vials that line the shelves. Lavender is the answer for my sleep issues, according to her, and sweet orange will not only eliminate pet odour but boost my happiness quotient. She leads me to a row of diffusers and I pick out the store's bestselling ultrasonic model ($79.95). I can't resist adding an essential oil travel kit, with five roll-on remedies strapped into a zippered travel pouch, a ready arsenal the priestess tells me will effectively battle multiple vacation issues, everything from jet lag to altitude sickness and Montezuma's Revenge.

Back at home, I examine my holy haul. I arrange some items on a narrow hall table I've pulled into the living room, put the crystal necklace in my jewellery box and plug in the diffuser. Before bed, I fill it with water, tap out fifteen drops of oil and drift off as puffs of lavender waft around my head. For the first time in weeks, I sleep through the night, like a newborn with a belly full of warm milk.

As for the rest of my purchases, it doesn't take long for disillusionment to set in. My allergy-prone husband and oldest daughter start sneezing as soon as I set a match to the sage. Every card in my Rumi oracle deck is a beautiful piece of artwork inscribed with a cryptic saying. My intent is to draw one on a daily basis and consult the accompanying guidebook for its meaning, but laziness sets in and I start giving the cards out to friends, who more often than not seem convinced Rumi is channelling a message directly to them. "*Enter the garden of delights?* I need to build more fun into my life!" "*Beware divine discontent?* This is the year I have to look for a new job!" The crystal necklace is lovely, but it has a fussy clasp so I never wear it. My youngest daughter takes a shine to the Himalayan salt lamp and asks if she can put it in her bedroom.

The shaman rattle stays on the altar, but once in a while I pick it up to bug my kids, who roll their eyes every time I give it a playful shake in their direction. This, I come to see, is wrong-headed. When I speak with some Unitarian friends about my altar, one of them asks if I understand the significance of the rattle; how it's an ancient instrument used to call forth spirits for help and healing and a tool for creating sacred space; how it incorporates elements of the three kingdoms (mineral, animal and plant). I realize I've been guilty of spiritual appropriation, the practice of engaging in sacred traditions or using religious objects from cultures that have been disenfranchised by the dominant group. The SBNR, who don't have a specific faith tradition to call their own, like to partake in the practices of various world religions, but before adopting a sacred tradition it's important to go deep, explains Mary

Mueller Shutan, the author of *The Spiritual Awakening Guide.* "If you don't fully understand all that is going on with the culture and the ceremonies or practices you are emulating, it's appropriation," she tells me. "Beyond that, it's just rude." Ouch. I consider other practices that are problematic if not observed properly; consider a non-Catholic receiving the Eucharist or someone casually wearing an unearned Purple Heart. Or a privileged white woman shaking a rattle traditionally used in Indigenous ceremonies as if it's some sort of whimsical novelty item.

My altar experiment hasn't altered me in any way. I realize a revamp is in order.

"The soul will attach itself," says the spiritual writer Thomas Moore. "We're attached to families and to our kids and to pets and to things— even objects . . . That's a sign of a real soulful life, that you're able to make that attachment." I clear my little altar of its store-bought purchases and start fresh. I display two photos of my late mother-in-law Clarice, one in which she is a young raven-haired beauty and one of her with glasses and grey hair. She has a wide smile in both. I prop up an old Polaroid of myself laughing with my two girls, a favourite memory from when they were little, taken on a cottage vacation while they were having a bath simultaneously in a two-sided kitchen sink. I add a small framed black-and-white photo of myself when I was little, too. I am smiling cautiously, standing on the sidewalk outside my childhood church, dressed in a smart woollen knee-length coat with a tartan purse on a silver chain over my shoulder. My mother always managed to dress me well, even when she had very little money. Next, I display a gilt-edged print with the title *Guardian of Motherhood*, depicting an ethereal young woman with golden angel wings who is protectively holding a large blue egg—a gift from my mother when I had my first child. I make room for a couple of books, too—*Goodnight Moon*, the simple childhood tale I must have read to my girls at least a thousand times, and which they loved to recite back to me, and a collection of poetry by Mary Oliver, with a famous line urging readers to account for their days by considering what it is they hope to accomplish with their "one wild and precious life." Just looking at Mary's wise and weathered face on the cover fills me with peace. I place my ukulele on a stand below the altar. I took up this joyful, simple instrument a few years ago, the only hobby I've ever really had. I hope displaying it will inspire me to play it more. I complete the tableau with a couple of candles and a bowlful of crystals.

Then I go searching for something I've kept stored in the basement. I dust off the old Dutch print, *De Brede Weg en de Smalle Weg*, and stare at it a good long while. I no longer believe its simplistic message that there are only two paths, the way of suffering and the way of indulgence. Life is more complicated than that. There's nothing wrong with the humble and heartfelt faith depicted on the narrow way, and yes, way stations of sorrow are inevitable on life's journey. But I have no quarrel with the spirited life of the dancehall, either. The fiery pit doesn't frighten me any longer. This picture was important to my grandparents, whom I loved. They cared enough about it to carry it with them across the ocean when they immigrated to Canada from Holland more than sixty-five years ago. I reclaim this inheritance and hang the print in my home as a way to honour Luink and Anna Luinge and the courage they had to take that overseas journey. Maybe it's more sentimental than spiritual, but it reminds me of where I've come from, the detours I've taken and the importance of finding my own way in the world.

Photo on next page: Wedding day, May 17, 1986, with the women in my family. Left to right: Oma, me, Aunt Lonny, my mother, and my sister in the foreground.

March

The Rigour of Ritual

"Rituals are so powerful because they provide structure
for the full spectrum of our emotional lives: the births,
and the deaths, the union and the disintegration."
—*Courtney Martin*

Q: "Do you acknowledge God's covenant promises, which have
been signified and sealed to you in your baptism? Do you truly
detest and humble yourself before God because of your sins
and seek your life outside of yourself in Jesus Christ?"
A: "I do."

I am nineteen years old, standing in front of the altar of Cornerstone Canadian Reformed Church in Hamilton, Ontario, and lying through my teeth. I'm participating in the ritual known as the Profession of Faith, my church's version of confirmation, the age-of-majority rite in which young adults make public their commitment to follow in the ways of the Lord and the teachings of the church. I am making promises I know I won't keep. In front of me stands Reverend Huizinga with a bench full of sombre elders, all men. Behind me is a congregation of more than three hundred that includes my parents and grandparents, who are looking on proudly. I am wearing a smart navy pinstriped jacket and matching modest knee-length skirt that my mom has bought for me. As they beam, I die a little inside.

This moment had been my destiny from the time my teenage parents, Henk and Aafke, had me baptized in this church. Actually, it went even further back than that, as prophesied in Jeremiah 1: "Before I formed you in the womb I knew you, and before you were born I set you apart." My indoctrination in the faith had been years in the making, and now I was expected to fulfill the promise of my birthright. My lower-middle-class mother and stepfather, a homemaker and a carpenter, went without family vacations so they could afford the tuition to keep me and my younger siblings out of public school, where we would have been subjected to worldly ideas like evolution and dancing. At our private Christian school, we had daily religion classes, and parents used Magic Markers to black out "sacrilegious" phrases such as "by Gosh" in children's books when they volunteered in the school library.

I listened to the Ten Commandments read out in church two thousand times over two decades. For three years my stepfather also made the long drive to our church every Wednesday night after work and waited in the parking lot while I attended a class with other teenagers, memorizing and then reciting the 129 prescribed questions and answers of the Heidelberg Catechism, the four-hundred-year-old doctrinal tract of our faith.

The cap to my religious education was a closed-door vetting by the elders to ensure I was ready to make public my Profession of Faith. An elder asked me if I had any intentions of ever leaving the Canadian Reformed Church for the nearly identical yet rival Christian Reformed Church, which was marginally more liberal (going to the movies was not a sin, for example), and thus suspect. I answered correctly and said no.

As I stood at the front of the church to participate in the Profession of Faith, I imagined myself as a runaway bride of Christ. I considered my escape route: down the red-carpeted centre aisle, past the pews of confused parishioners, including my horrified parents and grandparents, and out through the large double doors. But once I got outside, where would I go? My history was here, inside, with these people. Out there was nothing but rootlessness. The story was that my biological father had been an unhappy wanderer ever since leaving this same church two decades earlier. I'd been told he went from city to city, woman to woman, a runaway husband, father and son who never found his way back home again. Wouldn't the same happen to me if I followed in his footsteps?

I stayed put, like a dutiful bride, answering the rest of the questions set before me:

Q: "Do you declare that you love the Lord God and that it is your heartfelt desire to serve him according to his Word, to forsake the world, and to crucify your old nature?"
A: "I do."
Q: "Do you firmly resolve to commit your whole life to the Lord's service as a living member of his church? Do you promise to submit willingly to the admonition and discipline of the church, if it should happen, and may God graciously prevent it, that you become delinquent either in doctrine or in conduct?"
A: "I do."

My lips spoke the words, but my fingers might as well have been crossed behind my back. I knew it was wrong when I made my way to the communion table and popped a small piece of bread from the communion platter into my mouth. When I raised the goblet of wine to my Judas lips to wash it down, I could taste the bitterness of hypocrisy on my tongue. My hand shook as I placed the goblet back down on the white tablecloth.

Not long after my Profession of Faith, my church attendance started to drop off. I'd graduated from journalism school, moved away from my small hometown and got my first job at a weekly newspaper in the big city of Hamilton, an hour away. My fellow newsroom employees, Paul, Norm, Denise, Jeff, Dan, Bruce, Melanie and John, became my new community (we remain close friends thirty-five years later). My absence from the pew was noted, and I was called to account. There were phone calls and letters, entreaties to meet with the minister, elders who hounded me on the phone. They all threatened excommunication if I didn't "repent and return." When I told my mother I was considering leaving the church, she was despairing. "You're just like your father," she said. I was in despair, too. But also resolute.

After a few months of this, I met with Reverend Huizinga, and did what I should have done before completing my Profession of Faith: I confessed my doubts about my denomination and my faith. I didn't believe ours was the "one true church" or that billions of decent people were doomed to hell because they weren't born Canadian Reformed. I didn't believe I had to attend this particular church in order to be saved. I wasn't even sure I was in need of saving. I had enrolled in a women's studies course at the local university and had just read *Outrageous Acts and Everyday Rebellions*, Gloria Steinem's 1983 collection of essays charting the experiences that resulted in her consciousness-raising. I had become a feminist, a definite F-word in the religion I was raised in.

Only men could be ministers, elders or deacons in the Canadian Reformed Church. Women were silenced in all kinds of ways, right down to being expected to sit in their cars in the parking lot while the men conducted the annual election of the church elders. The only church business women could attend to was housekeeping tasks such as dusting the pews, arranging the flowers and ensuring a sufficient supply of fresh coffee after the service. Church members were regularly reminded to conduct their domestic arrangements in accordance with the words of Ephesians 5: "Wives, submit yourselves to your own husbands as you do to the Lord. For the husband is the head of the wife as Christ is the head of the church." I'd always thought that a bit of a joke, since neither my formidable Oma nor my strong-minded mother was the type to easily acquiesce to her husband's will, no matter what her church might say. I suspected it was the same in many Canadian Reformed households. But in public at least, women were expected to nod along, their tolerance of inequality touted as a badge of belief.

When I told Reverend Huizinga I had problems with how our church treated women, he referred to the oft-cited 1 Corinthians 14 as the final word on the subject: "Women are to be silent in the churches. They are not permitted to speak, but must be in submission, as the Law says. If they wish to inquire about something, they are to ask their own husbands at home; for it is dishonourable for a woman to speak in the church."

Thanks to my years of religious indoctrination, I knew my Bible. I pointed to Corinthians 11, just three chapters earlier: "And every woman who prays or prophesies with her head uncovered dishonours her head, for it is just as if her head were shaved." I didn't understand why some rules applied and not others, I said. Women in our church weren't expected to cover their heads during worship. "Isn't the church just picking and choosing whatever suits its point of view?"

Reverend Huizinga was taken aback. "Head coverings were a cultural tradition of the time," he said.

"Couldn't the same be said about women not speaking in church? Besides, that verse talks about women prophesying."

Reverend Huizinga sighed. "The Bible is the final authority," he said, effectively ending our discussion. "It is not for us to question. You must have faith like a child."

It would be years before I fully understood how my religious education had failed me by effectively censoring the many examples of strong female leaders in the Bible—apostles, deacons, heads of churches, warriors, queens and a judge among them. Women such as Esther, Junia, Phoebe, Priscilla, Nympha, Lydia, Chloe, Sheba and Deborah. Jesus challenged the patriarchal culture by regularly interacting with women, including Susanna, Mary Magdalene, Martha and all manner of unnamed widows, mothers-in-laws and "fallen women." I never once heard a sermon about how God had used Jael, mentioned in the book of Judges, to inspire the Israelites to victory in a battle during which she hammers a tent peg into the temple of an enemy soldier while he is sleeping. Women like Jael are the disappeared. They don't fit the ideal model of womanhood that's been drummed into us. Instead, the focus is on women such as Eve, the temptress responsible for the fall of man, the scheming Jezebel, who is eaten by dogs, and the disobedient and nameless Lot's wife, who dared to look back over her shoulder at the smouldering Sodom and is turned into a pillar of salt.

I wrote a letter withdrawing my membership in the Canadian Reformed Church. I knew this meant there was a good chance I'd also lose my family and would have to create a new life without them. Not long after sending my letter, I got one back from the consistory:

Dear Sister Bokma,

The Consistory, with great sorrow, received your letter of withdrawal. With a single paragraph you sever a relationship for which Christ suffered unimaginable agony.

Do you fully realize the consequences, for your life here and into eternity?

In the name of Christ we write you in a last attempt to call you back from this act of disloyalty to God the Father and His Son, an act by which you place yourself in an environment where God the Spirit cannot reach you. If you do not repent and return, that one paragraph letter will become a document which may have eternal repercussions.

Eternal repercussions meant hell, of course. But that threat no longer held any power over me. My idea of hell was alienation from my family. My parents were angry and ashamed, and our relationship started to fall apart.

What had happened between the time I lied in church and the time I told the truth in the minister's office? I had met a man. Jeff was from a large, loving Catholic family in Montreal. He'd never once seen his parents fight or have any kind of squabble. Perhaps that was why he had a deep-seated aversion to conflict. I couldn't believe my good fortune at meeting this handsome, funny, smart and agreeable guy who said yes to everything—including me when I asked him to marry me just a few months after we started dating. Rootless no longer, I'd found someone to hold on to—and I hung on for dear life.

Jeff moved into my apartment, and I hid the fact that we were living together from my family for two years. It helped that I rarely saw them. He agreed never to answer the phone, and on the couple of times my parents did visit, he accommodatingly left the apartment; I cleared out his razor from the bathroom and hid his guitar. Sex before marriage was a sin—not quite as evil as murder, but maybe as bad as manslaughter. I envisioned my mother having a heart attack if she learned we were shacked up. Self-preservation kept me quiet—along with a lack of courage. I was afraid of her disappointment. As bad as it would be if she found out we were living together, it would be even worse if she knew I was involved with a Catholic, just about the most heretical thing a Calvinist-raised girl like me could do.

To understand the animosity my family had against Catholics you have to go back a few centuries to the Protestant Reformation, when John Calvin challenged the teachings of the Catholic Church, which in turn persecuted and executed Protestants under heresy laws. More than five hundred years later, this religious grudge was kept alive and well in my family through contempt and inexplicable stories. "They worship in round churches because they're afraid of the devil getting in the corner," said my Oma. My siblings and I were told Catholics bought their way into heaven, that they worshipped the Pope instead of God. When a Catholic friend's father died, my mother said it was doubly sad because now he was in hell.

I told my mother Jeff and I were engaged.

"I will never be happy as long as you are with a Catholic," she said.

Anxiety grabbed hold of my gut. But I held firm. I loved Jeff.

"We're getting married, Mom."

"We won't be coming to the wedding."

I didn't see my parents for months after this conversation. Then, a few weeks before the wedding, they came for a visit. We hid the razor and the guitar. One of the first things my mother said to Jeff when she met him for the first time was, "You know, the Catholics burned us at the stake."

I held my breath. I was certain that once Jeff witnessed first-hand the religious fervor that ran in my family like a consuming fever, he would be out the door. Then I would be truly rootless.

"I know, Mrs. Bokma, and I'm truly sorry," he said.

Jeff's willingness to apologize for events on the other side of the world during the Middle Ages seemed to placate my mother. Either that, or he stunned her into silence. My parents agreed at the last minute to come to our wedding.

Jeff had actually been a lapsed Catholic for years before I met him. He identified as an atheist. Even though I was in the process of leaving my church when I met him, I still clung to some of the falsehoods I'd been taught. On one of our first dates, Jeff and I got into an evolution-versus-creationism debate. He couldn't believe that I still thought Adam and Eve were the grandparents of all of humanity. I couldn't believe he thought we'd descended from apes. What can I say? The sex was good. It helped us overlook our differences.

DESPITE, OR MAYBE BECAUSE OF, THE NASTY THINGS I GREW UP hearing about Catholics, I have remained curious about their religion. For one thing, I envy Catholics the instant absolution of the confessional. Protestants fret under a cloud of doubt and guilt, robbed of the relief that comes with knowing all is forgiven. Jeff describes the confessional as being like a therapist's couch: sometimes he wasn't sure what he would say when he got there, but he could usually come up with something. If not, he'd make up run-of-the-mill misdemeanors: "I hit my sister." "I lied to my mother." When he was ten, he confessed to the priest that he and his friends had stolen Beatles wigs from a Montreal department store. When he was fourteen, he confessed to impure thoughts about Catwoman (Eartha Kitt's version). A few Hail Marys and all was generally right with his world. There were, however, some ideas he'd been exposed to that I didn't envy, among them purgatory, exorcism, transubstantiation, and the Holy Prepuce, the weird worship of Jesus' foreskin. At sixteen, Jeff was the last in his family to leave the church. Even his parents had stopped going. "I was just so afraid of going to hell," he told me. "Until finally I wasn't anymore."

Most religious rituals don't make a lot of sense. A fantastic suspension of logic is required, for example, to buy the idea that wafers and wine can turn into flesh and blood. But millions of people will engage in even the most bizarre of behaviours if the brainwashing begins early enough. Consider the traditional Kaparot ceremony of ultra-Orthodox

Jews, which involves waving a live chicken above the head and reciting verses from a holy book to transfer one's sins on to the bird. Or the kaya klesh rite of Jain monks and nuns, which compels them to spread an ash made of dried cow dung over their heads before painfully pulling out each strand of their hair in a symbolic gesture of renouncing worldly attachments. Or the horrific baby-tossing practice of both Hindus and Muslims at the Grishneshwar Temple in the Indian state of Maharashtra, in which children between the ages of one and three are thrown from a fifteen-metre tower and caught in sheets by men below. The seven-hundred-year-old ceremony is thought to make the children smarter and healthier.

For centuries, religious institutions have had a monopoly on rituals and sacraments, attracting even non-believers who participate to mark significant transitions such as births and weddings. But life is not a straight line from birth through marriage to death. There are glorious byways and painful detours along the way, and many of these other passages, including adoption, the onset of menstruation, career change, becoming a grandparent, miscarriage, divorce, milestone birthdays, retirement, menopause, coming out and transitioning to a new gender, are increasingly being recognized with secular rituals.

Lately, the holy ritual of Lent, in which millions of believers forgo candy or cable to get closer to God, has been co-opted by the nonreligious. The *New York Times* has reported on the practice, describing secular Lent as an "eccentric observance," but more than 80 percent of non-Christians celebrate Christmas, so why not Lent as well? Surely everyone could benefit from a little self-denial. As the month of March dawns, I wonder if this forty-day period that begins with sombre Ash Wednesday, when believers mark their foreheads with grey dust as a reminder of their eventual death, might be a way to deepen my spiritual life. There's something appealing about the sacrifice that Lent requires. I could hit the reset button on failed New Year's resolutions and introduce a new deliberateness to my days. Besides, I want to see if I can give up drinking for a few weeks. Over the past several years, my wine consumption has risen steadily, and it seems like a good time to stabilize the situation. Or, in Catholic parlance: to mortify the flesh. Lent is calling on me to change my ways.

A clever Catholic technicality allows one to "break the fast" on each of the six Sabbaths of Lent. This convenient escape hatch makes it easier for me to commit. If not for those impending cheat days, I'm not sure I'd consider depriving myself of something I enjoy so much. I'm in full agreement with the Biblical view of wine, which along with olive oil and bread is considered an essential dietary staple: It "maketh glad the heart of man" (Psalm 104:15). Even Rumi, the beloved Persian poet and Sufi mystic, extols its carnal virtues: "Either give me more wine or leave me alone." The Buddha had a different take on alcohol and other intoxicants, explaining, "The mind is confused enough as it is and doesn't need any help."

Jesus spent forty days wandering in the Judean Desert, avoiding people. Surely I can spend forty days avoiding liquor. Maybe forgoing wine for a time will have a sobering effect on my soul and lead me to a greater state of grace. There's a reason fasting is ubiquitous in the world's religions, from Yom Kippur to Ramadan: giving up stuff is good for us.

Also, there was the blackout. Two full hours lost, never to be retrieved from my memory bank again. The previous summer, after a raucous evening at a campground with friends—during which both the wine and the conversation were flowing freely—I woke up with a hangover and couldn't recall how I had gotten back to my tent. When I discovered that a friend had escorted me, I asked her if I'd done or said anything stupid. According to her, I had told—and repeatedly retold—a story my husband had shared with me on the phone earlier that day about his flight home from a wedding in Cuba. The crew didn't speak English and the pilot, circling the airport for hours during a rough storm, offered no words of consolation to the agitated passengers other than a desperately enthusiastic, "Good luck!" I had taken particular relish in pronouncing the words "Good luck!" in a Spanish accent, my friend informed me. And I had been loud. "I think the whole campground heard you," she said. She was laughing, but I was mortified.

Until that blackout, I didn't think I had a problem with alcohol—not a big one, anyway. Sure, I drank more than most of my friends, and I often woke up on the weekend with a low-grade headache from imbibing the night before. But I never threw up, never passed out or missed work because of it. I thought of wine as simply my way to unwind. It was both a reward and a relief. But now I recalled something Caroline Knapp had said in her bestselling memoir, *Drinking: A Love Story*: "To a drinker the sensation is real and pure and akin to something spiritual: you seek; in the bottle, you find."

When I was young, I only drank at parties with friends. In my late thirties, after having two kids, a glass of wine was a reward after a long day at the office and a second shift of toddler time at home. The sound of a cork popping and the glug-glug of liquid being poured into a wide-brimmed goblet was music to my ears. Home life became less demanding as my kids got older, but by then I had started working as a freelance writer, and wine released the steam on pressure-cooker deadlines. By the time I thought about giving it up, two or three glasses of wine had become an almost daily habit. On weekends it was sometimes more. This put me well over the low-risk drinking guidelines recommended by Canadian health agencies for women: no more than two drinks a day on most days, to a maximum of ten drinks a week.

I wasn't a falling-down drunk, and yet there were times when I lost my balance. Once, at a backyard summer barbecue, my wild dancing—fuelled by tequila—caused me to topple into a rose bush and come home with unsightly scratches across my forearms. Another time, at the end of a long and engaging dinner party, I slid off the ottoman in my friend's living room when I was putting on my boots to walk home. And then there was that blackout. Maybe I was in a fallen state after all.

Women drink at all stages of our lives, from the sorority sisterhood days of university to the after-work drink rituals of our twenties to the time-starved, sleep-deprived, mommy-needs-a-martini years of early parenting—and it doesn't stop there. Drinking is progressive, and for some it can escalate in mid-life, says Dr. Vivien Brown, a Toronto family physician. "Women often drink when they are lonely, after the kids leave home or after a separation or divorce," she says. She has female patients in their seventies who have "a sherry in the late afternoon, followed by a couple of glasses of wine at dinner and a hot toddy before bed." That's twenty-eight drinks a week, almost three times the recommended guidelines. Why do they do it? "When women feel vulnerable, they may think alcohol is a safe thing to turn to," says Brown. "To some women, drinking at home seems acceptable and safer than taking drugs or going to bars."

In my case I worried that my love for wine was partly hereditary. Over the years I'd heard stories about my biological father's boozing. Shortly after my parents were married, my mother had frantically slit the tires of his Ford pickup with a steak knife to keep him from going out to the bars. My last contact with my father had been ten years before he died. He called our home, and I was the one who picked up the phone. It was obvious to me, at age fifteen, that he had fortified himself with alcohol. "Did you know that when you were a little girl, you used to wrap your arms around my neck and say, 'I want to marry you when I grow up, Daddy'?" he asked me. I didn't know what to say and handed the phone to my mother. His words made me sad. I was forever frozen in his mind as an adoring toddler. He had no sense of the young woman I was becoming, and never would.

Shortly after that, I had my first drink. My mother and stepfather were hosting a party with all my aunts and uncles, and there were several bottles of wine open in the kitchen. I helped myself to a few glasses, and later that night I threw up. From then on I spent many weekend nights at the local park drinking cheap white wine with the kids from the neighbourhood. I'd get tipsy and then come home and tiptoe up the stairs to avoid waking my parents.

One of the worst things about my drinking was that it made me crave cigarettes. I still occasionally sneak them on the back porch late at night when the kids are asleep. I had hidden my habit from them until they were teenagers, when they figured it out from the telltale evidence of lighters and ashtrays. From the moment when my best friend in Grade 9 handed over her pack of Du Maurier Lights in the schoolyard, smoking became an addiction, one I'd managed to give up from time to time, sometimes even for years, but then would go back to. It was like a no-good lover I couldn't resist. Cigarettes were the elegantly slim, extra-long filtered pals I packed along on the ride of my life. They added a lift to good days and took the edge off bad ones. Like many women, I was a social smoker. But what began as a social habit had morphed into an antisocial one. I am ashamed that I still smoke at all when everyone else I know has long ago kicked the habit. I know it will be easier to quit once and for all if I curtail my drinking.

I burn a bit of sage in my abalone shell and smear my forehead with ash to mark the start of my period of abstinence. The first Friday night without wine is hard: work has wrapped up, the kids are out and I am making a nice dinner, listening to music, ready to relax. The phantom drink is a palpable absence. I overcompensate for the days of deprivation by downing almost an entire bottle of wine that first Sunday. The hammering in my head the next morning pounds the message home.

I figure I'll have more success if I conscript others to join me in my Lenten challenge, so I create a private Facebook group. Within a few days forty people have signed on. Two weeks in, one of the members posts that she no longer misses the glass of wine she used to have every day at 5:00 p.m. on the dot. Another member is finding the no-booze challenge impossible and decides to give up. As for me, by the second week I am sleeping more soundly than I have in years. I wake in the morning feeling clear-headed and energized. I've also stopped my late-night snacking on guacamole and chips, nuts or cheese and crackers, a habit when my defenses are down after a few drinks. Three weeks in, I brace for the deprivation I'm sure I'll feel during late-night confessional conversations over topped-up glasses of wine when I head off to a long-planned weekend getaway with girlfriends. To my surprise, I manage to breeze through it, buzzing on the pleasure of being in the company of lively friends. Never before have I said no to alcohol in that kind of social situation. It feels like progress.

Members of the Facebook group provide updates on how they're faring, sharing tips for non-alcoholic drinks and stop-drinking strategies—everything from thinking of cravings as a wave with a crest and a fall to mentally superimposing the skull-and-crossbones symbol for toxic substances over the image of a favourite drink. One person is stunned when he figures out what his long-term drinking has cost him over thirty years: about $60,000. Another feels she's being a better role model for her teenage daughter. We confess when we fall off the wagon by sipping champagne at a birthday party (that's me), throwing back a couple of beers to celebrate winning a sailing race or having a swill of Scotch on a cold night. Every Sunday I allow myself two glasses of wine. It always tastes like more.

Maybe I can boost my chances of long-term success, I think, if I meet other drinkers who are trying to stop. That's how I find myself one Monday morning sitting in an orange plastic chair and drinking lukewarm coffee from a styrofoam cup at my first ever Alcoholics Anonymous meeting in my city's gritty east end. To my mind at least, a cloud of shame seems to hang over the room full of thirty people who talk about their "character defects," the importance of taking a "fearless moral inventory" of their misdeeds and "surrendering to a higher power." A man who looks like he could be in a motorcycle gang says he has done such terrible things he can't even tell his sponsor about them. Another, who's been sober for twenty years, speaks of the relief he feels now that his binging days are over. "AA might not get me into heaven, but it sure got me out of hell," he says. It's as though he's channelling Rumi when he compassionately describes the new AA arrivals who walk through the door: "I see the tombstones in their eyes."

Sobriety coins representing the amount of time everyone has remained sober are handed out at the end. Ever the keener, I step forward to collect a silver coin and receive a big round of applause. But I feel like a phony, especially at the end of the meeting when everyone holds hands and says the Lord's Prayer. When I leave the meeting, a man comes running after me down the street. I'd forgotten my sobriety coin on the table. He pushes the plastic keepsake into the palm of my hand and I put it in my coat pocket.

All of the God talk at my first meeting turns me off, but then I discover there are ten agnostic AA groups in the Toronto area. In 2017 they settled a three-year Ontario Human Rights Tribunal challenge against the AA organizing body, which tried to stop them from offering a secular interpretation of the twelve-step program. I discover a decidedly different demographic from my previous meeting at the We Are Not Saints agnostic AA meeting I attend. The two dozen people who assemble at a Toronto Unitarian Church are well heeled, outfitted in Patagonia jackets, Gap sweaters and expensive footwear. But their problem is the same. It's St. Patrick's Day, and several people talk about how, in years past, they would have spent this night in a bar, not a church basement. An atheist social worker just out of rehab says he's thankful this meeting doesn't reference a higher power. He doesn't need God, he says. What he needs is other people: "I cannot connect to myself unless I can connect to others. I need you guys."

Larry Knight is also here. Sober since 1993, he's the guy who launched the human rights challenge against AA after realizing many of his non-Christian friends weren't comfortable talking about their addiction in religious terms. He seconds what the social worker says: "When we aren't connected, we get sicker. When we are connected, we get better." I see the truth in his words. Drink can make us sick. But so can loneliness. I ask myself the question again: Do I have a problem with alcohol? Some of the folks in this room share stories of things I've never experienced: days-long benders, jobs and relationships lost due to drinking, rehab. But I'm reminded of Dr. Brown's warning about how drinking is progressive, and how mid-life women are especially vulnerable. I may have more in common with the people here than I'd like to admit.

Larry's been dry for over twenty-five years. "I could never stop at two," he tells me. I don't want to give up drinking entirely, but I know that when I start on a third drink, there's a good chance it will lead to a fourth. I realize that unless I can stop at two drinks, maybe I shouldn't be drinking at all. Here in this room, among these people, I experience what feels like a communion of saints. It makes me think of the words of the Unitarian minister George E. Odell, who wrote, "We need one another when we are in despair, in temptation, and need to be recalled to our best selves again."

Perhaps that's what observing Lent does: recall us to our best selves. I had figured that giving up alcohol, even temporarily, would be like saying goodbye to a dear friend. Instead, I feel like I am spending less time with an old pal who was starting to drain me.

Some people take issue with the nonreligious reclaiming the ritual of Lent. "Lent is one of the most profoundly anti-humanistic features of Christianity . . . It's all about reminding ourselves of how depraved and sinful we are, and taking on added sacrifices so we can purify ourselves," writes Tom Flynn, executive director of the US Council for Secular Humanism. "If I've been a bad person, if I've harmed others, then it is ludicrous to imagine that the best way for me to try to make things right is to take on some arbitrary, unrelated privation."

I'm with Flynn on the pointlessness of self-flagellation to address a sinful nature I don't believe we have. But what if my drinking is standing in the way of me leading a more spiritual life? What if I'm hoping giving it up for a while will help me connect not with God but with myself? "We associate ritual with a major life passage, the crossing of a critical threshold, or in other words, with transformation," says the American writer and physician Abraham Verghese. Do I dare believe that transformation lies at the end of this year for me?

Photo on next page: Getting away from it all in a treehouse in Port Perry, Ontario.

April

The Quiet Centre

"Loneliness is the poverty of self; solitude is richness of self."
—*May Sarton*

I'VE NEVER BEEN VERY GOOD AT KEEPING QUIET. THE TEACHERS always said the same thing in my mediocre grade school report cards: "Anne talks too much in class." I had trouble shutting up then, and I have trouble shutting up now. I think a good conversation is as satisfying as good sex: expressive, energetic, definitely not one-sided, maybe a bit messy. And it should last longer than ten minutes. I can sympathize with the garrulous Anne Shirley of *Anne of Green Gables* who laments,

"I say far too much, yet if you only knew how much I want to say and don't, you'd give me some credit for it." It hurts when I bite my tongue.

This compulsion to fill the air with words started early. The first time I remember being disciplined by my mother was when I was five or six and repeatedly interrupted her, tugging at her skirt, while she was talking with a neighbour on the sidewalk outside our apartment. As soon as the neighbour walked away, my mother turned to me and snapped, "Don't *ever* do that again." I wasn't disciplined often, and all these years later I can still see the flash of anger in her eyes.

In Grade 7 at John Calvin Christian School I was hit for talking in class. Our teacher, an ill-tempered bear of a man, Mr. Torenvliet, executed a reign of terror on the classroom; his prescient Donald Trump blond combover fell dramatically across his beet-red face when he lashed out at his pupils. Once, he actually held the pint-sized John Schellenberg upside down by his ankles in one hand and slapped his face with the other because John had talked back to him. When poor John started crying, Torenvliet scoffed at his "crocodile tears." We students were stuck in our desks, helpless and dumbfounded, certain no one would come to our rescue; it was tacitly understood that parental permission for discipline had been freely handed to our teacher overlords because of the school's spare-the-rod-spoil-the-child ethos. That teacher was the first person I ever hated, maybe the only one. I challenged him the only way I knew how, wordlessly, by squinting my eyes in contempt whenever he looked in my direction. Maybe that's why he hit me when he caught me talking to my best friend, Margaret Van Andel, in class. He approached from behind, taking me by surprise, and walloped me across the head so hard I fell out of my desk and onto the floor. That night, it was my stepfather's face that turned beet-red when I told my parents what had happened. I can still picture him, ranting and pacing, his hand twisting around the black kitchen telephone cord as he yelled at Torenvliet: "Are you crazy? Who the hell do you think you are? Don't ever touch her again!"

Maybe my chattiness is a cultural legacy—the Dutch are generally known for their extreme extroversion. Or maybe it was a trait inherited from my biological father. Apparently he could talk anyone into anything. My mother used to describe him as "a real good talker," and she didn't mean that in a positive way. Years later, she'd say to me when we argued, "You're so good with your words. Just like him." In her eyes, it was a suspicious business, this being good with words.

My mom was only twenty-one when my father abandoned our family. She was left to raise me and my baby brother, spending the lonely evening hours reading library books and listening to plaintive songs from the Ray Charles *A Man and His Soul* double album my father had left behind. I don't remember ever seeing my mother cry back then, but I knew she was sad. My father's departure—from our family, our church and our small town—was a rare occurrence in 1965. It was the first divorce in our Canadian Reformed denomination of more than three hundred people, where families trotted out their broods of six or seven or eight children on Sunday mornings, filling entire church pews as proof of their obedience to the Biblical directive to be fruitful and multiply. It raised eyebrows too in our small town of Fenwick, population one thousand, where marital separation was about as rare as violent crime. My mother had no car, no TV, no means of support except for welfare (or mother's allowance, as it was diplomatically called back then) and odd jobs picking fruit and cleaning other people's houses. She didn't even have a bank account, keeping whatever cash she earned rolled up in elastic bands in the freezer section of our fridge. The rent for our two-bedroom apartment on the first floor of an old yellow clapboard house was $80. She got a discount for cleaning the upstairs apartment of the landlady, a lonely old woman named Mrs. Leopard, who would announce her arrival while coming down the internal staircase of the house by yelling out, "Yoo-hoo! Anybody home?" My mom and I would roll our eyes at each other and share a conspiratorial laugh.

I felt protective of my mom and didn't want to do anything to upset her. I worked on the charm, always ready with a smile, obedient and willing to do as I was told, whether it was helping to dry the dishes or going to bed on time. I sang "Jesus Loves Me" with gusto, convinced of the enduring approval of this substitute father figure, especially if I behaved like a good girl should. I was born and bred a people pleaser, outwardly directed, allowing others to project their personalities onto me to put them at ease.

Extroverts struggle with extended silence. Lulls make us nervous. We're prone to jump in to fill any awkward gap in conversation. We bloom in the company of others and droop like week-old roses if we go too long without human contact. I've lived on my own only once, for less than six months when I was a twenty-year-old fledgling reporter, before happily moving in with Jeff. Even today I don't care for my own company all that much. I overbook my weekends with social stuff. I turn on the radio as soon as I get in the car. I go for a walk with headphones dangling from my ears. It's a struggle to be still long enough to get through ten minutes of meditation.

It isn't just extroverts who have this problem. Noise increasingly invades our lives. Doom and disaster blare from twenty-four-hour news channels, and emails, social media channels and game screens compete for our increasingly divided attention. Our cell phones ping with persistent notifications. A study of students from Australia's Charles Sturt University found many young people fear the sound of silence because they have grown up with constant media-generated background noise. A 2017 study from Rhode Island's Brown University reported that meditation was disquieting for some participants because sitting in silence made them panicky.

All this discord is actually killing us. The World Health Organization says excessive noise seriously harms human health, and the effects of constant sensory input are devastating. Noise pollution is a modern plague that can lead to high blood pressure and heart attacks, not to mention hearing loss, insomnia, anxiety and depression. We can barely even recognize what silence sounds like anymore. Any kind of lull—whether it's waiting at the grocery checkout or hurtling up an elevator—makes us fidgety. We're too digitally connected to dawdle or daydream.

Even when all our gadgets are turned off, it can be difficult to still the chaos in our minds. Because it's not just external noise that distracts us. The internal chatter can be just as oppressive. And usually that chatter isn't very kind. Mine, for instance. That I'm a bad daughter for hurting my parents. When my kids roll their eyes or don't help around the house when I ask them to, the voice in my head tells me I'm not a good enough mom. When my marriage feels like it lacks the kind of intimate connection I long for, the voice tells me I'll never be truly loved. When I'm morose, the voice accuses me of self-pity. My inside voice is rarely on my side. I may have long ceased thinking of myself as a wretch in need of saving, but there are times when the sense of unlovability runs deep. Maybe this is the legacy of growing up in a fundamentalist religion that teaches you're born depraved. Or I could blame it on being born female. The average woman criticizes herself at least eight times a day, according to a 2016 British survey of two thousand women aged eighteen to sixty. (The most common zingers? "You're too fat." "Your hair is a mess." "Your belly looks big." Even, "You're not wearing enough makeup.") If we talked to our friends the way we talk to ourselves, we probably wouldn't have any friends.

I decide to enrol in a popular "Life Reboot" program run by Kimberly Carroll (who calls herself a "soul coach"). One of the first things Carroll addresses with our group, which meets at her home once a week for seven weeks, is the importance of positive self-talk. She says learning to speak more kindly to herself has had such a revolutionary impact on her personal growth that the first thing she now asks her coaching clients is, "How shitty is your inner dialogue?" In reply, most of them will first look down at the floor. Guilty. "Think about it this way," she says. "If you had a child and you told that child day in and day out how much they sucked, picked on everything they did or said, and were constantly beating up on them, do you think they'd feel encouraged to grow and take flight in life? Of course not. Instead they'd be in a corner rocking back and forth in the fetal position. Or one day they'd just start yelling, 'Screw you! I'm not going to do anything you want me to!' That's exactly what happens when we constantly beat up on ourselves. We either get stuck in that fetal ball or end up rebelling and sabotaging ourselves."

Carroll asks her clients to consider how a loving parent speaks, how they might be tender with their child, encouraging and playful, acknowledging the child's pain, soothing them and helping them look at things in a more positive light. If that child is doing something damaging to themselves or others, a loving parent will call them on it from a place of gentle concern rather than angry recrimination. "Every time you notice that you're beating up on yourself, you need to stop and ask, 'Would I treat my own child this way?' Then, tap into that energy of the loving parent in the way you speak to yourself. That might sound like: 'What's hurting you, my dear?' Or 'I will love you no matter what' or 'Let's figure this out together.'"

Deep-seated shame can be a legacy of harmful religion and represents "a turning against the self," according to psychologist Marlene Winell. She observes that self-compassion is difficult for those of us who have had the doctrine of original sin drummed into us from birth. "Recovering from this unloving assumption is perhaps the core task when you leave the fold. It's a discovery of great joy—to permit unconditional love for yourself and others."

For women, being overly self-critical is also a legacy of growing up in a sexist culture. Women aren't supposed to get too full of themselves or take up too much space, in our physical size, our personalities or our ability to accomplish things. The world is most approving when we stay small, compliant and humble.

I resolve to work on quieting the critic in my head. Internal criticism can be relentless, self-compassion elusive. It takes practice to speak more kindly to ourselves, but I hope it will mean I'll learn to enjoy my own company a little more. After all, who wants to live with a constant commentator who is always reminding us of the many ways we don't measure up? Not me. Not anymore.

ALONG WITH SHUSHING THE NEGATIVE VOICE IN MY HEAD, I AM eager to find ways to cultivate more quiet time. I can relate to the predicament of Kyo Maclear, who contemplates her unease with silence in her memoir *Birds Art Life*:

> I have come to realize that a lull is not just an occupational problem. It is an emotional, intellectual and existential one as well. If I ever find an answer, I figure I will feel less fatalistic about intervals, periods of unemployment or dormancy, fallow times. I might be easier on myself and engage in less-anxious behavior. I might achieve the kind of Zen serenity that allows one to sit with unresolved and sometimes aching emptiness, to feel the silence and immensity of the universe without being too rattled by it.

Silence can restore our energy and help us better understand ourselves. Our souls suffer when we are disconnected from ourselves. One way to restore the connection is by turning our attention inward.

There's lots of evidence that shows quiet time is a balm for the body and mind, boosting creativity and making us smarter and happier. A study on mice in the journal *Brain Structure and Function* found that two hours of daily silence can literally create new cells in the hippocampus, an area of the brain that helps us learn, remember things and regulate our emotions. Dr. Leo Chalupa, a neurobiologist and vice-president of research at George Washington University, has advocated for a national day of absolute silence that he says "would do more to improve the brains of all Americans than any other one-day program."

In *Zero Decibels: The Quest for Absolute Silence*, author George Michelsen Foy, overwhelmed by the incessant noise of New York City, escapes to the Parisian catacombs, visits Joseph Pulitzer's "silent vault" and spends an unprecedented forty-five minutes in the pitch-black interior of a Minnesota laboratory's anechoic chamber, which the *Guinness Book of World Records* calls "the quietest place on earth."

My quest for a little peace and quiet isn't quite as ambitious. I start with a sensory-deprivation chamber. It's a float tank, purported to expand consciousness and creativity, and it's back in vogue again after a surge of popularity in the hippie era and then a fall from favour during the '80s AIDS crisis because of (unwarranted) public health fears. Through endorsements from celebrities like comedian Russell Brand and actor Kristin Wiig, these water-filled pods are making a splash again. Practically every major city has float centres, and you can even buy your own personal tank (they range in price from $2,000 to more than $30,000). The Bright Float Pod, for example, is a sleek, modern sanctuary with a cavernous interior and piped-in sound. In Sweden, where there are more float tanks per capita than anywhere else in the world, bobbing around in water is considered so therapeutic that physicians are allowed to write prescriptions for time in the tank.

It's a fifteen-minute bike ride from my house to Zee Float, where owner Jay Ziebarth tells me his clients rave about how floating has changed their lives. "A guy came in the other day for back pain, and when he came out he said it was the most transcendent experience of his life," says Ziebarth. "Some people see visions, and others go back to their early childhood memories." I strip down and shower in a room called the Oasis that features a chamber about four feet tall and two feet longer than a coffin. I climb in gingerly and lie down in nearly three feet of water that's been heated to body temperature and saturated with four hundred kilograms of Epsom salts, making it twice as buoyant as the Dead Sea. The closed container blocks all light and sound, although there is the option of letting some light in by keeping the door open. I opt for total blackness and settle into my liquid cocoon, swirling my hands through the water, gently pushing off from the wall with my toes, stretching my limbs into a pentagram. At first my mind reverts, as always, to my cursed to-do list. I have to pick up groceries for dinner, pay my cell phone bill, finish a piece for tomorrow's deadline and remember to check in with my daughter who's stressed about a university exam. I try to settle my mind by listening to the silence. It's so quiet I can hear my heartbeat in my ears and the gentle trickle of water as I slowly move my feet and hands. I'm naked in the dark, floating like a fetus in an amniotic pool of water. The last time I was in this position was probably in my mother's womb. I'd considered delivering my own babies in one of those hospital birthing pools. Now, I imagine each of my daughters emerging easily from my body, happily bobbing to the surface, instead of arriving the way they did, wailing into the hands of an anonymous doctor while I writhed in pain on a cranked-up hospital bed with Jeff standing beside me, anxiously twirling the hair on the crown of his head. I remember how scared I was giving birth for the first time at thirty-five. It must have been so much more frightening for my mother. She was only eighteen and alone, my father having been banished from the delivery room as men were back then.

There's nothing to do in this float tank but drift. Soon, incredibly, I lose track of time and space, and my mind stays blissfully empty. It's thought that time in the tank allows brain waves to transition from the logical beta state to the dreamlike theta state. Some people take years to achieve a deep theta state in meditation. "With floating, you can get there in forty-five minutes," Ziebarth says. The research is thin, but a meta-analysis of twenty-seven small studies indicates that float therapy has a positive impact on mood, blood pressure and stress levels.

I've brought a teenage friend of my daughter's with me, and when I finish my sixty-minute session, I learn she only lasted fifteen minutes. "I couldn't stand it," she says. "It was too quiet." Ziebarth says younger people often exit the tank early. There's a good chance they're suffering from nomophobia: separation anxiety from their phones.

SINCE MY QUIET EXPERIMENT WAS A POSITIVE ONE, I'M EAGER FOR A longer stretch of silence. I log on to Airbnb and book myself into a secluded treehouse a few hours from home. Never in my life have I gone forty-eight hours without talking to someone or tuning in to some sort of electronic device. This little getaway is the stuff of fantasy for a lot of working moms, the chance to be blissfully free of responsibility. I'm quite certain my family will not starve without me—of course they won't. Just to be on the safe side, I stock the fridge with a home-made lasagna and a pot of sweet potato soup.

Two days is hardly a monkish retreat, but it's something. I've long admired people perfectly content with their own company. Virginia Woolf, the pioneering feminist and great observer of everyday life, advocated "a room of one's own" (as well as a little money) for women if they are to be truly independent and creative. Emily Dickinson, a famous recluse, wrote 1,800 poems during her fifty-five years and didn't leave her property for the last two decades of her life. She spoke to visitors through doors and offered treats to local children by lowering a basket from her bedroom window. Mary Oliver, the beloved poet, found her solace and inspiration through hours-long walks in the woods. Woolf and Oliver had a shared secret torment that may have led them to seek out the solitary life: sexual abuse. Oliver was abused by her father,

Woolf by her older stepbrothers. There is scholarly speculation that some of Dickinson's poems also detail experiences of being violated.

Isolation may have been a survival mechanism for these writers. But sometimes solitude doesn't offer any kind of solace. Being alone is hard when it's not by choice. Perhaps the worst kind of solitude is feeling that sense of aloneness in the company of others—with a self-absorbed friend, say, or in a marriage that's grown cold. Sometimes we stay in unsatisfying relationships because we believe that some company is better than no company at all. In his book *Waking Up: A Guide to Spirituality without Religion*, Sam Harris writes about the contrast between solitude as punishment and solitude as a path to enlightenment: "Even when forced to live among murderers and rapists, most people still prefer the company of others to spending any significant amount of time alone in a room. And yet contemplatives in many traditions claim to experience extraordinary depths of psychological well-being while living in isolation for vast stretches of time."

For company in my treehouse, I bring along two books: *Upstream*, Mary Oliver's last collection of essays, and *The Illustrated Walden*, a special bicentennial edition that documents Henry David Thoreau's retreat to a tiny cabin on Walden Pond in Concord, Massachusetts.

The main floor of the retreat I've booked has dimensions equal to Thoreau's ten-foot-by-fifteen-foot cabin, but that's where any similarity ends. Thoreau's abode, situated on his friend Ralph Waldo Emerson's property and made of white pine, cost him a mere $28 to build and contained only a bed, a desk and three chairs. My upscale cedar treehouse, an octagonal structure some six metres off the ground and encircled by towering pines, is situated on 121 hectares of private forest. It has a loft bed, skylights, a wraparound porch, floor-to-ceiling windows, a wrought-iron spiral staircase, a glass shower and a kitchen equipped with a gas stove, a microwave and long-stemmed wine glasses. It costs ten times a night what Thoreau paid in total for his humble home.

Like Thoreau, I also have a very large pond at my disposal. It's not nearly as big as the twenty-six-hectare Walden that Thoreau regularly canoed and bathed in, but it's crystal clear and spring-fed. I dip a toe in. In late April the water is frigid, and snaky-looking weeds line its edges, camouflaging what I suspect are leeches and water snakes.

Thoreau lived in his cabin for two years, two months and two days. My three days and two nights are paltry in comparison. Still, I've untethered myself from digital distractions—no TV, computer or tablet, not even a radio. Birdsong will be my playlist, the view of the swaying pines outside the windows my screen time. My phone is on standby in case of emergency, but I do not allow myself any texting, messaging, phone calls or random Google searches. It feels like a Quaker boot camp.

Thoreau advocated for having as few possessions as possible. "A man is rich in proportion to the number of things which he can afford to let alone," he wrote in *Walden*. I haul a knapsack, small suitcase, cooler, book bag, hiking gear, box of dry goods and cosmetics case (yes, I've brought a blow dryer) up the steps of the treehouse. I'm sure the great naturalist, who mocked those "who can hardly venture to go a-huckleberrying without taking a medicine chest along," would disapprove of my inability to pack light.

Nevertheless, I commit to spending my time much as Thoreau did: hiking, reading, journalling and daydreaming. I pack a small knapsack for a long walk in the woods. I come upon a screened-in gazebo where I while away several afternoon hours with a book in my lap—something I haven't done in years—until a liquid drowsiness pours over me and I head back to the treehouse, climb to the loft bed and settle into a drooling, intoxicating slumber. When I awake, there's nothing to do but read some more. The branches of the evergreens outside of the window glimmer in the sunlight, seeming to offer up lush applause, as if saying, "Good for you!" I have no deadlines, no demands on my time and no dishes to clean except a single fork and plate. Nobody needs me, and it feels great.

I keep virtuous hours: 10:30 p.m. to bed and 6:30 a.m. to rise. I rely on nature's cues: the croaking bullfrogs trumpet the dinner hour with a sound like a rubber band being thumbed, and when the inky outline of trees disappears into the dark I climb into bed at the end of the day. The silence amplifies sounds I normally wouldn't notice: the click-click-click-hiss of gas from the stove when I make my tea, the slight rustle of a book page turning. "The quieter you become, the more you can hear," says the mystic poet Rumi. I notice the absence of sound, too; the futon I'm sleeping on doesn't squeak the way my mattress does at home. I try to distinguish the songs of birds. I can recognize the harsh caw of the redwing and the owl's haunting hoot, but I can't identify who is responsible for the merry tin whistle and soft warble in the distance.

I deeply examine whatever presents itself: the tiny ant crawling around my upper arm when I'm sunning myself on an Adirondack chair, the deposit of small pebbles (what I assume is raccoon poop) outside my deck door in the morning, the skittering water bug sliding back and forth in a small stream as if looking for some kind of opening. Mary Oliver wrote that she believed the soul is built completely out of attentiveness. It's not until I'm quiet and alone that I realize how much I usually miss in my everyday life.

Meals mark the morning, noon and evening. I make a simple dinner of comfort food—Campbell's tomato soup and a tuna sandwich, taking my time mashing the fish, adding a teaspoon of mayonnaise, cutting an onion fine, adding celery, salt, pepper and a dash of curry. I savour it as if it were a four-star feast. I think of all the time-consuming meals I've made for my family over thirty years of marriage and twenty years of parenting. I did the math once. It came to ten thousand meals. Mostly, I was happy to do this. I puréed baby food, marinated tofu and peeled potatoes. I sent my daughters to school with sandwiches wrapped in neatly folded wax paper. I lit candles every night at dinner because I believed the supper hour held special curative powers that would both bond our clan and keep vitamin deficiency at bay. But sometimes I hated it, too. I hated it when no one came to the table when I repeatedly hollered, "Dinner!" like a fishwife from the bottom of the stairs. I hated it when my kids argued practically *every single night* about doing the dishes. Once, my husband put a pizza in the oven upside down in what I took as a purposeful act of culinary sabotage so I'd stop asking him for help. I wanted my family to pitch in, but it was tough to convince them since I had done everything for years. I was the one who continued to cut up apple slices for my kids as a bedtime snack well into puberty. I was the one who elbowed my husband out of the way when he burned the eggs.

Sometimes I wonder if I spent too much of my life in front of the stove. I am not a fancy cook—I've never made risotto or a béchamel sauce. Essentially, I prepared the same seven dinners for decades. But I rarely missed a meal. In my mind, I was a great and powerful kitchen magician, Oz in an apron, waving a spatula so the smell of home cooking wafted through the house, a protective potion against the ills of the world. I don't think my children will remember much about my food when they leave home. I don't have a signature dish like my mother's seven-layer salad or my mother-in-law's beef bourguignon. But I hope they'll carry with them a sense of belonging that comes with having a seat at the table and nourishment from more than the mashed potatoes. The philosopher Emerson said, "I cannot remember the books I've read any more than the meals I have eaten; even so, they have made me." Even Thoreau's mother was known to bring dinner to his cabin in the woods.

On my last day, I lie on my back on the grass beside the pond and dreamily make out shapes in the cotton-ball clouds in the sky. A swallow zooms in to dip its tail in the water just a few metres away. In the late afternoon the sun is still bright enough that I need to shade my eyes, but the sky also holds the faint outline of a half-moon. The sun and moon appearing together is an everyday miracle that I rarely stop to notice. "Attention," wrote Oliver, "is the beginning of devotion."

As I get in the car to head home, I turn on my phone. There's a message from my husband asking if I've managed to survive my own company. There's a text from one of my daughters asking if I can transfer her some money. A couple of friends have checked in. It feels good not to be forgotten.

Even Thoreau, cast inaccurately as a hermit divorced from the world, needed to connect with others. He writes in *Walden* about making the thirty-minute stroll into Concord from his cabin every other day or so "to hear some of the gossip . . . which, taken in homeopathic doses, was really as refreshing in its way as the rustle of leaves and the peeping of frogs." I could easily have spent a few more days here without feeling lonesome, and that revelation comes as a surprise. But I've missed my daughters, and I'm looking forward to weekend plans with friends. As I drive away from the treehouse, I'm thankful there are people to whom I can return.

Photo on next page: Channelling Thoreau at Walden Pond.

May

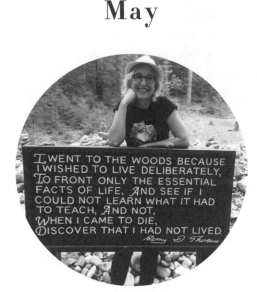

Into the Woods

"It is not so much for its beauty that the forest makes
a claim upon [our] hearts, as for that subtle something,
that quality of air, that emanation from old trees, that so
wonderfully changes and renews a weary spirit."
—*Robert Louis Stevenson*

I'M TAKING A WALK IN THE WOODS, BUT IT'S NO ORDINARY WALK.
It's an excursion in forest bathing, a slow and deliberate stroll—covering perhaps half a kilometre over three hours—designed to enhance well-being through connection with the natural world. You don't have

to get naked for this particular type of immersion. Since this is not an energetic stride in the woods, it's more meander than march. There's no point bringing a Fitbit. Ben Porchuk, one of Canada's first certified nature therapy guides, who is leading our group of four, says talking to trees is also part of the experience. Not only does he want us to actually introduce ourselves to a tree, he wants us to *ask it a question.* Outwardly, I act like I'm game, but I'm already thinking: *awkward!* Turns out, though, that you never know whom—or what—you might befriend in the forest. "We've lost our intimacy with the natural world, and this is a way to get that connection back," says Porchuk. "The guide simply opens the door. The forest is the therapist."

Forest bathing (literally translated from *shinrin-yoku*) began in Japan in the 1980s as a way to calm stressed-out urbanites. The Japan Forest Society, which oversees more than sixty certified bases, has poured millions into forest-bathing research to demonstrate how it can calm the mind, lift the soul and decrease blood pressure. The idea is catching on elsewhere, too: the US Parks Rx program encourages doctors to prescribe time in nature to improve physical and mental health. A host of clinical studies proves that a simple stroll under a lush green canopy helps us drop our worldly woes the way a maple sheds its leaves in the fall. That's because trees emit the natural pharmaceutical phytoncide, an essential oil that protects them from germs and insects. It's the serotonin of the forest. Its mechanism of delivery? Deep inhalation.

Porchuk begins our walk through Toronto's 70-hectare Sunnybrook Park with a pagan prayer ("Holy Mother in whom we live, move and have our being / From you all things emerge and unto you all things return") and then asks us to recall a favourite childhood "sit spot" in nature. As a boy, his favourite sit spot was a log that had fallen across a creek on his family's farm. "I could look down and see the fish spawning. It was so peaceful," he tells us. This makes me remember how, during the tender and trying years from eleven to fourteen, I used to ride my powder-blue ten-speed to a stream beside a remote gravel road a few kilometres from the house my stepfather built for us in the country after he and my mother got married. There, under the graceful arms of a willow, I would daydream and write poetry. It was my own secret garden, a place where I could be alone with my thoughts. Sky Maria Buitenhuis, co-founder of the Global Institute of Forest Therapy, says a sit spot is something most of us have lost in our adult lives. "We often believe we can think or worry our way out of a problem, but what we really need is quiet time in nature so that our inner wisdom and intuition can arise."

Porchuk plays a wooden flute as we wander through the park, leading us through a series of "invitations." In one called Notice of Motion, he sends us off wandering for fifteen minutes, telling us to look for any type of movement in nature. As I poke around some bushes, I spot a couple of flitting damselflies and get so close I can see their shadows dancing on a broad leaf. I look up and catch sight of the tops of a bank of elderly pines swaying languidly as if saying, "What's your hurry?" Below us, the Don River maintains its eternal movement, crashing into jutting rock and stone, its surface punctuated by whirling commas and curlicues.

During the Pleasure of Presence exercise, we are instructed to stand perfectly still to experience the forest through all of our senses. When Porchuk suggests we stick out our tongues to see if we can taste anything, I notice the tang of morning coffee lingering in my mouth. When I open my eyes, I catch sight of a single dewdrop glimmering so brightly on the tip of a leaf I can see it from two metres away. How like that dewdrop we are, I think, so often trembling and hanging on for dear life.

When it's time for Introduction to a Tree, our group links hands and walks across a rocky stream to a small sandy shore. I take off my shoes, lie down and put my feet in the cool water while I survey the party of trees gathered before me. I pass over the spindly-looking one that's clearly suffering from drought and settle on a tall, muscular oak with a crown full of leafy branches. I stare at it for a good long time—its dark base rooted in the dank soil and its quivering leaves some thirty metres in the air. As I prepare to officially greet this tree, a name pops, unbidden, into my head: Tree of Darkness and Lightness. The oak survives thanks to the black earth and the bright sunshine. It needs both. I remember Porchuk's directive to ask the tree a specific question. Any self-consciousness I expected to feel has been shed. It helps that no one is watching. Not one for small talk, I go deep: "How do I make my life matter?"

I study the oak's half-dozen large branches, each with a cluster of smaller branches that in turn sprout dozens more leafy offshoots. My chin is tilted upwards, my hands open, my head empty. My heart feels full, sitting here before this tree. Incredibly, the Tree of Darkness and Lightness sends me a message. Or maybe the message is just from me. Does it matter? The tree is showing me there's no single way to make my life meaningful, no solitary achievement. Rather, there are dozens— hundreds—of ways to do it. Every tiny offshoot represents a decision, a conscious action—the choice to have children, to make art, to work hard, to connect with others, to perform some act of kindness, to say or do something in the face of fear. In all my life I've never talked to a tree. I've never hugged one either, but that's what I do now, spreading my arms in gratitude around its trunk, resting my cheek against the rough bark. It feels like we're related. Trees give us so much: oxygen, shelter, shade. They're always providing for others, like a mighty mother offering consolation. Through some alchemy of person-to-perennial connection, this tree has passed some of its wisdom on to me.

Our forest-bathing session ends with a ceremonial tea made from plants Porchuk has been collecting during our walk, including eastern hemlock, white cedar and nuts from the American beech, which, he explains, is the only lightning-resistant tree in the world. A skilled wildlife biologist and ecologist, he has no trouble telling the difference between a hickory and a hawthorn. I can barely distinguish a fern from a fig leaf. In spite of the advancing years, I'm still a seedling with a lot to learn.

PORCHUK ALSO LEADS EXCURSIONS IN WHICH HE TEACHES PEOPLE
how to scale trees. "Tree climbing gives us new vantage points, opens
our hearts to joy and playfulness, and reconnects us to the value of
measuring every step in life as though it is our last," he writes in his
blog, *Lost and Found in Nature.* He recounts the story of a sixteen-
year-old boy with ADHD who climbed a Norway spruce during one of
his sessions. "His mom had died ten years earlier, and when he asked
for a sign from her, the tree told him to go higher. While he was swaying at the top, he received a message—she told him she was proud of
him and was supporting him as much as she could. When he shared
this with the group, the other kids stood up in tears and embraced him."

City trees can also be healing agents. In 1984 renowned researcher
Roger Ulrich published a seminal study that found that hospital patients
who could see trees outside their window had shorter stays and took fewer
pain medications than those viewing a brick wall. Those results have
held up when tested by others, including a recent University of Chicago
study of more than thirty thousand Toronto residents, which found that
people feel better and have fewer health problems when they have more
trees on their street. *The Tree Climber's Guide,* in which author Jack
Cooke details his year spent climbing eighty trees in London, England,
sparked a bidding war among publishers. Cooke's book enthusiastically
promotes the idea of adults climbing trees. Doing so, he says, offers a
fresh perspective on life and connects us to the natural world in a pri-
mal way, much like a chimpanzee swinging on a branch. To address the
fear of heights, he suggests starting with trees such as oak, ash, pine and
cedar that offer "ladder-like ascents on firm boughs." Self-consciousness
may be trickier to manage. There's the perception that climbing trees is
"just not what grownups do," he writes. "An adult in a tree is [considered]
either drunk, deranged, suicidal—or a combination of all three."

As I'm reading Cooke's book, I recall an incident from when I was about five. My mother had hired a professional photographer to come to our home to take a family photo. It was going to cost her $25, a fortune back in 1967, but she wanted to document our new family configuration—the three of us, my mom, my brother Henry and me—now that my father was gone. Before the photographer arrived, I wandered through an apple orchard far behind our house. It was the end of September, and the trees were ripe with fruit, the ground below them strewn with rotting apples. I grabbed the low branch of a tree, hoisted myself up, and found a broad beam to settle on. I picked some apples within arm's reach and threw them as far as I could.

When I heard a crackling sound down below, I realized I wasn't alone. An older boy was standing there, staring at me. I didn't recognize him from the neighbourhood. I got a bad feeling and thought about yelling for my mom, but she was too far away. When I looked at the boy again, he was undoing his belt. His pants dropped to the ground, and I could see he wasn't wearing underwear. His body was white, except for the dark place where something was sticking out, and his hand was on it, moving back and forth.

I jumped, fell, rolled, got up and ran. A branch cut across the bridge of my nose, and when I got home I was bleeding. My mom was upset. I was supposed to be neat and clean for the family portrait. I told her I'd fallen out of a tree but nothing else.

After I'd washed up and put on a dress, I joined my mother and brother on the couch. The photographer asked us to smile, but it was as though I'd forgotten how. My mother looked at me. "Come on, smile," she said. And I did. I still have a copy of that photo, and every time I look at it, I wonder about the impulse that stops children from telling the truth about what happens to them. Shame is embedded early.

That was the last time I climbed a tree, but maybe I can reclaim the experience. Is it unbecoming behaviour for a fifty-five-year-old woman? I decide not to care. Robert Frost, after all, said that "one could do worse than be a swinger of birches."

I head out into the woods near my house and find a perfect "entry-level" climbing tree, a low old oak. It has two large trunks splitting off diagonally at its base and requires more scampering than climbing to reach a spot where I can perch myself among the branches. Below me, there's a nest of rotting crab apples on the ground, along with a torn condom package. (Apparently, I'm not the only one who has sought repose here.) Above me, the birds are in full choir mode. The branches of dozens of tall trees around me stretch toward the sky in eternal optimism. I feel connected to everything. I'm no longer lithe-limbed, but up here in this tree I feel young again.

A LAPSED UNITARIAN, HENRY DAVID THOREAU CHOSE THE WOODS over the church, trading the hard pew of the cathedral for the spires of white pines. He believed the best cure for just about anything was being in the woods. He spent his two years at Walden Pond walking, playing his flute, writing in his journal and scrupulously examining every bit of flora and fauna. He had a scientist's eye and a poet's soul. He once told his young neighbour, Louisa May Alcott, who would go on to write *Little Women*, that a cobweb in the grass was really a handkerchief dropped by a fairy. The initial print run of *Walden* was two thousand copies, but in the years since its publication it's become a spiritual guide for millions, beloved for its indictments of modern society.

One of the resolutions from my April treehouse visit was to make the eight-hour drive to Concord to pay homage to Thoreau, whose ideas are as relevant now as they were 150 years ago. He's considered a major influence on modern ecology and the grandfather of the simplicity movement. Thoreau's presence is still felt in Concord, the small New England town half an hour from Boston where he lived most of his life. It attracts 700,000 visitors a year, many of them pilgrims who swarm the famous pond in summer, creating the kind of crowd Thoreau did his best to avoid. They head to the Walden Pond State Reservation to walk the 2.7-kilometre trail circling the 25-hectare pond and line up to see an exact replica of his cabin, its only furniture a bed, desk and three chairs ("one for solitude, two for friendship, three for society"). The Concord Museum houses 250 Thoreau artifacts, including his walking stick, flute and spyglass, as well as the simple green desk where he wrote each day. Thoreau quit First Parish, a Unitarian congregation, when he was twenty-three, preferring to spend his Sabbaths searching for chestnuts or leading a huckleberry party. Still, when he died of tuberculosis in 1862, the church honoured him by ringing its bell forty-four times, one for each year of his life. "Though it stings a little to realize that Henry did not want to join us, we have forgiven him his standoffishness because we like the other things that he did and said," Rev. Howard Dana preached from the pulpit of First Parish on the bicentennial of Thoreau's birth. "We like how his love of nature calls us to the woods ourselves. This favorite son, this wayward child, this prophet in our midst—this much-loved Thoreau—also represents a deep ambivalence towards organized religion that we also share."

First Parish stands in the centre of a town that's famous for two revolutions. It's the site of the first battle of the American Revolution—the notorious "shot heard round the world" fired between the British and local militiamen on April 19, 1775, on the North Bridge, now part of Minute Man National Historic Park. It's also the birthplace of transcendentalism, the nineteenth-century philosophical, spiritual and literary movement centred on a close-knit group of writers and intellectuals who represented the most original minds of their time. Led by Emerson, they included Thoreau, the educator Bronson Alcott, his daughter Louisa May Alcott, journalist Margaret Fuller and Nathaniel Hawthorne, author of *The Scarlet Letter*. The lives of this "genius cluster" were deeply intertwined, and this remarkable circle prompted the writer Henry James to call Concord "the biggest little place in America."

These great thinkers were also idealists. "To be yourself in a world that is constantly trying to make you something else is the greatest accomplishment," wrote Emerson. The transcendentalists believed morality was innate; that God is in nature rather than church and the real miracles were "the blowing clover and the falling rain," as Emerson put it. Instead of relying on biblical authority, they relied on themselves, insisting that spiritual truth is known intuitively rather than learned through institutions. "Make your own Bible," Emerson urged.

"The transcendentalists were responsible for introducing the distinction between religion and spirituality," says Rev. Barry Andrews, author of *Transcendentalism and the Cultivation of the Soul*. "Thoreau eschewed religious institutions, but was a deeply spiritual person. And this is one of the reasons that many people today find him so appealing. He may have been decried as a heretic and an atheist in his own time, but now he is viewed as the avatar of an alternative way of being religious in the world."

They were nature-loving dreamers, but the transcendentalists were people of action, too. Thoreau sheltered slaves on the Underground Railroad and gave speeches and published articles calling for the abolition of slavery. Margaret Fuller advocated for women's rights to work and to higher education. Bronson Alcott was a founding member of the Non-Resistance Society, which opposed all forms of violence, including killing animals for food.

In death, as in life, Thoreau's cluster of friends remains close. The transcendentalist movement faded when they died, but their graves are separated by mere metres in the section of Concord's Sleepy Hollow Cemetery known as Authors Ridge. Thoreau's tiny stone, marked simply "Henry," is a big draw for pilgrims who leave offerings of pine cones, rocks, pennies and notes inscribed with his popular sayings. They stab pencils into the earth around his headstone, a tender gesture to this pencil-maker's son whose written words have left such a lasting impression. From beyond the grave, "Thoreau speaks to us like a prophet," says Lori Erickson, who includes Walden Pond as one of a dozen sacred sites in her book, *Holy Rover: Journeys in Search of Mystery, Miracles, and God.* One of Thoreau's most important lessons, says Erickson, is that he proved one doesn't have to go far to be a pilgrim. "You can go to Jerusalem, but you can also go to the nearby woods."

My own pilgrimage to Concord ends at Walden Pond, a five-minute drive from Thoreau's grave. A few children scamper along its shore, and a couple of boaters cast lines into its clear depths. I pass a dozen or so hikers as I make my way around the pond's circumference to lay a stone, like many before, at a memorial cairn of rocks near the original site where Thoreau's cabin once stood. A large wooden sign proclaims his intention for his sojourn here: "I went to the woods because I wished to live deliberately, to front only the essential facts of life, and see if I could not learn what it had to teach, and not, when I came to die, discover that I had not lived."

There's nothing unique about the geography of Walden Pond. It is an ordinary place in nature made extraordinary because of the loving attention Thoreau paid to it. He often began his days here with an early-morning swim. "I got up early and bathed in the pond; that was a religious exercise," he writes in *Walden.* Standing on its shore, I consider Thoreau's particular talents: how he was so connected to nature that he could summon a woodchuck with a whistle and distinguish the calls of the wood thrush, the scarlet tanager, the field sparrow and the whippoorwill—all the "thrilling songsters of the forest." I'm startled when a heron flying overhead is followed a few minutes later by a trio of helicopters headed for the local airbase. Soon the air is still again. I brace myself for immersion and wade into the cool, refreshing water.

Photo on next page: My first solo. At my parents' wedding in 1971.

June

Finding My Voice

"Singing is a way of escaping. It's another
world. I'm no longer on earth."
—*Edith Piaf*

FOR MANY OF US, SINGING IN UNISON WITH OTHERS IS AS CLOSE TO
holy as we can get. Communal singing forms intense social bonds,
which is why it's one of the things people miss most when they stop
going to religious services. After my recent quiet sojourns in the woods,
I'm ready to raise my voice. The popular Choir! Choir! Choir! duo of
Nobu Adilman and Daveed Goldman is coming to town, with their

unique concept of gathering large groups of strangers to learn pop songs in three-part harmony. "The simplicity of it is kind of frightening in this day and age," Goldman said in an interview with the *New Yorker*. "You sell yourself short by connecting with ten thousand people in 140 characters over the Internet. People don't even go to movies anymore. People feel something in that room that we're in."

It's true. They do. I join about 150 people who have paid $5 each to sing Leonard Cohen's beloved ballad "Hallelujah," with its prayer-like incantation, its blaze of light in every lyric. For two hours we rehearse this song that conjures up a cast of Biblical characters, including King David, Bathsheba, Samson and Delilah, and draws a parallel between religious experience and what I've always assumed was Cohen's own adventurous sex life. The American singer Jeff Buckley, who covered Cohen's masterpiece, describes the song as a "hallelujah to the orgasm." Cohen himself explained it differently. "I wanted to push the hallelujah deep into the ordinary world," he said. "I wanted to indicate that hallelujah can come out of things that have nothing to do with religion." Carnal and sacred. Secular and spiritual. That's how it feels singing this erotic anthem alongside a bunch of strangers, our eyes glassy with emotion, the secret chord pulling at our secret places. No wonder the Choir! experience has been likened to a "choirgasm." At the end of the night I feel filled with wanton affection for every fellow songster in the room.

Singing is at the heart of all kinds of sacred traditions and gatherings, whether it's a religious service, a funeral, a campfire, a choir practice, a birthday party or a protest march. Singing unites us not only with each other but maybe even with some aspect of the divine. It can keep us in the present moment, transport us into the past, make heartbreak more bearable and lift us out of the mundane.

These days community singing groups like Choir! are popping up all over the place. There are queer choirs and Parkinson's choirs, homeless choirs, pop choirs, women's choirs, deathbed choirs and intergenerational choirs. In my neighbourhood, the Tuesday Choir, a weekly drop-in group, meets on the top floor of a pub called the Winking Judge. I arrive a few minutes late, put $5 in the donation bucket being passed around and scan the faces of the thirty or so people standing in a circle. Someone gives me a songbook, and I try to contain my ego and manage my fear. Turns out the tunes are familiar and easy to sing: "Jolene," "Wagon Wheel," "Ring of Fire," "Fifty Ways to Leave Your Lover." I don't even need to look at the song sheets. Initially, I barely open my mouth so no one will hear my wobbly efforts, but two hours in my self-consciousness is tossed aside like a bouquet thrown by a drunken bride. I'm swept up in the energy as the group belts out its final number, the Beatles' lyrically simple "Don't Let Me Down," written by John Lennon as a pleading love song to Yoko Ono. Despite the anguished nature of the song, I feel so much better for singing it. I came in here preoccupied, and now I feel free. When I leave the pub, I'm walking on air, just as Edith Piaf promised.

ALL THE FIRST SONGS I LEARNED WERE RELIGIOUS ONES. WHEN I sang "Jesus Loves Me" I did so with the conviction that I was indeed loved by the kind-faced, long-haired man in sandals and a white robe on the cover of *The Golden Children's Bible*. My mother taught me many songs in the same vein: "He's Got the Whole World in His Hands," "Jesus Loves the Little Children," "Jesus Wants Me for a Sunbeam" and "This Little Light of Mine," a favourite still. When I sang that song as a child, I wanted my light to shine bright for my mother. More than half a century later, it makes me think how dark the world can seem, how fragile our small candle, and yet how persistent our inner light can be.

Beyond the Bible tunes, there was "You Are My Sunshine," an eighty-year-old tune second only to "Happy Birthday" as one of the most popular pieces of music of the twentieth century. It was at once comforting and melancholy, and I remember my mother singing it to me often. Ray Charles had a hit with the song in 1962, the year I was born. I didn't realize then how much the lyrics about lost love must have resonated for my mother after my father left.

I lost my love for solo singing when I was nine. My mom asked me to sing the hymn "The Lord Is My Shepherd" on stage at her wedding to my stepfather at the local community hall. In the Canadian Reformed Dutch tradition, homespun wedding entertainment includes games, skits and songs, though no dancing. (Everything from the hustle to the hokey pokey is considered the work of the devil—or at least a possible prelude to illicit sex.) On that stage I discovered that singing into a microphone in front of 150 guests was an entirely different thing from singing into a hairbrush in front of my bedroom dresser. My prepubescent self sang earnestly, but I cringed at the sound of my thin, breathy voice, and self-consciousness settled on me like a dark cloud. It would be decades before I tried to sing solo again—at a karaoke bar when I was in my late forties. I hopped impulsively on stage to perform a favourite Beatles song, "Eight Days a Week," and instantly regretted it. Even though it's a simple song and I had the assistance of recorded music, I started in the wrong key and could not get back on track. I stumbled through my discordant delivery until friends jumped on stage to rescue me. I vowed then and there: no more solo singing for me. I stopped even singing in the shower.

One of my goals this year is to boost my vocal confidence. I book a singing lesson with Jocelyn Rasmussen, a London, Ontario, recording artist who has taught at Julliard. As she explains in her book *Meant to Be Heard*, her lifelong love affair with voice and music began when she was three years old and her father cut a section of railing off the outdoor steps of the family home so he could move a new upright grand piano into the sun porch of their farmhouse.

As I stand in front of Rasmussen's own grand piano in the rehearsal room of her elegant apartment, I feel much like the nervous schoolgirl I was at my parents' wedding. She gets me to warm up by singing primary vowels over and over: "Ahhh . . . Ehhh . . . Eeee . . . Oooo . . ." "Pretend you have a mango in your mouth," she instructs. I feel even more foolish as I open wide and make sounds around the fruit. But I repeat the warm-up until my cheeks practically start to vibrate, and then I'm surprised at what comes out—a ringing like the sound of singing crystal when you run a wet finger along its rim. Next we do the vocal workout: lip trills, humming, squeaking like Minnie Mouse and growling like an angry bear. All this helps to shape the articulators, stabilize the larynx and morph sound into song, explains Rasmussen. When she tells me I'm a mezzo, the most common female singing voice, it's a relief to finally know my musical identity. Lower than a soprano, higher than a contralto, being a mezzo puts me in the good company of Beyoncé, Ethel Merman and Madonna. Mezzos sing with sopranos, not altos, and when the two split up, mezzos tackle the lower melody. At the end of the lesson Rasmussen offers her assessment. I have a solid choral voice, but if I want to make it stronger, there's only one thing to do: practice. She suggests fitting singing into my life any way I can, including in the car ("no one's around"), along with the vacuum ("it has lots of overtones") and in the shower ("the bathroom has magnificent resonance").

Her final bit of advice: "Don't sing to be good, just sing for the joy of it."

As I leave her apartment she gives me a copy of her CD, *Singing Is Praying Twice*, which she produced for charity after being diagnosed with ovarian cancer. The CD features songs that helped her get through her treatment, including "The Serenity Prayer," "Abide with Me," "Amazing Grace," and "An Irish Blessing." I sing along with her CD on the ride home, and when it's run its course, I keep on singing, going back through my musical memory bank right back to those early songs my mother taught me.

"The only thing better than singing is more singing," said jazz great Ella Fitzgerald. I go in search of more singing.

A friend tells me about a new choir called Singin' Women that meets at the Good Shepherd Centre, a local social services agency offering emergency shelter, food and clothing for people in need. When I go to a regular Thursday night practice, there are about two dozen women there. Some of them have experienced homelessness or precarious housing. Others work in the social services sector or, like me, just live in the neighbourhood. No previous choral experience is necessary, despite the fact that the choir is run by Laura Thomas, a celebrated local musician who conducts two orchestras, leads two choirs and is the principal percussionist of a local symphony. Under her direction we spend most of the evening muddling our way through a complicated piece, "Begone Dull Care," based on an anonymous poem from the late eighteenth century. "It's the 'Don't Worry, Be Happy' of the English Renaissance," Thomas jokes. As I scan the faces around me, I have no doubt many of these women carry a load of care, but I can see that, right now, they are happy to be here singing together. I'd read the words of one of them, Anne Thompson, in an interview with a local newspaper about the new choir. "It's a great healer for me," she said. "Even when I'm at home feeling depressed or sad, it's the music that gets me. It's like taking my medicine."

A fear of singing badly and looking foolish stops a lot of us from engaging in one of life's most pleasurable pursuits. And that's a shame, because singing makes us feel better in just about every way. It lets our troubles melt like lemon drops, spiking dopamine, serotonin, oxytocin and other feel-good neurochemicals in the brain's pleasure centre, creating a flood of positivity even when we sing the blues. It boosts the immune system, improves sleep and increases our social connections.

In search of more of that good medicine, my friend Donna and I sign up for a weekend choral gathering at Unicamp, a Unitarian campground an hour and a half north of Toronto. We wake up early to chant before breakfast and sing a cappella under the midday sun on the dining room porch. Our group numbers about a dozen, and we go around the circle in a democratic fashion, each person picking a tune from a collated songbook. Once again, I'm taken aback by the big emotions that surface as I sing. I'm glad I'm wearing dark sunglasses, because the tears flow as I harmonize about going down to the river to pray and needing somebody to lean on and being captive on the carousel of time. These songs touch every emotional button like a run of notes on a scale. I get what the neurologist Oliver Sacks meant when he said music is the one thing that "can pierce the heart directly."

We finish our afternoon session with a rousing rendition of "I'll Fly Away," and this group of non-theistic Unitarians sings as rapturously as I imagine evangelicals would about flying off to a land where joy will never end. Hymns may be dated and dirge-like, filled with centuries-old sexist language and repressive concepts of sin and salvation, and offered up to a deity we don't believe in, but they can still hijack our emotions. Such songs bypass our normal skeptical reasoning and directly target the tender amygdala in our brain's limbic system, unleashing primitive feelings. "Amazing Grace" has the potential to shatter even a stubborn atheist. Maybe that's partly because these old melodies create an ache for the time when they first landed on our ears. I'm sure that's true for me. When I flash back forty years, I can see my mother standing beside me in the pew, dressed in her smart, for-Sundays-only shimmering grey mink, singing her favourite hymn, "What a Friend We Have in Jesus" with her eyes closed in a kind of rapture. I can picture my stepfather beside her, in his usual loud tie, singing "Abide with Me" in his tuneless yet enthusiastic voice. My parents only ever sang in church; what impressed me was that they seemed so full of feeling. "Where words fail, music speaks," wrote Hans Christian Anderson.

That evening at Unicamp our group forms a circle again, this time around the blazing flames of a firepit. We are far from the city, and the dark sky is bright with stars. We begin an impromptu singalong of favourite tunes from the '70s, when the mid-life members of our group were grappling with the mood swings of adolescence: Helen Reddy's "Delta Dawn," Three Dog Night's "Joy to the World," Terry Jacks' "Seasons in the Sun," the theme songs from *The Mary Tyler Moore Show* and *The Brady Bunch*. And the Coke commercial "I'd Like to Teach the World to Sing." The lyrics come back to us with stunning accuracy, which seems surprising considering most of us are in our fifties and prone to immediately forgetting the names of people we've just met. But in this perfect moment we are free-spirited fourteen-year-olds again, minus the acne and the insecurity, and anything seems possible.

THE PLAYLISTS OF OUR LIVES ARE PERSONAL. EVERY TIME I HEAR Stevie Wonder sing "Isn't She Lovely," I remember looking down at Ruby, my tiny firstborn, born a month premature. She weighed less than a bag of sugar and immediately took up all the space in my heart. I've listened to Elton John's "Benny and the Jets" hundreds of times, and every single time I do, it brings to mind my first fumbling kiss with Stephen Levasseur, the boy next door. I can sometimes still feel the phantom form of my daughter Lucy resting trustingly on my shoulder as I sang "I See the Moon," the lullaby that soothed her to sleep every night of her first few years. "It Had to Be You"? That song makes my chest squeeze because it was the one Jeff and I chose for the first dance at our wedding. "Sunday Morning Coming Down" brings on sadness and regret for the father I never knew—after his death I learned that Kris Kristofferson was his favourite singer. Certain songs in certain circumstances can practically bring us to our knees.

It's the songs of our youth that are wired most deeply into our psyches. This is why I can remember every word of Meatloaf's eight-and-a-half-minute "Paradise by the Dashboard Light" but can't name a single top Billboard hit from last year. Researchers and neuroscientists have discovered that these early songs leave such a lasting imprint because of the rapid neurological development that occurs during the dramatic years of puberty. Songs from their younger days can put a smile on the faces of old, cranky people, allowing happy memories to be accessed even by those with dementia. No matter how our tastes evolve over time, musical nostalgia connects us most strongly to the songs of our formative years.

Singing songs we love with others is an antidote to despair, and science proves it. In the world's first randomized controlled trial on community singing with depressed older adults, a year-long study by the Sidney de Haan Research Centre for Arts and Health at Canterbury University found that 60 percent of participants had markedly less mental-health distress a year after joining a singing group. Some no longer even met the diagnostic criteria for clinical depression. Could a prescription for singing be an effective remedy for a sadness of the spirit? The UK government thinks so. It's planning an innovative initiative called the National Academy for Social Prescribing, which will see doctors guide patients toward activities such as singing. "I don't sing because I'm happy," said the American philosopher William James. "I'm happy because I sing."

In a 2017 study, "Searching for Spirituality in the U.S.," the Public Religion Research Institute found music was the single most popular practice among Americans who describe themselves as spiritual but not religious. Even Kurt Vonnegut, the atheist writer and honorary president of the American Humanist Association, indicated he would like his epitaph to read: "The only proof he needed for the existence of God was music." For those who identify as SBNR, praise music doesn't cut it. Communications scholars at Brigham Young University found that for non-churchgoers, secular hymns fill the space that religious music once did. "While nonreligious in nature or intent," they write, "the secular hymn is a pop song that allows the listener to experience the numinous by creating an affective state that parallels a spiritual or religious state of mind." These songs don't preach or try to convert.

They acknowledge the difficulties of life and offer solace, and, like the enduring hymns of old, they encourage us to persevere. The secular hymn at the top of the researchers' list? Cohen's "Hallelujah." Other such spiritual anthems include "Somewhere over the Rainbow," "Don't Stop Believing," "Imagine," "What a Wonderful World," "Bridge over Troubled Water," "Let It Be," "Fire and Rain," "I Can See Clearly Now," "Lean on Me" and "Stand by Me." The perfect SBNR playlist.

Music gives full expression to all the emotions of our lives. But it may be most poignant in periods of grief. Kate Munger understood this when she founded the Threshold Choir, a small group of people who gathered to sing at the bedsides of the dying in San Francisco almost twenty years ago. The concept has since spread to 150 chapters throughout Canada and the US and involves thousands of volunteers who sing to those on the threshold of life as a way to ease their pain, anxiety and loneliness. "We sing very softly and quite close," Kate told *Reader's Digest* in an interview. "We're trying to re-create the distance between a mother's mouth and a baby's ear."

There isn't a Threshold Choir in Hamilton, but in nearby Toronto the Comfort Choir sings every Friday afternoon in the chronic care and palliative wards of a large Toronto hospital. It was co-founded ten years ago by Suzanne Maziarz, the music director of a Toronto Unitarian congregation, with a mission to "bring comfort, calm, spirit, and a soul-connection to the bedsides of patients." I join their group of four for an afternoon, donning a purple vest and toting a thick green binder with the music and lyrics to everything from folk songs to hymns and pop tunes. Before we venture down the fifth-floor hallway, we gather in a quiet room where we close our eyes for a few minutes to centre ourselves in preparation. "Let's remember this may be the last song they hear," says Maziarz. She will gently knock on the door of each room to check whether the patient or any visitors present would like us to sing, she explains for my benefit. If a patient requests a song that's not in the binder, the choir will make a point to learn it and perform it the following week. (Unusual requests have included "Black Hole Sun" by the rock band Soundgarden and Paul Anka's "[You're] Having My Baby.")

I have not been up close with death and suffering very often, and I'm not prepared for what I see. Several of the patients in the chronic care section are unconscious, kept alive by machines attached to their windpipes. The first woman is about my age. Her eyes are closed and her mouth hangs slack. She is missing several teeth, and as we gather around her bed I can see from the outline of her form under the covers that she is also missing her legs from the knees down. A car accident, I wonder? Her blue hospital gown is thin, and I can see one breast is gone. Breast cancer. So many missing pieces. But the window ledge in her room is full—there are plants in bloom, cards and photos from another life. In one she looks vibrant and carefree, standing on a tropical beach with what I assume is her grown son and a grandchild. There's a Mother's Day card addressed "To a Special Mom." I naively hope for some slight movement in her face as we sing, but it doesn't come. I don't know what's happened to this woman, but I do know she is loved.

As we enter the room of a patient who looks to be in her early forties, her elderly mother is standing next to her bed. "Yes, please sing," says the mother, and we launch into a short selection. The mother never stops touching her daughter, patting her shiny black hair, adjusting the cotton padding around her trach tube, lifting her hand to check if her daughter's already perfectly manicured fingernails need further trimming. When we finish our last song the mother claps her hands and looks brightly over at her daughter, but there's no response. Afterward, I'll learn that the daughter has been in hospital for seven years, nonresponsive for the last few. At first I wonder why the parents have kept her artificially alive. But then I imagine that this is one of my daughters, in a silent coma for years, her heart still beating, fingernails still growing, still needing her mother, her mother still needing her.

Machines hiss and beep as we make our way from room to room. Wheelchairs crowd the hallways, and some rooms have a foul smell. In the palliative care ward we find a woman, toothless and tiny, dwarfed under a big afghan. A small stuffed electronic dog on the table beside her yaps manically. She looks at the dog, then at us, then back at the dog with a blank expression. We sing a full-throated rendition of "Go Tell It on the Mountain" and I suddenly remember my mother at my Oma's nursing-home bedside as she lay dying almost twenty years ago, singing this hymn into her ear. I held Oma's hand and was shocked when she squeezed mine, as if in a final goodbye, because she had been unconscious for a couple of days. Today, when we wrap up our last song and say goodbye, a faint voice pipes up from under the afghan. "Thank you," says the woman. "Thank you."

As we head back to the volunteer room to put our vests and song-books away, we pass a large room with half a dozen elderly women in it, some in hospital beds and some bent over in wheelchairs. A young male orderly at one end of the room is holding an iPhone that's playing a tinny version of John Lennon's "Imagine." He's singing to the women, a few of whom follow along in quavery voices. When the orderly sees us, he invites us to sing for the group. We oblige, and some patients from the hallway also manoeuvre into the room. Soon there are patients all around us. Some clap their hands, some know all the lyrics, a few continue sleeping. One woman in a wheelchair raises her bent head every once in a while, looks at us, and moans. Some of these women are barefoot. Some have brightly painted toenails, which I take as a hopeful sign. Their legs are thin and fragile, like the limbs of schoolgirls dangling from monkey bars. More women in wheelchairs are congregating in the hallway, jockeying like bumper cars, following the call of our voices. We've practically got a concert going on here. A middle-aged woman comes into the room and goes over to the moaning woman in the wheelchair—she strokes her thin, grey hair and whispers gently into her ear, which quiets her momentarily.

There is certainly despair here, among those who are confused and feeble and dying, but there is love, too. Music soothes us at the beginning of life and comforts us at the end. It achieves the miraculous task of simultaneously expressing our suffering and offering solace.

Our little choir moves into the hallway because the room is getting overcrowded. As we line up against the wall, the moaning woman gestures to her daughter to move her wheelchair closer to us. As we sing she begins to mouth the words slowly. In her confused and innocent face I can imagine the young girl she once was. And also the old woman I'll become—if I'm lucky enough to live another thirty years. All these mothers and daughters administering so tenderly to each other makes me think of my own mother and what it will be like for her at the end, whether she'd want me to stroke her hair. I think of my daughters and how I hope they'll outlive me by decades. How I hope I can hold their hands when my time comes. How I hope there will be music to mark my ending. Maybe even "This Little Light of Mine," the song my mother once sang to me. That would be a comfort, I believe, as my particular candle goes from a flame to a flicker and then is extinguished. If we're lucky, our lives begin with someone singing to us and end that way, too.

SOON AFTER THIS EXPERIENCE I RECEIVE AN UNEXPECTED INVITA-tion that arrives by email: a week-long, all-expenses-paid "singcation" on the rugged coast of the North Atlantic in Newfoundland. It's from Susan Knight, the founder of Growing the Voices, a non-profit dedicated to getting people to sing more. The group hosts an annual singing retreat called Come All Ye, held in the village of Port Rexton. This year they have received a small grant to pay for a journalist to report on the singing retreat and help publicize it. Would I like to come? Definitely. A few weeks later I'm on a plane for the three-hour flight to St. John's, and then it's another three-hour drive to Port Rexton. Here our group of thirty or so singers will sleep, eat and rehearse at Fisher's Loft, an isolated and elegant inn that played host to luminaries Dame Judy Dench, Julianne Moore and Cate Blanchett when they were here to film the 2002 adaptation of Annie Proulx's Pulitzer Prize–winning novel, *The Shipping News*, shot among the foggy coves and picturesque seascapes of the area known as Trinity Bight.

When I have dinner with Susan Knight the evening before the retreat, she explains that when her seventy-eight-year-old mother was dying of cancer thirty years earlier, Knight asked her if she had any regrets. "That I was a mute in a household of songbirds" came the reply. It was at that moment that Knight, a celebrated choral director and chancellor of Newfoundland's Memorial University, learned that when her mother was six years old, a nun had pronounced her tone deaf and instructed her to stand in the back row of the choir and simply mouth the words. "All five of my mother's children loved to sing, and all four of her siblings sang, but she never did," says Knight, who is still angered by the memory of her mother's voice being silenced. "There are so many people who can tell you with great clarity the exact moment they began to believe they couldn't sing." I nod, thinking back to my nine-year-old self at my parents' wedding. To honour her mother, Knight made it her life's mission to help people discover or recover their ability to sing.

Self-diagnosed bad singers are never as inept as they think, Knight tells me. In fact, only a tiny portion of the population has congenital amusia, the technical term for the innate inability to hear pitch properly. "We are born with the developmental capacity for singing," says Knight. "It's an essential part of the human condition." She believes the world would be a better place if we all sang more.

The retreat is designed for insecure non-singers like me. The first lesson our music director, Doug Dunsmore, teaches us is simple: "When in doubt, open your mouth." Specifically, we should be able to stack two fingers on top of each other between our teeth as we sing, because this immediately helps improve vocal range. And keep your tongue soft, he instructs. Use your eyebrows to animate your face. His many singing instructions double as sound advice for life: "Be sure to breathe." "Stand tall." "Don't let yourself get small." "Do it over and over until you get it right." "If you screw up, just keep going."

For the next few days we open our mouths wide and then spend hours practising the repertoire of Broadway show tunes, Beatles hits and rousing Newfoundland folk songs that we'll perform in front of a live audience at the historic Garrick Theatre in nearby Bonavista. Dunsmore assures us there's no need to be nervous. "Anyone can sing," he insists. "It's 90 percent brains, 10 percent talent." I'm not so sure. I've spent almost a lifetime thinking my voice is as monotonous as the lonely foghorn outside my bedroom window.

There are a handful of pros assisting our group, including Julia Halfyard, who has performed across Canada as a professional cabaret singer. She's sympathetic when I confess my trepidation about performing on stage. "Singing is such a naked experience, and when you're naked you tend to be judgemental about yourself," she says. Ted Rowe, a member of Crooked Stovepipe, the oldest bluegrass band in the province, advises me to focus on connecting with my fellow choristers and not worry about the audience. "When you sing with others," he says, "you immediately create a bond that's lasting." This is something I'm beginning to understand. And I learn something new: people's heartbeats synchronize when they join voices. Communal singing offers one of life's rare opportunities for "truly sublime moments," says Dunsmore. "We're better together."

At the final night's performance, tears spring to my eyes, the way they have so often when I've been singing passionately with others. I get especially weepy during "You're My Best Friend." I'm overcome with a sweet connection of intimacy with my fellow songsters, strangers just days ago. Before our performance, someone in our group read us a few lines from *The Elegance of the Hedgehog* by Muriel Barbery: "There's this life we're struggling through, full of shouting and tears and laughter and fights and break-ups and dashed hopes and unexpected luck—it all disappears, just like that, when the choir begins to sing. Everyday life vanishes into song, you are suddenly overcome with a feeling of brotherhood, of deep solidarity, even love, and it diffuses the ugliness of everyday life into a spirit of perfect communion. Even the singers' faces are transformed."

I look at the flushed and happy faces that surround me here on what feels like the edge of the world. As our performance comes to a close, we strain together to reach the high notes of the final words of Leonard Cohen's "Anthem," the phrase about ringing the bells that's repeated eight times in a rising crescendo. There's a famous line in that song, about the crack in everything that lets the light shine in. My voice falters, but I carry on. It doesn't have to be a perfect offering. What matters is I've finally found my voice.

Photo on next page: Psilocybe cubensis, *the most popular species of magic mushrooms, also known as "Golden Teacher."*

July

Tripping

"Going to the grave without having a psychedelic experience
is like going to the grave without ever having sex. It
means that you never figured out what it is all about."
—*Terence McKenna*

AT FIFTY-FIVE I'M FAR TOO OLD TO BE GIVING BIRTH. AND YET HERE
I am, pushing my daughter out of my body. I lift my head, look down
and there she is—a delicate rosy sheen of a head emerging from
between my raised knees. There isn't even a split second of pain, only
searing joy. It's something I've always longed for—to go back in time

for just a brief moment and hold one of my babies again, fresh from the womb. My arms shake as I stretch them out toward her. I bring her carefully to my chest and look down in wonder, in love as if for the first time. There's something wet on her forehead. When I go to wipe it away, I see it's my tears, plopping down onto her face.

I slide my eye mask up to my forehead and glance around the room. There are three other women here with me. One is lying down like me, and the two others are watching over us. Pounding drum music, so loud I can feel it thrumming in my chest, blares from a speaker. I slide the eye mask back down and resume breathing fast and heavily, as we've been instructed to. I am desperate to return to my beautiful dream or trance or hallucination or whatever it was, back to the vision of my newborn's exquisite loveliness. But before long, I enter another world. In this one I'm travelling through a long, dark, winding tunnel.

I'm in this altered state of consciousness thanks to something called holotropic breathwork—a type of therapy featuring accelerated breathing and evocative music that leads to psychologically cathartic experiences. The materials I read in advance said you could enter a whole new realm—a "non-ordinary state of consciousness"—and relive key life experiences, both good and bad, simply by breathing intensely in this kind of guided setting. Apparently it was possible to have fantastic visions, unearth buried trauma, morph into an animal, visit past lives and, yes, go back to your own birth.

I'd arrived at my session smug and skeptical, convinced it was all quackery. There was no way this breathing stuff would work on me. I came out incredulous. This was unlike anything I'd ever encountered.

Allow me to backtrack.

Before I'd ever heard about holotropic breathwork, I was curious about ayahuasca, the powerful psychedelic brew made from indigenous vines and leaves that's been used for centuries in Amazonian religious ceremonies. Today thousands of Westerners, from footloose millennials to mid-life bankers, are spending millions on ayahuasca retreats to induce visionary states, spiritual epiphanies and psychological healing. Famous folks love the trippy tea. Sting claims it gave him his single most powerful spiritual experience. Actor Lindsay Lohan says it keeps her sober, and American TV host Chelsea Handler, who puked into a bowl on camera after taking ayahuasca at a retreat in Peru (the plant induces gut-wrenching vomiting and nausea), says it healed her relationship with her sister. It's not just celebrities who are enamoured of the "medicine." I'd had lots of regular folks tell me about life-changing experiences at ayahuasca ceremonies. My friend Rochelle, a forty-six-year-old nurse in Hamilton, said it helped break her addiction to busyness and perfectionism: "I was someone who never sat on the couch. Now I can enjoy just doing nothing." Dan, a thirty-seven-year-old Toronto actor, told me it helped him make amends with his alcoholic father. For Dan, "Taking ayahuasca over five hours was equal to five years of psychotherapy."

Sean's story also impressed me. At the time he sought out ayahuasca, he was a sixty-one-year-old physician who had everything he'd ever wanted: a happy marriage, a successful career and enough money to buy a small sheep farm in the Quebec countryside, where he planned to spend his retirement producing artisanal cheese. Still, the Peggy Lee tune that plagues angst-ridden baby boomers the world over kept looping in his head: "Is That All There Is?" In search of an answer, he flew to Mexico for a ten-day, $2,500 ayahuasca retreat led by Vancouver physician and addictions specialist Dr. Gabor Maté, author of the bestselling *In the Realm of Hungry Ghosts*. Maté used the illegal substance to treat addicts in Canada for two years before the government threatened to revoke his medical licence in 2011. Sean ingested ayahuasca and, after experiencing kaleidoscopic hallucinations that included fireworks, flowers with exploding tendrils and a sense that his heart was "a puddle of molten gold," he came to the realization that the world is a beneficent place. "I could see love everywhere . . . The plant gave me a glimpse that there is more meaning to the universe than I had comprehended before."

Where did I sign up? I called Maté to enquire if he would consider having a journalist attend one of the retreats he runs twice a year with a local shaman. But he didn't need the publicity—there was already a long wait list. Maté told me ayahuasca can be an "antidote to Western psychological distress and cultural alienation." Offering ayahuasca to people who are suffering is the most exciting work of his career, he said. "Properly used, it opens up parts of yourself that you usually have no access to."

You don't have to fly to an expensive foreign destination to try ayahuasca: there's a network of underground ceremonies offered right across North America. Tabitha runs one at an Ontario farm not far from where I live, charging groups of fifteen participants $250 each for dusk-till-dawn sleepovers. Ayahuasca offers such profound insights, she told me, that she's seen marriages saved, parents forgiven, anxiety lessened and passions pursued. One of her clients gave up his job in finance to become an acupuncturist after a ceremony. I was tempted to enrol, but leery about the prospect of barfing into a bucket in front of a group of strangers. I was not keen on the idea of having the runs simultaneously with fifteen other people, either. Then there were the bigger concerns. Two years earlier, a Winnipeg man had killed a British friend who attacked him during an ayahuasca-induced hallucination in Peru. I'd read reports of sexual abuse and negligence by unscrupulous shamans. Some argue ayahuasca's use by non-Indigenous people is also a form of cultural appropriation. When I spoke to Maté, he insisted the medicine itself is safe, free of the risk of overdose: "It isn't possible to take enough ayahuasca to kill you." Antidepressants, he said, are more dangerous. When I told him I was curious but nervous about taking a drug, he suggested a safe way to start my psychedelic experimentation would be with holotropic breathwork. "It has similar effects to ayahuasca," he explained. "Just make sure you find a trained practitioner."

Holotropic breathwork has its roots in ancient Indian and Tibetan yogic traditions. It experienced a North American revival in the '70s thanks to the pioneering efforts of Dr. Stanislav Grof. Grof was an assistant professor of psychiatry at Johns Hopkins University and chief of psychiatric research at the Maryland Psychiatric Research Center, where he studied the effects of LSD before his research was made illegal by the US government as part of the backlash against the hippie counterculture. Convinced of the therapeutic value of psychedelic experiences, Grof developed holotropic (literally translated as "moving toward wholeness") breathwork as a drug-free way to access the subconscious.

There are a thousand certified breathworkers around the world trained in Grof's method. As luck would have it, one of them lives a ten-minute walk from my house. Susan McBride, a Gestalt therapist with a master's degree in theological studies, leads monthly day-long breathwork sessions in her home for $175. She had an opening for me in her next session, she said. First I would have to fill out an extensive medical form. The experience can result in strong physical and emotional reactions and is contraindicated for some. After I verified that I didn't have cardiovascular problems, a history of aneurisms, retinal detachment or severe psychiatric issues, I was in. A couple of weeks later, at eight on a Friday morning, I arrived on the doorstep of the three-storey century-old home she shares with her physician husband. I would leave precisely twelve hours later, profoundly affected.

McBride spends two hours preparing our group of four mid-life women for what was about to happen, explaining that we would work in pairs, taking turns being "breathers" and "sitters." The sitter ensures the breather is supported during her three-hour session with sips of water, extra blankets, a helping hand to go to the bathroom and oversized cushions to rein in the breather in the event she is swept up in a kind of yogic flight and literally bounces off the bed, which has been known to happen.

Now we are ready to begin. As the lights dim, I lie down on a memory foam mattress, pull a fleece blanket up to my chin and slip on an eye mask. McBride starts us off with a short visualization. When a chorus of chanting monks blares over the sound system, I start breathing as hard and as fast as I can, in and out of my nose, as McBride has demonstrated. Huffing and puffing in this pseudo sleepover set-up feels incredibly silly, and I have to concentrate to contain a giggle. I tell myself to keep an open mind. I focus on my breath, thrusting it out of my nose like an angry bull. In and out. In and out. In and out. Our heavy breathing is so loud you'd think there was an orgy going on. Once again, I have to stop myself from giggling. Then, after about ten minutes, something weird starts to happen. My body tingles as if I'm being pricked with a thousand pins. What the hell? My brain is on high alert, and I'm buzzing with electric energy. My hands knot up, claw-like, and shoot straight into the air. McBride warned us about this. It's called tetany, an involuntary contraction of muscles that results from low levels of carbon dioxide caused by hyperventilating. It's an uncomfortable feeling, but it passes within a minute or two.

This is when I start to see things. Hazy, swirling purple and pink feminine figures—angels?—appear on the insides of my eyelids. They beckon me to follow them and I do, my form morphing into winged flight. I notice a pinprick of light in the distance. Then another. Soon, there are thousands of lightbulbs turning on in a blue-black night sky. I stand amazed, struck with the revelation that I am but a tiny speck in this enchanting, sparkling universe, insignificant yet part of it all.

I am having the most clichéd day-glo psychedelic experience ever.

As I grapple with this sense of cosmic unity, something stirs in my body. This is when I feel the urge to push and rebirth my daughter.

I never wanted to have children. I was so certain of this fact that, when I was twenty-one, I asked a doctor to sterilize me with a tubal ligation. When he refused, saying I'd likely change my mind, I was annoyed that he hadn't taken my request seriously. Why didn't I want kids? I wasn't sure I'd be a good mom. The world was already over-populated. I was also afraid I'd love a child too fiercely, that I'd become obsessed with worry and wreck the poor kid. During the first fourteen years Jeff and I were together, I was scrupulous about birth control—I did not want any surprises. Then, when I hit thirty-four, some inner wiring rearranged itself and overnight I was desperate for a child. We got lucky and had Ruby.

I did love her fiercely. So did my husband. He didn't worry, but I sure did—right from the moment I got pregnant and began reading *What to Expect When You're Expecting.* I read its list of horrors, glued to the pages as if it were a Stephen King novel: toxoplasmosis from touching kitty litter, blighted ovums, listeriosis from chewing on brie, uterine rupture, the possibility that the baby's hiccups could mean a knotted umbilical cord. My anxiety ramped up with the turn of every page.

Ruby was not an "easy" child. She had a head of fiery red curls and a temper to match. As a baby, she screamed with colic for hours. She resisted tidying up after playtime in preschool. She was sent to the principal's office in kindergarten for getting into a slugfest with her best friend. She'd rage at me if she didn't get what she wanted. I bought more books: *Raise Your Kid Without Raising Your Voice, The Explosive Child* and *How to Talk So Kids Will Listen & Listen So Kids Will Talk.*

In Grade 3 she was identified as having dyslexia. In Grade 4, after a year of constantly clearing her throat for no known reason, she was diagnosed with Tourette's syndrome. She didn't get asked on many play dates, so I arranged them for her. I compared myself to the other mothers, who seemed so much more carefree, and wondered what I was doing wrong. Instead of admiring my daughter's willful streak, her tough-minded attitude and her seeming disdain for what other people thought, I just wanted her to fit in—to try and please others a little more. The way I always had.

Three years after Ruby was born, we had Lucy. She went to sleep without a peep, woke with a smile, and generally did what was expected of her. Agreeable and positive, Lucy got along with everyone. I never had to orchestrate play dates for her. When the girls were about five and eight,

I had an epiphany in a Chinese restaurant in Montreal. Lucy was thrilled to be sampling Chinese food, while Ruby complained there wasn't anything she liked on the fifty-item menu. As I sat across from them, the words "light and dark, light and dark" kept repeating themselves in my mind. For Lucy, the glass was always half full. Maybe it always would be. The same wasn't true for Ruby. Two kids, same parents, two completely different temperaments. That's when it hit me—I could fight Ruby's innate nature, or I could accept it. Better yet, I could celebrate it.

I began to understand that worry was useless but action was helpful. I got Ruby remedial help for her dyslexia. She went on medication for a year to reduce her tics, which eventually disappeared just as mysteriously as they had arrived. By the time she was in middle school, I was a different kind of mother. I didn't get involved in her school work or offer advice on clothing or suggest which kids she should hang out with. If she was in a bad mood, I tried to just let her be that way, confident it would blow over.

It took me a while to figure out that parenting isn't about product development, but rather about loving and accepting your kids for who they are. Now that my girls are young adults, I know I can't protect them from the challenges life will throw at them. All I can do is provide security and love, the foundational ingredients all children need. Accepting that there's little I can do to change the outcome is a kind of relief. Their lives are out of my hands.

But now, in my breathing session, here is Ruby as a newborn, her life in my hands once again. She and Lucy are each moving into a new stage of life, and so am I; maybe my vision is a final chance to say goodbye to this part of motherhood. In the beginning, our mother is our world, her womb our home, her breast our sustenance. But separation is inevitable—first when the umbilical cord is cut, then when the nest is left behind. This is as it should be. A week after this breathwork session, I'll miss my regular-as-clockwork period for the first time in forty years, another marker that my intense mothering years are behind me.

I fall into a deep sleep for maybe thirty minutes, and when I awake I immediately start huffing and puffing again; I'm eager to see what will happen next. It doesn't take long before I'm transported once more. This time I am moving through the dark tunnel. I have no idea where I'm headed, but it feels safe, not scary. Then I sense the presence of my mother. My right hand involuntarily clamps over my mouth, as if it's a mask. Don't ask me how, but I know the mask is delivering ether. It's as though I've morphed into my mother and am giving birth to myself. I hungrily suck the anesthetic in gulps as the labour pains mount.

I see my mother as a teenager, alone in a sterile room, frightened about what's happening, and am overcome with empathy for her. It's my birthday in a week and here I am, witness to how intimately we were connected fifty-six years ago, my body in hers, kept alive by the supple rope that gave me all the nourishment I needed. Once she gave me everything. Now I feel the need to comfort her. And I still want her to comfort me. When does it stop, this longing to be mothered? "The materials are here for the deepest mutuality and the most painful estrangement," Adrienne Rich wrote of the mother–daughter bond.

When I get home, I can't wait to tell my husband what's happened. But even as I say the words, "I held Ruby as a baby!" "I saw my mother giving birth to me!" I know how incomprehensible it sounds. "Really?" he says. "Are you sure it wasn't just a dream?" It's difficult to describe the experience to anyone without appearing unhinged. I even feel a little queasy recording it here. And yet a psychological shift occurred in me.

Entering that altered state felt paranormal, but I know there is a physiological explanation: continuous rapid breathing delivers more oxygen to the lungs and at the same time decreases carbon dioxide, which leads to a rise in blood pH. This, in turn, has an effect on the brain that, according to breathwork practitioners, makes the unconscious more accessible. But how to explain the specificity of my visions? "The process of self-exploration and therapy in holotropic breathwork is spontaneous and autonomous; it is governed by inner healing intelligence rather than following the instructions and guidelines of a particular school of psychotherapy." This explanation comes from the Esalen Institute, the retreat centre in Big Sur, California, where Grof originated the method. Even as I write this, I'm still trying to decipher the "inner healing intelligence" of my own experience with breathwork, but it obviously has something to do with the everlasting bond between mothers and daughters. I'm so thankful that doctor didn't agree to render me infertile all those years ago. I'm so thankful I had the chance to become a mother.

AFTER THE HOLOTROPIC BREATHWORK SESSION, ANY TREPIDATION I have about trying psychedelics goes up in smoke. An article in the *New Yorker,* "The Trip Treatment" by Michael Pollan, examines the resurging interest in the therapeutic use of hallucinogenic drugs. It fuels my curiosity even further. Pollan interviewed researchers at New York and Johns Hopkins Universities who found that a solitary dose of psilocybin, more commonly known as magic mushrooms, dramatically reduced distress in end-stage cancer patients, with the positive results lasting for months and in some cases eliminating their fear of death altogether.

Pollan's article inspired his 2018 bestseller *How to Change Your Mind: What the New Science of Psychedelics Teaches Us About Consciousness, Dying, Addiction, Depression, and Transcendence,* which carefully details the emerging research and also looks back to the '50s and '60s, when the use of these compounds was widespread. For example, between 1950 and 1965, some forty thousand patients were prescribed one form of LSD therapy or another for mental health disorders. More than a thousand scientific papers and six international conferences were devoted to examining LSD's therapeutic use. Imaging studies show that psychedelics can set the brain ablaze by intensifying the connection between neural pathways, allowing for a higher state of consciousness, introspection and greater access to deep emotion. Many think this gives people under the influence of psychedelics an opportunity to confront significant past events and any self-destructive behaviours.

For example, hallucinogens have a long history of being used as a treatment for alcoholism. Bill Wilson, the co-founder of Alcoholics Anonymous, was undergoing therapy in a New York City hospital in the 1930s with the Belladonna Cure, made from the nightshade plant, when he had the epiphany that helped him stop drinking. Wilson also experimented with LSD in supervised settings. (He tried but failed to get his organization to endorse its use for alcoholics.) In his biography, *Pass It On*, he is quoted as saying, "It is a generally acknowledged fact in spiritual development that ego reduction makes the influx of God's grace possible."

The newfound popularity of psychedelic research was evident in April 2017 when more than 2,500 physicians, scientists and other health care providers gathered in Oakland, California, for the historic six-day Psychedelic Science conference to explore the role of psychedelics such as ayahuasca, LSD, psilocybin (also known as magic mushrooms) and MDMA in relieving conditions such as depression, anxiety and addiction, and enhancing well-being among healthy people. Gabor Maté was there. So was my breathwork guide, Susan McBride. And so was eighty-five-year-old Stanislav Grof. Among the presenters were Paul Summergrad, past president of the American Psychiatric Association, and Dr. Thomas R. Insel, the former head of the US National Institute for Mental Health. Attendees were buzzing about the FDA's recent decision to move ahead with large-scale clinical trials of MDMA (also known as Ecstasy) to treat PTSD, a disorder that affects 8 percent of Americans, nearly twenty-five million people. All this lends credence to *Scientific American's* pronouncement that "psychedelic drugs are poised to be the next major breakthrough in mental health care."

I'm still wary about the nasty side effects of ayahuasca. LSD has a connotation that scares me, and I think of MDMA as a party drug. But magic mushrooms sound earthy, relatively safe and, well, *magic*. Unlike many friends who sampled shrooms when they were in their teens and twenties, I've never tried them. Now I'm keen to get my hands on some. But how?

In the course of researching and writing an article on psychedelics, I interview Miranda, who tells me psilocybin helped fast-track her recovery through the grief of her recent divorce. Turns out she can get me some. Even better, she offers to supervise my "trip." I make a plan to spend the afternoon in her master bedroom, which she describes as having hardwood floors, a classic brick fireplace and bay windows facing a large maple tree on the street. "You'll feel like you're in a tree-house," she says. "You'll have lots of visual stimulation, but you can also pull the drapes if you need to." She emails me instructions on what to bring: a bell in case I want to ring for her assistance (she'll be downstairs cooking for a dinner party that night), a water bottle with a straw (I may be too uncoordinated to unscrew a lid) and a bowl in case I have to throw up. Her final advice: "Come with an open mind. Approach the experience with curiosity to see what you might discover."

There are about two hundred species of mushrooms containing psilocybin, a chemical that interacts with serotonin receptors in the brain to cause hallucinations and a flood of euphoria (and occasionally paranoia), growing naturally in many parts of the world. They are non-addictive and are considered among the safest psychoactive compounds available—safer, many believe, than alcohol. These humble fungi have been used in religious ceremonies for thousands of years to create visions, produce revelations and communicate with the gods— dating as far back as 7000 BC with the Saharan Indigenous tribes of Africa, then in Mayan and Aztec cultures. There's even academic speculation that psychedelics were the impetus for Biblical miracles such as the flash of light seen by Paul on the road to Damascus, the burning bush witnessed by Moses, and Jacob's vision of angels ascending a ladder to heaven.

The most famous study on magic mushrooms took place in a chapel on the campus of Boston University and involved twenty theological students. It happened on Easter weekend in 1962, so it was called the Good Friday Experiment. In the annals of psychedelic study, it's a doozy. The students gathered for a two-and-a-half-hour worship service as part of a double-blind study designed by Harvard Divinity School graduate student Walter Pahnke, under the direction of the infamous Timothy Leary, to test whether psychedelics could induce spiritual experiences among believers. In a twenty-five-year follow-up study, the subjects continued to characterize the event as a high point in their spiritual lives. Several went on to become ministers and one, religious scholar Huston Smith, wrote *The World's Religions*, which sold over three million copies and is still a popular introduction to comparative religion. Smith called the experiment "the most powerful cosmic homecoming I have ever experienced." Such studies would be shut down by the administration of Richard Nixon, who labelled Leary "the most dangerous man in America."

More than half a century later, Dr. William Richards, a Johns Hopkins researcher who specializes in the psychology of religion and has an MDiv from Yale Divinity School, is reprising the Good Friday Experiment. He's enlisted two dozen religious leaders (priests, ministers, rabbis and a Buddhist among them) to assess how a psilocybin-induced experience will affect their religious thinking. At the time I'm writing, the study has yet to be completed, but already Richards has observed that through their psychedelic experience participants gained a greater openness to and appreciation of other religions. Richards himself had a transformative experience when he volunteered to be part of a lab experiment with psychedelics in the early 1960s and wrote that he felt flooded with a sense of love, beauty and contentment that were beyond anything he had ever experienced.

Just as with holotropic breathwork, there are some contraindications to using psychedelics like psilocybin, the most significant being a history of severe mental illness. The potency of psilocybin-containing mushrooms is unpredictable, and so are the results. According to the US Center for Substance Abuse Treatment, a person high on mushrooms can experience extreme tension, anxiety and restlessness and have adverse reactions to the drug, including frightening hallucinations, confusion, disorientation, paranoia, agitation, depression, panic and terror that can lead to suicidal thoughts. All of this points to the extreme importance of what psychedelic researchers term "set and setting"—having a prepared, open frame of mind when you ingest the mushrooms and being in a safe environment, preferably with a guide to help ensure a positive experience. I feel confident in my own set and setting. Miranda is a registered nurse who will know what to do if I'm overcome by panic or psychosis. And she's promised to call 9-1-1 if there's any sort of emergency.

When I arrive at her home, she's carefully laid out nine mushrooms of various sizes next to a china mug decorated with tiny blue roses and the words "Good Luck." The dried stems are nearly ten centimetres long, and their sturdy, perfectly rounded caps serve as protection for the dark underbelly of delicately divided gills. They make an exquisite botanical tableau on her stainless-steel kitchen island. These are *Psilocybe cubensis,* she tells me, the most popular species of psychedelic mushrooms, also known as "Golden Teacher." She's prepared a dose of 6.5 grams. I find out later this is exceedingly high—you can feel the effects of psilocybin after ingesting just one gram, and a typical dose is about 3.5 grams—but Miranda says the amount will ensure a memorable trip. Some experts, I read afterwards, think a strong dose like this can help the user bypass anxiety and plunge right into a spiritual state. Others recommend a much more conservative dose for beginners.

Miranda chops the mushrooms into small pieces, then adds boiling water and a heaping teaspoon of honey. I cradle the teacup as I carry it upstairs to her bedroom and sip the concoction slowly, wincing as little chunks of fungi pass my lips. It tastes godawful, like wet sawdust. A few minutes later, Miranda comes to get the cup and sees that I've left a bit of detritus at the bottom. "You want to be sure to take it all," she says, and scoops out the last bits with a teaspoon that she slides into my mouth. I prop myself against a nest of pillows on her queen-sized bed and take in the bay-window view of the massive maple tree. I'm ready for anything and everything.

What I get is everything.

This will turn out to be the single most memorable experience of my life: ridiculously joyous (several long bouts of nonsensical, hysterical laughter so intense they make my stomach hurt), incredibly euphoric (undulating waves of electric energy course from the tips of my toes to the crown of my head, stopping at all points in between), filled with exotic sightings and definitely spiritual (I don't see the face of God, but I do see an angel in a corner of the room). Most significantly, it will provide much longed-for clarity on matters I've been stewing over. I could have spent thousands in therapy or simply stayed in an unhappy state. Instead, I lie down on a friend's bed, ingest some plant life and, like Paul on the road to Damascus, see the light. It isn't a conversion, exactly. More like an awakening.

Miranda had told me music was an essential part of the mushroom experience, and I found the official psilocybin playlist—the one used by researcher William Richards with his Johns Hopkins study participants—on Spotify. It's about five hours long and includes lots of classical music, some Hindu chants, a little Enya ("Storms in Africa"), a Beatles tune ("Here Comes the Sun") and an African American spiritual ("Swing Low, Sweet Chariot"). One of the longest pieces, at twenty-four minutes and forty seconds, is *Tod und Verklärung* (*Death and Transfiguration*), an 1880s orchestral piece by Richard Strauss, in which an artist sees the fleeting images of his life—from the wonder of his childhood to his years of struggle and eventual success and, finally, transformation of his spirit—as he lies dying. (When he himself was on his deathbed in 1949, Strauss said to his daughter-in-law, "It's a funny thing, Alice, dying is just the way I composed it in *Tod und Verklärung*.")

Since I'm a digital klutz, I asked Ruby for help downloading the playlist. "What's it for?" she asked. "Just something I'm writing about," I replied, trying to sound casual. She pressed further. "Psilocybin?" she said, noting the word in the title of the playlist. When I spilled the beans, she didn't like it one bit. "That's crazy, Mom! You're going to do magic mushrooms?" protested my hyper-responsible, straight-A economics major. When Lucy overheard the conversation, she chimed in. "Mom's a grown woman, Ruby. She can do whatever she wants." I assured them that I'd be doing this very safely, under medical supervision and for journalistic purposes. They let it go, but I was left to wonder about Lucy's ringing endorsement.

Once I'm settled on Miranda's bed—earbuds in, bell at the ready, a fresh eight-by-ten notebook in hand—it doesn't take long for something to happen. Within a few minutes my toes are tingling. A few minutes later the potted fern at the foot of the bed starts to sway wildly. Outside the window, the leaves on the maple pulsate in purple neon. Then I see the angel in my peripheral vision. If I didn't know Miranda was keeping watch downstairs, I'd probably start to freak out. When I become concerned that the visions will get overwhelming, I flip open my notebook. I write for four of the five hours of my trip. At some points it's so difficult to get the words down that I print in large block letters like a kid in kindergarten. I fill eighty-two pages.

Thoughts come on like an onslaught. Time feels distorted, so I consult the digital clock at the bedside. It feels as if I'm holding a thought for hours, but when I look at the clock only a minute or two has passed. Everything I write seems incredibly profound and I want to document as much as I can. Afterwards, much of it reads like drivel. Herewith, a real-time sampling:

10:00 a.m.: I am trying to write on the lines. It is hard.

10:12 a.m.: Is this joy for real?

10:20 a.m.: I feel warm all over.

10:22 a.m.: I love everyone.

10:37 a.m.: Alcohol is stupid compared to this.

10:44 a.m.: This is the best feeling I have ever known.

11:01 a.m.: Writing is a useless way to document this experience.

11:16 a.m.: I give in.

11:32 a.m.: Everyone should do this.

11:40 a.m.: Everything is beautiful.

11:44 a.m.: We need to love as we want to be loved.

12:01 p.m.: I don't want to waste my life on dumb stuff like Netflix.

12:09 p.m.: I'm not even going to have a hangover?!

12:27 p.m.: What's that I smell? Is something baking?

12:40 p.m.: Suffering is so unnecessary.

12:58 p.m.: How am I going to write about this?

1:05 p.m.: What if my pen runs out of ink?

1:10 p.m.: I have to pee but I don't want to get up.

1:12 p.m.: I should play the ukulele again.

1:25 p.m.: We should sell the house. It's too big. I can be happy anywhere.

1:55 p.m.: Any unhappiness I feel is self-inflicted.

2:10 p.m.: I have to pee.

2:20 p.m.: It's like I'm healed.

2:30 p.m.: I don't want this feeling to end.

2:35 p.m.: Anything is bearable if you feel like this, even death.

2:42 p.m.: I am awakened.

2:47 p.m.: It's like I've figured out all my problems. What the heck?

3:02 p.m.: I really need to pee.

Everyday vocabulary is woefully insufficient. What feels profound comes out platitudinous.

Various writers have encountered similar challenges trying to explain how they were affected by psychedelics. The Harvard University philosopher William James, considered the father of American psychology, said the first hallmark of a mystical experience is that it is marked by ineffability; it "defies expression . . . no adequate report of its contents can be given in words . . . its quality must be directly experienced; it cannot be imparted or transferred to others." This did not stop him from trying to express his conclusions about his own hallucinogenic experiments inhaling large amounts of nitrous oxide (also known as laughing gas). "Our normal waking consciousness, rational consciousness as we call it, is but one special type of consciousness, whilst all about it, parted from it by the flimsiest of screens, there lie potential forms of consciousness entirely different," he wrote in his seminal 1902 work, *The Varieties of Religious Experience*.

Aldous Huxley, author of *Brave New World*, documented his transcendent experience induced by four-tenths of a gram of mescaline in his 1954 book *The Doors of Perception*. He saw the world in a whole new light, as "Adam had seen on the morning of his creation." Everything was imbued with deep meaning, even the seams in his pants: "Those folds in the trousers—what a labyrinth of endlessly significant complexity! And the texture of the grey flannel—how rich, how deeply, mysteriously sumptuous!" This from a man who in 1962 was elected a Companion by the Royal Society of Literature.

Huxley was remarkably prescient about the potential for psychedelics. Some seventy years before contemporary clinical studies used psilocybin and LSD to reduce the existential distress of those with end-stage cancer, Huxley proposed a research project to administer LSD to terminal cancer patients. He also had his wife inject him with the drug before his death from cancer at age sixty-nine. In addition,

Huxley saw the potential of psychedelics for spiritual growth: "Those who are offended by the idea that the swallowing of a pill may contribute to a genuinely religious experience should remember that all the standard mortifications—fasting, voluntary sleeplessness and self-torture—inflicted upon themselves by the ascetics of every religion for the purpose of acquiring merit, are also, like the mind-changing drugs, powerful devices for altering the chemistry of the body in general and the nervous system in particular."

I'm not sure how religious my mushroom trip is, but it is certainly illuminating. All of my insights have to do with my closest family members. Not surprising, perhaps, since our once-intact little family of four (actually five now, since my daughter Lucy's friend Dori has recently moved in with us permanently) is in a state of flux. When I start recording my insights, I focus on Lucy, who is seventeen and has plans to go to film school. She's got a talent for creating elaborate calligraphic compositions in which the words are perfectly spaced, the letters embellished with curlicues and little bursts of colour. Over the past years she's presented me with artful pieces of writing on special occasions such as Mother's Day and Christmas, and I treasure them. As I try to form words in my notebook, I'm amazed by what happens. My usually sloppy scrawl takes on the shape of Lucy's beautifully scripted letters, complete with tiny flowers punctuating the ends of sentences and vines twirling around and through the words. The writing is exquisitely beautiful, yet I know I'm not capable of producing this kind of artistry. When I look up from the page and then back down, I see my usual messy style. Then, in the next moment, it morphs once again into letters that are as perfectly formed as Lucy's careful artwork. I'll learn later that this is a hallucinatory effect known as synesthesia (seeing colours and shapes in words), yet it seems stunningly real. It's in this moment that I realize Lucy has done mushrooms herself; that she's replicated the psychedelic writing she's seen while tripping. Initially, I'm alarmed. But I soon soften, acknowledging how wondrous this psilocybin experience is, how it must enhance her already creative spirit. I imagine myself as she must sometimes see me: an uptight mom who spends too much time trying to impose order on the household, instead of giving in to the inevitable chaos of life. "I'm more like you than you might think, Lucy," I write. "When I was your age, I used to write poetry all the time. I should do more of that. Sorry I've been such a doofus." And then, because the helicopter mom in me can't resist, I add, "Just remember, this isn't the real world. So be careful. And remember . . . Oops, I forget! Love, Mom." And just like that I know things will get better between us. Because from now on I'm going to be much less uptight. At least that's the plan.

Next, I turn my attention to my oldest daughter, a young woman prone, like her mother, to perfectionism. I hope she'll learn to relax, to take life less seriously, to consider taking a break from her intense studying and go on a trip somewhere. Maybe even a trip like this. "It will be good for you, Ruby," I write. "It will help you loosen up a little, so you aren't so much like me."

Is it irresponsible to advise your kids to take a hallucinogenic? Maybe. But I'm with the neuroscientist Sam Harris who observes in *Waking Up* that if his daughters "don't try a psychedelic like psilocybin or LSD at least once in their adult lives, I will wonder whether they had missed one of the most important rites of passage a human being can experience." He bemoans the fact that one can be sent to prison for trying a drug such as psilocybin, which is generally well tolerated and has no risk of addiction, while booze and cigarettes are acceptable addictions that have taken millions of lives.

I consider my relationship with my husband and the barricade of resentments I've built up toward him. We're not the only couple who has constructed such a heap after decades of marriage. There have been disappointments on both sides. But I appreciate what's good about him, especially his easygoing nature and a sense of humour that can make me laugh even when it's the last thing I feel like doing. I want more couple time, he's more solitary. I begrudge the fact that he seems to go out of his way to please people who are peripheral in our lives. He doesn't like my emotionalism. There is still admiration, but the decades of domesticity have taken a toll on passion. We've come close to breaking up more than once—we even had a quiet week-long separation last summer. But now I have a new understanding: I can accept my disappointment around all this or figure out a way to make a change. Now I can see that whatever happens, our family will stay intact, in one form or another. Just like that, the well-constructed barricade I've erected starts to crumble.

It's 2:43 p.m., almost five hours into my trip, before I think about my parents and how we've broken ties. I have a vision of them trapped in a cage. My arms aren't long enough to reach them through the bars. It's futile to even try. Their belief system may seem rigid to me, but it offers a comforting parameter for their lives. Who knows? Maybe one day they'll reach out to me. My sadness over this feels settled. I look at the clock—it's 2:46 p.m.

I feel happy. Pee-my-pants happy. And I do have to pee. I reluctantly get out of bed and make my way carefully down the long hallway to the bathroom. I'm laughing so hard I'm practically doubled over. I don't want to worry Miranda, so I yell down to her, "I'm OK! It's just all so funny!" I can barely get the words out, because at this point I'm snorting through my nose. She hollers up: "OK, then!" The smells that float up the stairs from the kitchen are exquisite—sizzling onions and garlic and something baking in the oven, which I'll find out later is carrot cake. I giggle at the sound of my pee trickling into the toilet. When I flush it's as loud as Niagara Falls. I look at my face in the mirror, and the woman looking back at me is glowing. I had no idea I had such a deep capacity for this kind of happiness. "I've only been living 10 percent of my joy," I'll write later in my notebook back in bed. "I am joy. Sadness is such a waste of time."

Pollan, the author of *How to Change Your Mind*, notes that great secrets of the universe become clear during these kinds of trips:

insights such as "love is all around," and "we are all one." "The usual ratio of wonder to banality in the adult mind is overturned, and such ideas acquire the force of revealed truth," he writes. "The result is a kind of conversion experience."

Was I converted, or did I just have a mind-altering drug trip? Whatever the case, it sure felt sacred to me. I've never felt such profound peace or such all-consuming heart-bursting love for my family, friends and the world in general, even myself. When I get home from my trip, I breeze in the door elated, despite the fact that I'm exhausted. I'm too tired to immediately explain to my family everything that's happened—I just want to nap. And eat carrot cake. I'd really like some carrot cake. Ruby, who looks relieved that I've come out of this experience the same mother as always, offers to bake one for me while I sleep. As I lie in a contented fetal ball in my own bed, I think about the doors that opened to me during this trip and my holotropic breathwork session. Did they lead to some great beyond, or just deeper into myself? While I did see some magical visions, my greatest lesson is that these experiences made me appreciate the relationships I have with the people closest to me, as well as allowing me to tap deeper into a reservoir of joy that has always been there—I was just skimming the surface before.

Weeks later, Lucy says I seem more lighthearted. (After I shared the revelations I had about her during my trip, she and I talked openly about her experience with mushrooms. It's been limited and positive, but she's aware that it's illegal and carries risks. I'm glad she could tell me about it.) Jeff notices I seem more able to see the big picture and not sweat the small stuff. Ruby is still skeptical about the whole thing. Whether or not this contentment lasts, I know the insights will stay with me, and I'm heartened by studies that show the positive neurological changes from psilocybin can last for a year or more.

Some experts, including Dr. Rick Strassman, associate clinical professor of psychiatry at the University of New Mexico School, are wary about the "messianic utopianism" they see pervading today's psyche-delic research community. Writing in *Scientific American*, Strassman cautions against "glorifying psychedelics' benefits and rendering innocuous their adverse effects."

Yet there are many like Rick Dobin, founder of the Multidisciplinary Association for Psychedelic Studies (MAPS), who believe the spiritual benefits of these substances could make us better people because they allow us access to a sense of the divine. Mysticism, he says, is the anti-dote to fundamentalism. As he told the *Washington Post*: "These drugs are a tool that can make people more compassionate, tolerant, more connected with other humans and the planet itself."

Mark Haden, chair of the Canadian branch of MAPS, expects psychedelic substances will be legalized for therapeutic and spiritual use sometime in the next couple of decades. He even envisions a col-lege of psychedelics where licensed practitioners, including therapists and spiritual leaders, will dispense them, perhaps in spiritual spas or even houses of worship. (The California Institute of Integral Studies— where Stanislav Grof is a professor—recently graduated its first class of forty-one psychedelic therapists.) The best part about using these treatments for spiritual purposes is that they can provide experiences tailor-made for diverse beliefs, says Haden: "Christians can meet the Christ, Buddhists the Buddha and atheists the universe."

The apostle Paul in 1 Corinthians 13 writes that in this life "we see through a glass, darkly" but one day we will see "face to face." I've had a glimpse into that mirror, and it brought clarity and bliss. I know now that there is a greater mystery beyond our everyday waking consciousness, and we can access it by methods that dismantle the barriers erected by the ego.

The last song on my psilocybin playlist was Louis Armstrong's "What a Wonderful World." Sometimes, when I think of all the things that are wrong—war, poverty, inequality, climate change, fractious rela-tionships—I'm not sure how wonderful this world really is. Sometimes it seems incredibly broken. But it can also be incredibly beautiful. And there's the paradox. Trees of green? I saw them as purple. But the colours of the rainbow? Yes, they really are so pretty in the sky.

Photo on next page: At the Women's March on Washington.

August

Finding My Tribe

"People must belong to a tribe; they yearn to have a
purpose larger than themselves. We are obligated by the
deepest drives of the human spirit to make ourselves
more than animated dust, and we must have a story to tell
about where we came from, and why we are here."
—*E.O. Wilson*

IT WAS 1974. I WAS PART OF SOMETHING, SOMETHING BIGGER THAN
me. There were five of us girls. We liked the Carpenters and the Bee
Gees, wore flared corduroys and striped turtlenecks. Eileen was the

queen bee in Grade 7, Jackie her aide-de-camp. As the new girl at John Calvin Christian School in Smithville, Ontario, I was initially granted access to this popular pack that roamed and owned the schoolyard. But a couple of weeks later, my social status plummeted when I approached them before the morning bell. Simultaneously, they turned their backs on me, effectively shunning me from the circle. I watched it all as if in slow motion. Standing at the edge of the clique, I wanted back in so badly I would have done anything to gain re-entry. They ignored my pathetic entreaties about what I had done wrong. Their backs remained cold and stayed that way. I was frozen out, friendless. Sick with shame, I spent an agonizing lunch hour sitting on the toilet in a cubicle in the girls' washroom, trying hard to swallow the cheese sandwich my mother had packed for me.

I'd lost my tribe, and I felt desperate. It was a carefully planned and executed form of girlhood torture. Psychologists call it indirect or social aggression. I called it hell. Some part of my twelve-year-old self still hasn't fully recovered.

Back then I was haunted by the question of why these girls had singled me out. Now I understand I was a target simply because I was different. Not just the new kid in school, but the only kid in this insular and rural Christian community whose parents had been divorced. The only one whose father had deserted his family. The only one who had scandalously worn pants on the first day of school. (Unbeknownst to me or my mother, the school had a "no pants policy" for girls, who were expected to dress in modest feminine attire. When I showed up in a pair of blue slacks, the teacher mocked me in front of the class: "What? You want to be a boy?")

Fifteen years later, when Margaret Atwood's novel *Cat's Eye* came out, I was struck by how accurately she depicted the menacing aspects of girlhood. In her story, ten-year-old Elaine Ridsley is the object of torment and manipulation by her group of friends, and yet she still desperately tries to please them. She despairs: "I don't want to see anyone.

I lie in the bedroom with the curtains drawn and nothingness washing over me like a sluggish wave. Whatever is happening to me is my own fault. I have done something wrong, something so huge I can't even see it, something that's drowning me. I am inadequate and stupid, without worth. I might as well be dead."

I too felt inadequate and stupid after my middle school rejection. Like Elaine, who has a vision of the Virgin Mary that guides her to safety after her so-called friends play a cruel and dangerous prank on her, I turned to a benevolent being for comfort in my misery. Feigning illness, I begged off school and stayed in bed for two days, clutching a miniature red-letter edition of the New Testament, certain that if I prayed hard enough and long enough, God in his everlasting mercy would deliver me back into the blessed embrace of that schoolyard cabal. He did not answer my prayers. Margaret Van Andel, another unpopular girl in the class, did. She sent me a note: "I don't have any friends and now you don't either. Wanna come over?"

It would be years before I was entirely comfortable in groups of women. There are legions of middle-aged women who still suffer the emotional scars of mean girl behaviour. As Rachel Simmons discovered in researching her book *Odd Girl Out: The Hidden Culture of Aggression in Girls*, "Women in their thirties, forties and fifties still carried with them the vestiges of victimization. They told stories with unusual clarity; they could remember the clothes they wore, the food they had eaten, the words they spoke on the hardest days of their girlhood . . . Even when the women had close friends, they reported not being able to shake a nagging feeling that these friends might at any moment and without explanation abandon them."

Expulsion from the group is one of our deepest human fears, and our suffering knows no end when we lose that sense of communion. This is the argument journalist Johann Hari makes in his book *Lost Connections*. Today, 40 percent of people say they are chronically lonely (compared to 20 percent twenty-five years ago). One in five

American adults (and one in four middle-aged women) is now taking at least one drug for a psychiatric problem.

Hari, who took antidepressants for thirteen years beginning at age eighteen, makes the case that soaring rates of depression and anxiety are not purely the result of low serotonin levels. None of us, he says, is meant to be an island. "We are told to seek happiness in all the wrong places. And to ignore the potential for human connections that are right in front of us," he writes. "What if changing the way we live—in specific, targeted evidence-based ways—could be seen as an antidepressant too?" What if, he asks, we "shifted from an individualistic vision of how to live—shut yourself off when you are home, accumulate stuff for yourself there—to a collectivist vision of how to live: we are a group; we belong together; we are connected?" What if, Hari asks, instead of being diagnosed with depression, people were diagnosed with disconnection?

This is, in fact, beginning to happen. Some experts say social prescribing—connecting people with community activities to address their need for social contact—is the next big wellness trend. Instead of giving people pills to feel better, physicians could soon refer their patients to a specialist who writes "prescriptions" for joining a choir, an art class or a volunteer group. Research has shown that being lonely has the same negative health consequences as smoking. And since one in five patients sees their doctor for social rather than medical problems, this has the potential to improve well-being and save on health-care costs at the same time.

"In all our searching, the only thing we've found that makes the emptiness bearable is each other," wrote James V. Hart and Michael Goldenberg for the 1997 film *Contact*, which was based on the novel by the astronomer Carl Sagan. In the prison system, solitary confinement is the worst punishment. In religions, the worst punishment is shunning. Rejecting someone from their human family creates such a state of hellish deprivation that many will suspend their disbelief to maintain their inclusion in the fold. The church I grew up in used the threat of excommunication—permanent banishment from the tribe—as a tool to keep members in line. "As long as he persists obstinately and impenitently in his sins, he . . . is therefore to be accounted by you as a Gentile and an outcast," reads its Form for Excommunication of Communicant Members. "Do not associate with him that he may be ashamed and come to repentance."

When I left the church, I pre-empted excommunication by taking the back-door route of withdrawing my membership. If I wasn't a member, the church couldn't discipline me or publicly pronounce me a sinner. I knew this would spare my parents some embarrassment, but I also found it satisfying to rob the church hierarchy of the opportunity to chastise me in front of the congregation. (The church leadership has since reconsidered whether they should let people like me off the hook quite so easily: "If the withdrawal is clearly a means of escape, the elders should inform the one who has withdrawn that the withdrawal is unacceptable and that church discipline will continue. After all, church discipline is not given to pester people but to show Christ's love to unrepentant sinners," a minister wrote in the *Clarion*, the magazine of the Canadian Reformed Church. "If withdrawal is an automatic way out, the sinner does not benefit [from] church discipline.")

I'll never understand how "Christ's love" is evident in urging a community to shun one of its own. This "sinner" snuck out, but leaving still came with a price. My actions ruptured the loving bond I'd had with my mother. At times, the guilt was overwhelming. She wasn't just sad about me leaving, she was angry, too. More than once she told me I was going to hell. That's what the theology of the "one true church" had taught her would happen to errant members like me.

After I got married, there was an uneasy truce. Still, visits to my parents were fraught with conflict and usually ended with me in tears on the drive home. I longed to repair our severed connection but didn't know how to do it. My Bible-believing family members, particularly my politically conservative stepfather, weren't the type to engage in superficial chit-chat. Rather, they had a tendency to deep dive into hot-button issues while we passed the potatoes at the supper table. No topic was off-limits: evolution, gay rights, abortion and "end times" events such as conflict in the Middle East and natural disasters. Our opinions diverged widely. During a provincial election, I debated taking down the New Democratic Party sign on my front lawn because my parents were coming for dinner. "Wait a minute," I told myself. "You're thirty-five years old. You don't have to apologize for how you vote." My stepfather saw the sign and avoided speaking to me that entire night.

I was in my forties when I learned about religious trauma syndrome. In *Leaving the Fold*, Marlene Winell explains that while we often think the worst damage is done by fringe cults, mainstream fundamentalist religions also employ brainwashing strategies that interfere with healthy development, including an enforced isolation from popular culture, a dismissal of science and psychology, and terror tactics that promote the idea that we are born sinful creatures in need of salvation. They threaten hell, the rapture, demonic possession, a vengeful god and expulsion from one's family. The indoctrination suppresses an individual's capacity for critical thinking and prevents the formation of a personal belief system. People suffering from religious trauma syndrome often exhibit mental health issues such as anxiety, depression, shame, guilt, perfectionism and a sense of being unlovable. Taken to its most extreme, some conservative sects deny life-saving medical treatment to children and take advantage of religious authority to sexually abuse children, procure their silence and cover up wide-scale abuse. Fundamentalist faiths require that children become secondary to a greater good, explains Winell. The Biblical precedent was set by Abraham, whose loyalty to God trumped his reluctance to bind his son to an altar and kill him. Religion hurts a whole lot of kids.

Adult children who manage to leave authoritarian religions experience extreme tension between two strong needs: their personal integrity and their need for intimacy and relationships. "The longing for closeness, belonging, acceptance and understanding from your family—especially your parents—is a primary need for any human being. That longing is deep and you shouldn't minimize it. The loss of this connection can feel like a death," says Winell. "Parents may feel hugely offended that their belief system is being rejected or they may feel a sense of failure because they were supposed to raise you to believe a certain way."

This described my struggle exactly. The question was, what to do about it? Should one ever have to earn their parents' love? Must a parent always accept their child, even when they despise what she thinks? Who owed what to whom? For me it was all fraught with so much despair. And after I rejected my religion, I was lost in a spiritual wilderness, too. Was it possible to find a religious community where I could feel at home? Who would have me when I was so full of doubt? I wasn't sure what I believed anymore, but I knew I still wanted to belong.

IN MY EARLY THIRTIES, I PHONED A LOCAL UNITED CHURCH AND asked if I could speak to a minister. I was in need of spiritual guidance to deal with the ongoing religious strife in my family, I explained. That's when I met Rev. Harry Oussoren, who, incredibly, had also been born into—and rejected—the Dutch Reformed Church. I shook and cried when I met with him. I could see his anger rising as he listened to my distress. "Churches like that should be kicked in the balls," he said when I had finished. "That's not what Christ's love is about." His words shocked me and offered a great measure of comfort.

I joined the United Church, embracing its liberal views on everything from gay ministers to right-to-die legislation. Both of my children were baptized in the United Church, and I found a happy home there for a number of years. I even taught Sunday school and led the children's choir. But as my kids got older and asked me about God, I wasn't sure what to tell them. Snuggling in bed one night, Ruby, six at the time, asked me if I really believed in God. I said something vague like, "I think God is the good in us." That didn't satisfy her any more than when she asked me sometime later if I believed in Santa Claus and I carefully explained that I believed in the "spirit of generosity" he represented. "You mean Santa's not real?" she cried. "Of course he is," I quickly responded in an effort to soothe her. It was one thing to fudge the truth about God. I wasn't going to rob her of Santa, too.

One Easter Sunday I sat taking in the scent of white lilies that lined the church aisle and listening to the hymns of the choir. Sunlight beamed through a stained-glass window with an image of Jesus on the cross, making the holes in his hands and feet look like bloodied jewels. Worried women stood gathered beneath him. I didn't believe any of it anymore, I realized. I could accept that Jesus was a good man. He'd fraternized with the marginalized, including lepers and prostitutes. But he hadn't died for my sins; he had died because he was a protester, a radical who challenged the authorities of the time. As I stared at that church window, any faith left over from my childhood disappeared.

As much as I cared for the good people of the United Church, I couldn't in good conscience remain a member. This time there were no elders haranguing me to repent and return, only pleasant and regretful handshakes goodbye.

As it turned out, the spiritual home I'd been seeking was literally just up the street: a large and active community of free-thinking Unitarians. I'd driven by their church hundreds of times without ever giving it a second look. When I walked through its doors that first Sunday (with my children and reluctant husband in tow) and heard a woman with the voice of an angel singing John Lennon's "Imagine," I knew I'd found a home.

Unitarians believe that personal experience, conscience and reason should guide people in their lives, rather than the Bible or other scripture. In other words: people should think for themselves. It's a church that doesn't ask me to believe the unbelievable. Instead of the Ten Commandments, they follow seven principles. These include the inherent worth and dignity of every person; a free and responsible search for truth and meaning; and respect for the interdependent web of all existence. The Unitarian hymn book was the first to combine African-American spirituals with folk songs, music from non-Christian religions and old Christian standbys such as "Amazing Grace" and "Rock of Ages." Readings are from poets such as Walt Whitman, Mary Oliver and Langston Hughes; activists such as Emma Goldman and Martin Luther King Jr.; religious leaders such as Mother Teresa and Gandhi; scientists such as Albert Schweitzer; and religious texts such as the Bhagavad-Gita, the Koran, the Torah—and, yes, the Bible.

Because Unitarians are creed-free and non-theistic, critics like to make fun of them. Hell, Unitarians make fun of themselves and have a bunch of jokes to prove it. There's the one about visitors on a tour of heaven who notice a group of Unitarians arguing about whether or not they are really there. The one about Unitarians praying, "Dear God, if there is a God, please save my soul, if I have a soul." And the one asking what you get when you cross a Jehovah's Witness with a Unitarian. Answer: Someone who knocks at your door for no particular reason.

Here's my favourite:

Q: How many Unitarians does it take to change a light bulb?
A: We choose not to make a statement either in favour of or against the need for a light bulb. However, if in your own journey you have found that light bulbs work for you, you are invited to write a poem or compose a modern dance about your light bulb for the next Sunday service, in which we will explore a number of light-bulb traditions, including incandescent, fluorescent, three-way, long-life and tinted, all of which are equally valid paths to luminescence.

Despite the jesting, Unitarian Universalism is a serious religion that's been at the forefront of the most significant social movements in history, from the abolition of slavery to civil rights, equal rights for women, prison reform, same-sex marriage and Black Lives Matter. UUs believe that ethical living is the whole point of religion and that our relationships with one another should be governed by justice, equity and compassion. Unitarian Universalism has its roots in Christianity, but it rejects the idea of the trinity, Jesus as a deity, the doctrine of original sin, the infallibility of the Bible and the idea of hell. Every religious idea I was brought up with.

So fearful was I of my parents' reaction that I didn't tell them for a year I had switched from the United Church to the Unitarians. Then, on one of our rare visits, my mother asked Ruby if she was still going to Sunday school at the United Church. "Oh no," Ruby replied brightly. "We go to the Unitarian Church now. We *never* talk about Jesus!"

All hell broke loose.

My mother paced the kitchen floor, her face by turns contorted with despair and inflamed with anger. My stepfather stood by with his arms crossed, silently furious.

"How could you do this to us?"

"You're turning your back on everything we've taught you."

"At least go back to the United Church!"

"Your grandparents would be rolling over in their grave."

"You're putting your children on the road to hell."

I wouldn't have been at all surprised if they'd accused me of selling secrets to the Russians.

It was wrenching. But even as my parents argued with me to return to the "one true church," there was a stubborn voice inside my head. *You can't make me,* it said.

A few weeks later I went into therapy.

"What's your bottom line for continuing a relationship with your mother?" the therapist asked me.

"I want to stop arguing about religion. I want us to be pleasant with each other," I said.

"Then that's what you have to tell her."

And that's what I finally did, in a phone call to my mother. I told her I didn't want to fight about religion any more.

"You're trying to muzzle me," she said. "I can't accept those conditions."

And, just like that, it seemed we were through. I felt a heaviness of spirit. But a strange lightness, too. I stopped blaming myself for all the conflict. Finally, the fighting could be over.

Today, almost fifteen years after telling my mom we were attending the Unitarian Church, I'm still an active member. You can find me there at least a couple Sundays a month. I sing hymns, light candles and listen to the minister preach on topics ranging from the spiritual practice of "paying it forward" to what it really means to love our neighbour as ourselves. I put money in the collection plate and nod at my fellow congregants, most of whom were not born into Unitarian Universalism but found their way here, like me, via a tortuous spiritual route. I usually stick around for coffee hour to share handshakes and hugs. A few times I've even climbed up to the pulpit myself to share a lay-led sermon, something that would have been considered an abomination in the church I grew up in.

It feels like a hopeful act to gather with intention in a world so often torn by the divisiveness of difference. I believe in the church's mission "to nurture each other, serve the community and inspire action that heals the world." I go for the liturgical uplift of listening to the choir, sharing both joys and sorrows, and celebrating traditions, whether it's the changing seasons of the earth or the changing seasons of our lives. But mostly, I go to church because it fulfills the most primitive and compelling of all human needs: the desire to belong. The journalist and social activist Dorothy Day said it best: "We have all known the long loneliness and we have learned that the only solution is love and that love comes with community."

In Unitarianism I have finally found what had seemed so elusive: a place that focuses on the celebration of the human spirit, rather than the stain of sin; a place where I can exercise my spiritual muscles without having to lift the dead weight of ancient dogma; a religious institution in which doubt is understood and even expected.

FINDING ONE ANOTHER IS THE GREATEST CHALLENGE FOR THOSE who are SBNR. Some, like me, are religious refugees who left the faith of their childhood. Others never had a religious home to begin with. There's also a growing trend of formal secular communities, including the Sunday Assembly, Oasis and independent groups such as the Calgary Secular Church and the Seattle Atheist Church, which appeal to those who want the structure of old-time religion without the doctrine. Call them sanctuaries for skeptics. There's a new breed of minister coming out from behind the collar, too, thanks to the trailblazing Gretta Vosper, a self-professed atheist and ordained minister with the United Church of Canada who has fought for and won the right to maintain her place in the pulpit. The divergence of belief among these spiritual seekers can be vast, and there's often no common pew to share, no building to gather in, no agreed-upon doctrine or set of practices that have been handed down through the generations. Writing in the *New York Times*, columnist David Brooks describes the dilemma: "Secular people have to choose their own communities and come up with their own practices to make them meaningful."

The decline in association with traditional religion corresponds with the simultaneous rise in the popularity of secular gatherings that create solidarity, enhance personal growth and allow for the kind of transcendence we usually associate with religious feeling. Such gatherings can be unconventional and wide-ranging, anything from drumming circles to community choirs, secular AA meetings, storytelling events, Death Cafes, SoulCycle classes, creative maker-spaces, book clubs, ecstatic dance sessions, co-housing initiatives, meditation groups, social justice organizations, music festivals, pilgrimages and spiritually-themed Meetup groups.

Some claim that secular spirituality is so individualistic, it encourages disengagement, especially from the public sphere. Dave Webster makes this argument in his book *Dispirited*, suggesting that those focused on an inner spiritual journey are not outwardly directed enough to care about the issues that need addressing to make the world a better place. Webster, who lectures in religion, philosophy and ethics at the University of Gloucestershire, seethes with anger at the SBNR, so much so that he opens his book with this line: "When someone tells me that they are not really religious, but that they are a very spiritual person, I want to punch their face. Hard." But Webster's idea that embracing secular spirituality is antithetical to living a moral and publicly engaged life doesn't hold up. It's an underestimation of human beings. One doesn't need God to be good. "I see with ever greater clarity that our spiritual well-being depends not on religion, but on our innate human nature—our affinity for goodness, compassion and caring for others," writes the Dalai Lama. "Regardless of whether or not we belong to a religion, we all have a fundamental and profoundly human wellspring of ethics within ourselves. We need to nurture that shared ethical basis."

GALEN WATTS, A PHD CANDIDATE IN CULTURAL STUDIES AT QUEEN'S University, researches the socio-political implications of contemporary spirituality. "The rise of [the] SBNR is bound up with the 1960s counterculture and the rights revolution: the civil rights, second-wave feminist and gay liberation movements," he writes. "Conservative commentators have generally denounced the SBNR, seeing them as narcissistic, lazy and without a clear sense of morality. Yet, this characterization is distorted and leaves out many attributes of the SBNR who display a robust sense of ethics [including] mutual respect and acceptance of difference. In fact, I believe the ethical core of SBNR spirituality holds human rights as sacred." He says one of the most meaningful expressions of secular spirituality is activism.

That's how my year began—by attending the largest single-day protest in US history. Like tens of millions of others, I felt a profound mix of anger and sadness when Donald Trump improbably became president in November 2016. Then the Women's March on Washington was announced. Never before had I so longed for the comfort of community; for the opportunity to stand shoulder to shoulder with like-minded citizens.

Some people take action in the face of despair. My friend Tracey Erin Smith is one of them. A writer, actor and teacher who runs Toronto's SoulOTheatre, Tracey wept when she woke up the day after the US election. Then she dried her tears, rented a sixty-seat Greyhound bus she dubbed the "Soulomobile" and invited her friends to climb aboard for the nine-hour drive from Toronto's Union Station to Washington, DC.

The march took place on January 21, 2017, the day after Trump's inauguration and drew a crowd of half a million. Initially, I was worried about it being targeted by feminist-hating snipers. Thankfully, there wasn't a single negative incident. The huge march was entirely peaceful and incredibly joyous, with a sense of spiritual vibrancy everywhere you looked. I shared handshakes and hugs with Americans who were stunned that Canadians would come to their capital to stand in solidarity with them. There were moving benedictions of song: a women's choir performed "Singing for Our Lives" along the National Mall, and a man with a guitar strummed "This Land Is Your Land" as we waited in an hour-long lineup for the porta-potties. Chanting took on the intensity of righteous fervour and included a call-and-response in front of the White House: "Whose house?" someone yelled. "Our house!" the crowd screamed back. Gloria Steinem rose to the podium like Moses to the mountain. Surveying the scene before her, she called out to her people: "I wish you could see yourselves. It's like an ocean."

An estimated five million people participated in close to seven hundred marches in eighty-five countries that day. It was an uprising, a global communion, a prayer for a more equitable world. Pussy hats became sacramental vestments, chants became liturgy and placards proclaimed sacred messages such as "Hate does not make us great" and "Love thy neighbor." Millions gathered in divine defiance, fortified by their interconnectedness.

Protests don't generally effect change right away. Consider that women didn't get the right to vote until seven years after the 1913 Suffrage Parade, which saw five thousand march in Washington, DC. Then again, sometimes they do. In 1990, sixty activists with disabilities abandoned their wheelchairs to crawl up the eighty-three stone steps of the US Capitol Building. Four months later, the long-fought-for Americans with Disabilities Act was passed. Whether or not they immediately change laws, marches allow us to choose action over apathy, to alter public opinion and challenge the divisiveness we see around us. Public protests can rouse us from our spiritual malaise by reminding us what it means to love our neighbour as ourself.

I'LL NEVER FORGET THE COMMUNAL POWER OF THE WOMEN'S MARCH. But a much smaller demonstration that occurred two years earlier made just as profound an impact. Some people had warned me not to get involved. Some were furious about my role in it.

It was January 2015, and Bill Cosby was on his way to town. He was set to appear in Hamilton for the third and final Canadian performance of his boldly titled "Far From Finished" North American tour. Fourteen theatres had already cancelled his shows due to the allegations of thirty women (the number would eventually climb to sixty) who said Cosby had drugged and sexually assaulted them. While there were a few small demonstrations outside his shows, no group had ventured inside the protected bubble of the venues where Cosby continued to be adored. As accusations against him reached their peak, a Florida audience greeted him with a standing ovation. That made me feel sick. And when I thought about him taking to the stage at FirstOntario Concert Hall, a venue where I'd seen legends such as Anne Murray, Gordon Lightfoot and Harry Belafonte perform, and where I'd brought my daughters to see Raffi and *The Nutcracker*, I also felt outrage. I wondered why somebody didn't do something. I wondered why that somebody shouldn't be me.

I told my husband I was so angry I was going to buy a $90 front-row ticket and yell "Rapist!" at the top of my lungs. He looked at me as if I had a strange kind of fever. I guess I did. When I calmed down, I hatched a different strategy, enlisting a few friends to purchase tickets with me. I consulted with a civil disobedience expert and a criminal lawyer on how to stage a peaceful protest inside the theatre without risking arrest or inciting an angry mob. The media caught wind of what was going to happen, and former fans donated their tickets to protesters.

I didn't want to keep quiet, but there were a lot of people who thought I should. News stories about the planned protest brought out the haters, most of whom hid behind anonymous online comments: "If Bokma opens her yap in the auditorium the hundreds there to enjoy the comedy icon will put her in her place quick and proper." "All men who go to that show should be ready to shut those man-haters down." "If I am there and she does anything I will willingly toss her ass out." "Stupid bitch." "Leave the old man alone. If he dies of stress his death will be on their hands."

Someone posted my email address online, and the vitriol spilled into my inbox. I was accused of "comedic terrorism" and told to "go to

Afghanistan to get some perspective." A newspaper columnist wrote that our protest efforts "reek[ed] of elitist contempt for the ability of individuals to think for themselves." I got into a heated argument with the relative of a friend who called Cosby's accusers opportunistic starlets in search of fame and money. I told him no woman has ever gotten rich from being raped.

What helped was that I wasn't alone. Thirty people joined me in taking a seat at the show. Many were friends, some complete strangers. Most were women, several were men (one the eighty-five-year-old father of a friend of mine), and I was heartened by the presence of a couple of fifteen-year-old girls. Outside the theatre another one hundred or so protesters gathered while a motley group of men's rights advocates protested our protest, saying we had created a "lynch mob" against Cosby.

Our group was scattered throughout the orchestra level, awaiting the fifteen-minute mark in the show when we would stand in unison to demonstrate our support for Cosby's accusers. Under old coats that we planned to leave in our seats, we were wearing white T-shirts emblazoned with the words "We believe the women." Rolled up under our clothes were posters with the same words. Rape whistles dangled around our necks. Cosby was aware of our protest and had taken precautions. The house lights never came down, and more than two dozen security and police officers roamed the aisles between the half-empty rows.

Cosby spoke to the audience in the tone of a tolerant grandfather: "Whatever happens here tonight, if there's some sort of outburst, we just have to remain calm and things will be taken care of. It oughtn't last that long." He facetiously saluted the protesters gathered outside the theatre in the January cold, acknowledging their "human spirit" for standing up for what they believed in, then dismissed them. "In two years when I'm back, they'll be inside," he said. (In fact, in three years he would be on the inside, confined to a cell in the State Correctional Institution of Phoenix, serving three to ten years for aggravated indecent assault.)

Cosby started his show with a joke about stealing from the collection plate when he was a boy. So as not to arouse suspicion, we clapped when the audience applauded, soundlessly banging the heels of our hands together. We felt watched. We were nervous. But we were ready.

The first rape whistle sounded, our cue to stand in unison. We peeled off our coats, unfurled our posters and rose up, chanting, "We believe the women!" over and over again. We made our way between the rows, walking slowly toward the aisles. The audience booed and hissed and yelled at us: "We believe Cosby!" and "Go believe outside!" Cosby, for his part, was eerily unflustered, urging calm.

Emboldened by the fact that police and security guards seemed to be parting a path for us, we blew our whistles harder. When a man blocked my friend Denise from getting out to the aisle, a police officer told him to move his leg and gently escorted her out. We emerged on the street jubilant, barely feeling the winter cold, still shouting, "We believe the women!" The next day, our small act of defiance made international headlines.

OUR GROUP OF THIRTY WILL BE FOREVER BOUND BY THE SHARED experience of standing up to Cosby. And while his eventual conviction was certainly a victory, what has stayed with me most is the fact that it prompted so many women in my circle to share stories of harassment, molestation and sexual abuse, often for the first time. One friend tells of literally being dragged off the street by a man when she was a teenager. Another says something so terrible happened to her when she was twelve she still can't talk about it. Yet another reveals that her Brownie leader's husband molested her when she was six. On and on it goes.

Healing can begin when we are empowered to tell what happened to us.

A WHILE BACK, MY NINETY-THREE-YEAR-OLD FRIEND VAL GOT UP in front of 250 people at a storytelling event and told a tale she'd kept secret for eighty years. Recalling her life as a girl in the 1930s, she spoke of running happily in the mornings to a one-room, red-brick schoolhouse with her twin brother. The two of them would collect hickory nuts and eat wild berries along the way as black-birds sang overhead. By the time she was thirteen, Val was no longer carefree. She dreaded going to school. Her teacher had taken an unseemly interest in her. When he insisted on driving her home after a Christmas concert practice, she leaped from the car when he tried to grab her. She ran for her front door, but the teacher fol-lowed her into the house, crushing her against the spines of the radiator in her front hall. She was too terrified to scream. "The last six months of school were a frightening game of cat and mouse," Val told the assembled. Not long after, the teacher was jailed for his unlawful involvement with another girl who had gotten pregnant. Haunted by what might have been her fate, Val would never again walk through the village of her childhood. Yet she still dreams of going back. "Perhaps the ghost of my twin brother will take my hand, and we'll skip as children safely from school to home," she said. "May blackbirds sing again for us."

Following the public telling of this private story, a number of people—many in mid-life and older—approached Val. They too had similar things happen to them, in some cases decades earlier. They too had never told a soul.

Personal storytelling is both confession and exorcism. "If I were to reinvent religion, I'd make it about storytelling," says Tracey Erin Smith, whose SoulOTheatre helps people craft stage performances based on pivotal experiences in their lives. "Two of the most important things to humans are community and meaning, and storytelling provides both.

When you know someone's story, you can't hate them. In fact, you might just fall a little bit in love with them."

In our secular age, people are more hungry for stories than for sermons. Credit for the current popularity of confessional-style storytelling goes to The Moth, which produces five hundred stage shows a year as well as a weekly podcast and an NPR radio show. Then there's the viral phenomenon of TED Talks, which follow a classic sermon structure (no more than twenty minutes) to deliver uplifting messages. The non-profit StoryCorps has a bank of sixty thousand recorded memories, accessible online, from storytellers who include veterans, people with Alzheimer's and 9/11 survivors.

At a certain point I became intrigued with the Six-Word Memoir, a project from *Smith Magazine*, which has published more than a million short, sharp tales online and in a series of bestselling books. The initiative was inspired by the legend of Ernest Hemingway responding to the challenge of creating a six-word story with "For sale: baby shoes, never worn." Many famous folks have contributed their tiny tales, called Celebrity Sixes. Some of my favorites: "Started small, grew, peaked, shrunk, vanished" (George Saunders), "Secret to life: marry an Italian" (Nora Ephron) and "The miserable childhood leads to royalties" (Frank McCourt). If you could summarize a life in six words, I thought, imagine how much ground could be covered if people had a bit more time. I asked a few friends and fellow writers to give it a whirl, telling a revealing tale about a "first" in their lives in six minutes or less. We staged a free event, with the option to donate to a local charity. More than one hundred people showed up, and the 6-Minute Memoir ("Speed storytelling for a cause") was born. That was six years ago. Since then there have been more than two dozen such events and more than two hundred stories, tales both heartbreaking and hilarious, have been shared. The mood in the room always feels holy. Sharing our stories is a sacred act.

I love what the Canadian Ojibway author Richard Wagamese had to say on this theme: "All that we are is story. From the moment we are born to the time we continue on our spirit journey, we are involved in the creation of the story of our time here. It is what we arrive with. It is all we leave behind. We are not the things we accumulate. We are not the things we deem important. We are story."

I knew exploring the idea of community would be an important part of my year of spiritual experimentation. It's one of the reasons I attended the Women's March. It's why I continue to engage in story-telling. And it's why I went to witch camp.

I don't exactly lie to get into Wild Ginger, but I do fudge the truth a little. The registration form asks for my "magical" name. I consider using my middle name, Celeste, which I've always thought is a lot more enchanting than my first. But I decide to leave the space blank and hope my true identity as a muggle won't get me cast out of the coven.

This five-day camp has been running for the past twenty years in south-central Ontario. I'm curious to learn how the sixty or so participants, most from Canada but a few from the US, manage to form an instant community once a year. My ideas about witches have been entirely formed by stereotypes in the overculture, from the con-spiratorial hags in *Macbeth* to the beautiful nose-twitching Samantha Stephens of *Bewitched*. My religious upbringing has also had an influ-ence, promoting the idea that witches are in league with the devil. The book of Revelation lumps them in with murderers, condemning them to the "fiery lake of burning sulfur." Exodus 22:18 puts it bluntly: "Do not allow a sorceress to live." It's safe to say *Harry Potter* would never have been allowed in the house I grew up in.

So I'm surprised when the orientation meeting looks like a grownup Brownie troop, only with more tie-dye and silver jewellery. Magical names abound: Daisy, Dandelion, Strix, Dragon Dancer. There are two Sages and three Ravens. A woman who looks to be in her seventies calls herself Becoming, which I find endearing. One of the perks of being a witch is picking a new name that symbolizes your rebirth. There's a practical reason for a magical name, too, since a lot of these women are still in the broom closet and don't want people to know their true identities. (There are far more witches than you might think—Wicca and similar pagan practices are among the fastest-growing religions, according to Pew Research. There are an estimated 1.5 million followers in the US. That's more than the 1.4 million members of the Presbyterian Church.)

There are as many tattoos at Wild Ginger as you'd expect to see in a correctional facility: dragonflies, butterflies, pentagrams and half moons. One young woman has several birds tattooed across her chest. Another, whom I learn holds down a government job in the energy sector, has her arms festooned with a myriad of female characters, from Tinker Bell to a tough-looking boxer. In the Middle Ages, witch hunters would inspect the bodies of suspected witches for the mark of the devil. A mere skin tag could do you in. Without a single tattoo, I stand out here.

The first person I meet is Rainbow, a social worker in the mental health field. I tell her that it's my first time at witch camp. "You're gonna love it here," she assures me. And you know what? I do. These witches are a warm and welcoming bunch. Most, like Rainbow, are in the helping professions: teaching, nursing and healing. And most seem to be involved in some sort of activism, including a Jewish professor who lobbies for Palestinian rights, a businesswoman who is working with her local Rotary Club to help a First Nations reserve improve access to water, and a therapist who created a sign campaign to welcome immigrants to her community.

I meet a theological student who is training to become one of Canada's first pagan chaplains, a nature therapy guide, a young woman who is the accounting manager in her father's medical marijuana plant and a few Unitarian Church members, including a lay chaplain. I'm introduced to Geof Thompson, a member of the United Church who is here to attend a memorial for the "beloved dead" that will pay respects to, among others, his wife, known as Luna, who died earlier this year.

I learn that she was the "kitchen witch" at Wild Ginger for a number of years and a much-loved member of the community. Geof tells me the church memorial for Luna included pagan elements, including a spiral dance and the United Church hymn "Called by Earth and Sky": "Precious these waters, endless seas, deep ocean's dream, waters of healing, rivers of rain / The wash of love again." That hymn might as well be a Wiccan chant, Geof says. I ask him if their differing religions ever caused problems in their relationship. "Not at all," he replies. "We helped each other in our understanding of spirituality. We had different ways of connecting with something larger than ourselves." Geof was raised Presbyterian, with the idea that man is the centre of the universe, having dominion over the earth. "But I know now that I am only a piece of creation," he says. "There is no hierarchy. I am no more important than a bird in the air or a leaf on the tree."

The folks gathered here are reclaiming a tradition of witchcraft that combines feminism with political activism. They aim to live by their version of the Golden Rule ("Do what you want, but harm no one") and follow the Principles of Unity: all life is interconnected, each person is their own ultimate spiritual authority, everyone is called to do service in the community, and the goddess is present in the earth's cycles of birth, growth, death, decay and regeneration. They believe the planet is sacred, and so it's their duty to do what they can to save it from environmental destruction and fractious politics. They do not speak the US president's name in full, referring to him only as "D.T."

Storytelling is central to the Wild Ginger gathering, and at this summer's retreat the focus is on Pandora, the goddess who, in Greek mythology, was the first woman on earth, and drew gifts for the world, including flowering trees, minerals and flint to make fire, out of a large jar known as a *pithos*. Over time, her story became the misogynistic tale of Pandora's Box, which blames the goddess for unleashing a load of troubles upon the world. (Replace the box with forbidden fruit and you've got a very similar Biblical narrative of woman as the origin of evil.)

The week includes a number of "path offerings," essentially small groups that meet for a couple of hours every morning. I join "sustainable magical activism," where the focus is on how to stay hopeful in the face of negative world events. In honour of Pandora, we each fashion a miniature pithos out of clay to represent the gifts we might offer to the world through our lives and work. We are also asked to write a spell, which really is a type of prayer. Mine is: "When I fall into despair, I will remind myself there are many helpful actions I can take to bring me back to balance, peace and joy." We pass around a smooth stone that's been "charged" by each member of the group and hold it while we read our spells aloud. The group responds by saying our name and repeating the words, "I honour your commitment and support you." When it's my turn and everyone in the circle chants this to me, I'm overcome by emotion.

I learn to cast a circle, invoke a deity and call in the four directions and the elements. In a nightly ritual in the woods around a roaring bonfire, I learn to "raise the vibration." People come dressed for the occasion. The evening ceremonies are a veritable fashion parade of pagan ritual wear, including high-waisted goddess gowns, flowing velvet capes with pointed hoods, flouncy skirts and loads of black. The ritual begins with a spiral dance, during which we hold hands, do a grapevine step and follow a leader. Our faces shine from the glow of the blazing fire as we chant loudly to the pounding of drums: "Earth my body / Water my blood / Air my breath / And fire my spirit."

Priestesses take turns circling the fire, speaking prophetic words to the assembled, retelling the myth of Pandora. We dance, chant, drum and sing for close to an hour. The air is punctuated by hoots and howls. Suddenly, the singing stops and the "toning" begins. Our sustained communal vocalization creates a powerful drone, sounding like thousands of bumblebees. I channel my voice with the others and raise my hands to the sky like they do. This is what witches call "raising a cone of power." It's believed the collective energy of the group swirls into a pinnacle similar to the vibrating funnel of a tornado, which is then psychically dispersed as a cloud of transformative and healing energy to the earth and its people, blowing over the tops of trees, cities and mountains until it hopefully sweeps right into D.T.'s combover and changes the world a little bit for the better.

At least, it works something like that.

A few hundred years ago, these women would have been risking their lives to do what they are doing out here in the woods. Scholars estimate that fifty thousand women were executed by hanging, drowning and burning for witchcraft in Europe and the American colonies between 1480 and 1750. Hanging was the preferred method of execution during the Salem witch trials. But burning was usually favoured because it was slow and more torturous.

When I arrived at Wild Ginger, I had the idea that witches must be a wild lot. By the time I leave, I realize they are a lot tamer than I expected. Wild Ginger is alcohol- and drug-free. No one gets naked and dances around the fire. (For that, you have to go to nearby Mansfield, Ontario, for the Wiccan Fest, where participants are free to roam in the buff.) The camp where the retreat is held does have a clothing-optional beach, and one hot afternoon I peel off my clothes and swim "skyclad" across the pond. Other than the nude swimming, the most hedonistic thing I see at Wild Ginger are the slabs of frosted chocolate cake served one night for dessert.

On my last morning of witch camp we play "tug of peace." The group of sixty gathers in a circle, holds on to a thick circle of rope and leans back. One woman proves how strong and steady the rope is by climbing on top of it. It's a much different experience from the usual tug of war, where the object is to humiliate the opposing team by dragging them into the dirt. The world could use a lot more witches, if you ask me.

Photo on next page: Before he became Mr. You Know Who: My mom, biological father, me and my brother Henry, 1965.

September

Supernatural States

"I have always held that people insist too much upon direct proof."
—*Sir Arthur Conan Doyle*

DEBBIE ANDERSON IS SHAKING A GOURD RATTLE UP AND DOWN MY body while periodically spitting an arc of "spirit water" from a glass bottle into the air. I'm lying on a treatment table in an upstairs room of her home, hoping none of her spittle lands on me.

Anderson, who calls herself The Country Shaman (her motto: "Bringing healing to the world, one person at a time"), is checking out my chakras. The good news, she says, is that I have four wheels of multicoloured spinning lights channelling life force energy through the upper half of my body. My crown, third eye, throat and heart chakras—representing enlightenment, intuition, expression and connection—are all in fine form, open and activated. "They're spinning beautifully," she says. The bad news is that my bottom half is blocked. My root, sacral and solar plexus chakras—representing groundedness, sexual energy and personal power—are cosmically constipated, filled with emotional gunk that's plugging up my prana, chi, qi, ki or whatever you want to call this metaphysical force. When I ask Anderson whether I should be worried about these stubborn closures, she assures me she's had clients with all seven chakras blocked. Still, if my lower chakras stay clogged like this, it could lead to an imbalance. I could get depressed or sick, she says. Her rattle shaking and spirit water spitting are meant to clear the blockages. It's the equivalent of a spiritual enema.

Welcome to the woo-woo chapter of my journey.

Chakras are invisible centres in the body. There's no scientific proof that they exist, but millions of people believe in them anyway. They were mentioned thousands of years ago in the authoritative Hindu Vedas and are also referenced in early Buddhist traditions. They were introduced to the West by New Age authors like Anodea Judith, best known for her 1987 book, *Wheels of Life*. Today, getting your chakras balanced is about as common as whitening your teeth. Amazon sells a "healing chakra wand" for $48, and Walmart has a chakra balancing stone kit that retails for $24.99. Or you can go the personal route and book an appointment with one of the army of mid-life women (many of whom, like Anderson, are white) who call themselves shamans, traditionally a spiritual healer in Indigenous cultures.

Anderson tells me she sometimes wonders if she should have called her practice The Last Resort, since people usually come to her when they are desperate. They might have anxiety or depression, phobias, chronic illnesses such as arthritis, even brain injuries or cancer. She tells me about a client with a tumour on her spine she'd been told needed to be surgically removed. Anderson claims to have gotten rid of it in four sessions. "It was an emotionally based tumour," she says. "In the third session it came out that she'd experienced childhood sexual abuse. We cleared out her root chakra."

I nod politely. Anderson seems like a perfectly nice woman, gentle and well-meaning. Despite the $60 she charges per session, I don't get the sense she's in this for the money. She lives in a beautifully appointed house outside Toronto and has a second home in Florida. She once had a high-profile six-figure career as a director of human resources, but after her first husband died when she was only fifty-one, she became restless and searched for a new path. When she read *Shaman, Healer, Sage: How to Heal Yourself and Others with the Energy Medicine of the Americas* by Alberto Villoldo, a California psychotherapist who spent time among the Q'ero shamans of Peru, she felt a calling and took courses with him. The first time she saw someone's chakras, she tells me, she burst into tears. "I felt like I had found my way home," she says. Like all body–mind practitioners, Anderson believes physical problems usually have underlying psychological causes, "unless you've been in a car accident or something." Once the emotional issues are cleared, the thinking goes, actual healing can begin. Certainly, there's scientific evidence to back up the idea that a person's state of mind can make them sick, but for me it strains credulity to think that a bit of hocus-pocus "cleansing" with magic water could have any real medical benefit. Believing that someone has the power not only to see invisible spinning discs in my body, but to actually pry them open, seems as silly as believing in TV faith healers who slam people on their foreheads and claim to make them walk again.

And yet something unsettling happens. Part of Anderson's process is clearing what she calls "crystalized" energy—places in the body where old injuries create a roadblock. As she moves around the table, grazing her hands over me, she stops at three specific spots: the baby toe on my left foot, the point of my right elbow and my left ankle. Injuries I haven't thought of in decades come back to me. I broke that toe playing baseball when I was twenty. A few years later I fell at a dance party and hurt my elbow so badly the pain flared up for years. The ankle injury stems from a incident when I was six, involving a surface cut that left a deep impression. It happened when my father came to see me and my brother Henry after he'd taken my mother to court to fight for visitation. We played Pick Up Sticks on the floor of my bedroom while my mother sat in the living room, smoking and reading the Bible. When I went to the kitchen to get a glass of water, the glass dropped from my hands, smashed to the floor and broke into shards, one of which stuck in the soft spot just below my left ankle. When I cried out, both my parents came. My father removed the shard and pressed a handkerchief on my foot, my mother smoothed on a Band-Aid, and for a moment they were united in their concern for me. My father left an hour or so later, and I never saw him again. After that we referred to him only as "Mr. You Know Who." His first $100 support check bounced, and his visiting rights were suspended.

Now Anderson is holding that ankle in both her hands. "I can feel little glass pieces in there," she says. She shakes her rattle over my foot, gives me a smooth stone to hold on to and tells me to breathe out hard, the way you do when you are giving birth. "Blow it out," she urges. "Just release it—you don't need it to go on." Every cell of our body holds memories, Anderson explains. "You won't forget this memory," she says afterwards, "but the emotional charge isn't living in your body any longer. The shards are gone." Lying there on her table I still feel plugged up, but that's because the tears sliding down the sides of my face have created tiny pools of water in my ears.

I can't deny I walk out of Anderson's home feeling something has shifted. Whether it's because my energy centres are spinning in happy alignment or because I've shed a few cathartic tears, I'm not sure. "A good cry is like a car wash for the soul," writes Bill Hayes in his memoir

Insomniac City. It does seem as though some kind of psychic cleansing has taken place.

THERE ARE LEGIONS OF "ENERGY MEDICINE" PRACTITIONERS WHO claim they can relieve emotional and physical issues by manipulating life force energy. These people are fond of terms like "raising the vibration" and "manifesting your destiny" and often believe in the Law of Attraction, the idea that positive thinking always results in positive outcomes.

I'm suspicious of anyone who claims they can unblock negative energy, but I'm curious, too. The popularity of certain alternative modalities—chakra balancing, reiki, crystal therapy, sound therapy, emotional freedom technique, biofeedback, reflexology, soul retrieval, past life regression, aura therapy, etc.—is linked with the declining interest in traditional religious practices. Religion used to offer comfort in an uncertain world. Now many people are looking for that security elsewhere. Instead of engaging in confession or communion, they're apt to flush out bad juju with a $100 colonic cleanse.

There's plenty of positive anecdotal evidence about alternative therapies, but solid research is lacking. These approaches may seem to work when in fact an ailment has run its natural course or the original diagnosis was incorrect. But the most compelling explanation may be the powerful placebo effect: if you expect a treatment to help you, there's a very good chance it will.

Reiki, one of the most popular complementary practices, promises to promote relaxation, speed healing and improve overall well-being. It's practically run-of-the-mill: one in ten Canadians have tried it, including, it seems, most of my friends, some of whom say it's helped them with everything from bad knees to crippling grief. The International Center for Reiki Training reports that four million people have been trained in the practice, and dozens of North American hospitals include reiki as part of their patient services. This traditional Japanese technique is gentle—it involves a practitioner lightly touching or hovering their palms above someone's body to manipulate the flow of energy. Fantastically, "absent" reiki can also be performed long-distance by connecting with a person's "energetic essence" across the miles.

Some consider Jesus the first reiki master. Rev. Coral Prebble, a minister at Toronto's St. James United Church, which has offered reiki provided by volunteers for more than twenty years, points to the forty-six Gospel accounts of Jesus healing people. She mentions Mark 16: 17-18, which indicates that one sign of a true believer is the laying on of hands to help the sick recover. (The other signs are the ability to cast out demons, speak in tongues, pick up serpents and drink deadly poison without getting ill.) "I don't know if these accounts are reiki-inspired, but they are healing-inspired, and that's what we want to reclaim," says Prebble.

Although many small studies show some positive effect, reiki has not scientifically been shown to improve significant health issues. Timothy Caulfield, a University of Alberta law professor and author of the bestselling *Is Gwyneth Paltrow Wrong about Everything?* is one of North America's highest-profile alternative medicine skeptics. He calls reiki "serious flat-Earth-level wackiness" and criticizes universities and hospitals that allow space for the practice. Yet even he understands its allure, telling me about a session he had (as part of a research trip to Kyoto, Japan), which he says was "thoroughly enjoyable and relaxing."

I post a request for reiki recommendations on Facebook, get dozens of suggestions for local practitioners and land in the living room of Debra Harding, a reiki master and "energy translator" who runs her Sacred Vibrations practice from her apartment not far from my home. "Enjoyable" and "relaxing" are not the adjectives I would use to describe my one-hour experience with Harding. More like "surreal" and "unnerving." Within five minutes of me lying down on her treatment table, Harding informs me that we are not alone but are, in fact, surrounded by spirit guides. "The room is filling up with beautiful divine beings," she says as casually as if she were describing the furniture in her apartment. I am primed for an hour of quiet time, not an incorporeal cocktail party. Harding tells me that an unnamed male "soul guide" has appeared to ask if he can speak through her. Her voice drops into a deep and enthusiastic register. "What a delicious feeling it is that you can sense me with your physical form!" this voice says before offering the kind of comfort anyone likes to hear ("You are very loved. You are never alone"), a few flattering comments ("You are a powerful human being. You have a strong calling"), some basic life advice ("The more you meditate, the more mindful you'll be. Listen to your intuition") and these parting words: "You can communicate with us and ask us for guidance and clarity any time. We look forward to the day when you can turn to us."

The first soul guide moves aside to make room for a "feminine goddess" bearing pink marigolds who, Harding says, is standing right beside me. "Her flowers are a symbol of the fleeting perfection of life— they come for a short period of time and then they go." Uh-oh. Could this be a forecast of my early demise? No. The message from the goddess is surprisingly superficial: "Your mission in life is to have fun, to be in the moment, to feel good. If it doesn't feel good, if it doesn't resonate, find another feeling until it feels good again."

Harding informs me that my chakras are whirling blissfully, that healing life force energy is coursing up and down my spine and, yes, that my "frequency is being raised." Whether or not my chakras are spinning, my mind certainly is. Just when my incredulity is strained to the point of snapping, she tells me that an Indian man, folded into the lotus position and decked out in a requisite turban, has plopped himself down on top of my navel, in the area of my solar plexus chakra, said to govern personal power, confidence and digestive function. I wriggle on the table. It's disconcerting, the idea of this man sitting on me. "You were a devotee of this guru. You used to sit at his feet," says Harding. She goes on to explain that I spent my days walking around barefoot and asking for food ("Not begging," she clarifies. "You were trusting the universe. When you needed nourishment, the food would just appear.") She writes the word TRUST in block letters on a piece of paper, as if taking dictation from this unseen guru, who soon disappears and is replaced by an Indian woman "from several centuries past." Says Harding: "As this female, you were not allowed to walk a spiritual path. You were not allowed to share wisdom. You were there to serve the men and children. This didn't sit well with you, even as a young girl. The men were reading the Vedas and you would hide in the bushes. You stole the book and read it and you were reprimanded viciously. This lifetime is being shown to you to remind you of your determination." I rather like this character, but she isn't in the picture long before my final visitors show up: a group of extraterrestrials she calls Palatians. "They are beautiful beings and they are all about love," she says. "Their message is simple. They don't mean this in a creepy way, but you are being watched. It means you are not alone. There are so many beings who are right behind you and pushing you forward."

The room is awfully crowded, and I won't be sorry when these guides take their leave. Harding must sense I've had enough. She bids the beings farewell and wraps up the session with a guided meditation.

What to make of all this? I've promised myself to keep an open mind throughout this year of experimentation—even with stuff I'd normally scoff at—so this is a good test. Harding seems nice. She runs what appears to be a busy practice of guided meditation circles and master's level reiki training courses, in addition to her part-time job managing a health-food store.

I try a direct approach. "This all seems unbelievable to me," I say. I'm pleasantly surprised when she doesn't take offense.

"I had a client the other day who said to me, 'You are really out there,'" she offers with a laugh. "I still have a little voice in my own head that says, 'This is really weird.'" Then she adds, "I've been doing this for so long that I know it's real. But it's still a little strange for me, too."

Despite her preternatural preoccupations, Harding is surprisingly down-to-earth—we commiserate over the challenges of raising teenagers. She also seems realistic about what she can do for her clients. She doesn't claim to heal the sick. "If you had a disease, my intention is not to cure you," she says. "I have no magical powers. My gift is in becoming a channel to allow your energy to flow." Her message, she says, is about love—love for self and love for others. "Love is your superpower," she tells me more than once. "Sometimes people just need a tune-up so that they can go back out into the world with a better sense of balance." At $90 for the hour, I leave her apartment feeling the experience has been more entertaining than enlightening.

Since this wasn't what I'd expected from a reiki treatment, I try another recommendation, but my visit with Dortmund Mattioli, who also runs his Peaceful Healer reiki practice out of his home, is more of the same. Mattioli tells me he sees chains around my feet that are causing me to feel stuck. Then he sees the archangel Michael, who has appeared holding the "sword of truth" to cut the chains so I can "speak my truth." Pegasus, the winged white horse, shows up too. "He represents freedom," says Mattioli. Just when it seems things can't get any more fantastic, a third party enters the scene—Quan Yin, the popular Buddhist deity known as the Goddess of Mercy and Compassion. Her message? "Go with the flow—let go of the struggle and trust that the universe is on your side." I'm sure Mattioli means well, but it's all so vague I don't believe any of it. His parting words do resonate, however. "Your energy is all in your head. All that worrying and thinking—it's too top heavy," he says. "You need to move that energy into your body to feel more centred and relaxed."

It isn't until I give reiki a third try that I finally get its appeal. Malia Ronderos, a reiki master at Toronto's Attuning for Wellness, comes recommended by a woman I met at a conference who tells me Ronderos' reiki sessions helped her keep her emotions on an even keel during her treatment for breast cancer. This time the session is offered in a professional office building, and no strange apparitions appear. Ronderos hands me an eye mask and instructs me to just relax for the next hour. I work to shut out the noise of the traffic on Bloor Street, and soon enough the soothing New Age music in the room almost lulls me to sleep. I never once feel Ronderos' hands on me. At one point I sneak a peek from under my eye mask to confirm she isn't sitting at her desk instead of tending to me. I see her moving with purpose, waving her hands as if scooping handfuls of air. Assured of her ministrations, I sink deeper into a relaxed state. My usual restlessness has evaporated. Maybe the reason so many women I know like reiki is because it gives them permission to lie down in the middle of the day and do absolutely nothing while someone pays loving attention to them. It's a way to quiet a roaring mind normally crammed with tasks related to children, caregiving and career. It's therapy without the bother of having to talk to someone. It's a hiatus from a hyper world.

When Ronderos rings a bell, I awaken with a half snore. She identifies a couple of places where I'm hurting and asks about the pain in my foot (plantar fasciitis) and my right shoulder (two weeks earlier I'd been diagnosed with a minor rotator cuff injury). "I think this pain is more about carrying a weight on your shoulders," she says. She asks what's weighing me down and we have an intimate chat. She opens up, too, telling me about how she first turned to reiki to help her cope during chemo and radiation treatments when she had breast cancer. "What I know is that it helped me manage the pain and the symptoms and helped give me a positive outlook. Reiki gave me the sensation of acceptance without thinking too much about the outcome. I felt [my illness] wasn't going to be fatal." Today she volunteers regularly at a centre called Wellspring, offering reiki to other women with breast cancer. "Cancer patients are anxious; they want peace of mind. Relaxation is a huge part of healing."

Ronderos doesn't charge me. The session is a gift, she says. Reiki might not be backed by science, but it sure was nice to rest for a while and spend time with this kind stranger who was as easy to talk to as a close friend.

ENERGY HEALING ISN'T THE ONLY PRACTICE THAT'S ON THE RISE AS mainstream religion descends into increasing irrelevance. There's a corresponding revival in the acceptance of paranormal phenomena. Christianity, itself defined by the acceptance of an all-powerful invisible being, the notion of the Holy Ghost and the concept of life after death, has some serious competition thanks to widespread belief in astrology, fortune-telling and past lives. A significant percentage of North Americans harbour some sort of supernatural belief: almost half believe in ghosts (about 20 percent say they've been in the presence of one), 41 percent believe in psychics, 33 percent in reincarnation and 29 percent in astrology.

The $2 billion a year psychic business is thriving, driven in part by celebrity psychics such as Colette Baron-Reid and Laura Day, "intuitive counsellors" who charge major corporations thousands of dollars for advice on how to direct their business dealings. Day is credited with predicting the financial crisis of 2008 and advising her Wall Street clients to pull out of the market.

It's not just secular folks who are superstitious—plenty of religious people embrace otherworldly ideas, too. A 2016 UK survey of twelve thousand self-identified Christians reveals they are more likely to believe in aliens than the devil, and more likely to believe in fate rather than in heaven. The same survey showed more Britons believe in ghosts than in a creator God.

Clay Routledge, a professor of psychology at North Dakota State University, writes that the popularity of paranormal beliefs is driven "by the same cognitive processes and motives that inspire religion." He credits their popularity to our desire to believe that "humans are not alone in the universe, that we might be part of a larger cosmic drama. As with traditional religious beliefs, many of these paranormal beliefs involve powerful beings watching over humans and the hope that they will rescue us from death and extinction."

No paranormal practice is as commonplace as tarot, a divination deck of seventy-eight cards. Tarot Biddy, the world's most popular tarot site, gets four million visitors a year, and there's an annual international TarotCon convention and a World Tarot Card Day. In 2017, the *New York Times* reported the highest tarot sales in half a century, largely attributed to the rise of feminist spirituality and witchcraft.

Tarot, along with its close cousins oracle cards and angel decks, is increasingly seen as a source of insight in times of need. For people who "don't go to church or consult a sacred text, tarot cards are becoming a popular devotional ritual and visual text used at home," says Rachelle Mee-Chapman, author of *Relig-ish*, who gives online readings as part of her spiritual coaching services. "They offer a way of slowing down, listening to the voice within and being guided. It's like a form of prayer."

Tarot cards don't so much predict the future as let practitioners listen to their inner wisdom. Carl Jung, the father of analytical psychology, saw tarot as a way to unveil the subconscious through the deck's use of archetypal symbols.

"You look at the images and make psychological connections between them and what's going on in your life—it helps you sort out your thoughts and feelings and provides perspective to make decisions," says Mee-Chapman, noting that many are unnecessarily spooked by the suspicious taint around tarot. "Even the Devil isn't a bad card—it's just a warning to watch out for tricksters."

I remember my Oma saying that tarot was from the devil (who, she also told me, lived behind the black grate of her fireplace and would come out and get me if I was bad). She wouldn't even allow regular playing cards in her house. Instead, she and I played Chinese Checkers. I never once beat her. She was a shark, my Oma.

I have no doubt she'd be shaking her fist at me if she could see me now, sitting across from Giselle Urech, a forty-year-old mother of five who reads tarot for a living in Hamilton. She charges $75 for a forty-five-minute session and averages three to four clients a day. Urech has a five-star rating on Facebook and also teaches tarot at a reputable local college.

There's a table between us laid with a violet cloth. The walls of this private back room in her modest house are mauve. A dreamcatcher hangs from the window, and a large angel sculpture in the corner, its wings flared, reminds me of the angel I saw during my magic mushroom trip. This one is holding a bowl filled with colourful gemstones. Soft music plays in the background. Urech's eyes close and her lids flutter. Then she opens them and turns over two cards: the Queen of Cups, depicting a dreamy woman sitting on a throne at the edge of the sea, and the Devil, a masked man with the curled horns of a ram. There's a pentagram in the background and flames lick at the edges of the card. This can't be good.

Urech advises me not to worry about the Devil card; it has nothing to do with evil forces, just the negative thoughts that can hold a person back. The Death card crops up too, but I shouldn't worry about that one either, it seems—it simply means the closing of one chapter and the opening of another. She draws a heart pierced by three swords. "I see heartache," she says. Next is the Chariot card reversed, which indicates I'm not moving forward and need to evaluate if I should change course. Without me telling her, Urech correctly guesses that

I've been married for decades and that the relationship hasn't always been smooth—not an unreasonable guess for a marriage as long as mine. We go over my allotted forty-five minutes and spend time talking about the challenges of intimate relationships. She only sees female clients, and most come to her because of romantic problems. "A lot of them believe they have to stick it out in their marriages, especially because of the kids. But what does that do to the soul?" she asks. "I'm seeing more and more women take back control of their lives." Urech considers herself a soothsayer for these sorrowful women. "I try my best to offer guidance through the cards that will empower them."

As with Malia Ronderos, I feel better after this conversation with a complete stranger. When I thank Urech, she says, "Most of the time, I'm just validating my clients' own intuition. Often, people come to me because they don't trust their gut. I don't have all the answers. I just try to give them a different perspective."

Curious to learn more about how tarot works, I sign up for a day-long beginner tarot session with Leslie Urquhart. She had a big IT job in Toronto before becoming a "lightworker" who runs workshops on drum-making and chakra painting at her Soul Escapes retreat in Grimsby, Ontario. Tarot is an ancient art based on intuition and interpretation, Urquhart stresses. "You might not believe it, but your whole life is in these cards. They've lasted for hundreds of years because they resonate with people."

She takes me through the twenty-two Major Arcana cards, including the Fool, the Empress, the Lovers and the Hanged Man, as well as the fifty-six cards in the Minor Arcana, comprising numbered and court cards in four suits: swords, wands, cups and coins/pentacles. Once I've figured out the basics, she encourages me to do a three-card reading around an issue I'm grappling with. I think about my daughter Lucy, who is pushing for more independence and sometimes pulls away from me, in the way that seventeen-year-olds do. I draw the Empress card (a woman sitting on a throne holding a scepter and wearing a crown of stars), the Sun (a blond child on a white horse holding an orange banner) and the King of Pentacles (a king in front of his castle, surrounded by verdant plant life and holding a golden coin). Urquhart interprets: "As the Empress, you still want to be the nurturing mother. Your daughter is the Sun; she's shining, exploring and testing limits. The King represents security and abundance. Don't worry. Your daughter is grounded, strong and independent. She's growing up, and you need to let her go." With that, I resolve to stop thinking of my youngest as my baby and acknowledge the young woman who will soon be out of the house, living a life of her own.

I purchase a Rider-Waite tarot deck from Urquhart, and at home I begin experimenting with pulling out the occasional card for guidance. One day, I draw the Four of Wands, which symbolizes domestic harmony, and spend a morning joyfully scrubbing down the kitchen. Another day, with a couple of deadlines looming, I pull out the King of Swords, which represents clear thinking and intellectual ability, and I sail through my work. I read cards for my kids and a couple of friends. It's an intimate and fun exercise as we explore the possible meanings together. Before accompanying a close friend to support her through what might be a scary diagnosis, I draw the Three of Cups. "It's a card of celebration," I tell her before heading to the doctor's office. She looks at me with a mixture of hope and skepticism. The news turns out to be good.

MY OMA, LIKE EVERYONE ELSE IN MY FAMILY, FERVENTLY BELIEVED IN life after death. Georgina Cannon, Canada's most prominent past-life regression therapist, also firmly believes the soul is eternal. I was raised with the idea that after you died you (most likely) went to heaven or (always a possibility) went to hell. Either way you lived forever, but in the same body. Cannon believes that though we live forever, our souls change into various forms throughout eternity: a princess or a pauper, a farmer or a midwife, a stealth leopard or a scrambling cockroach. Cannon has a lot of credentials in the paranormal world. She's the founder of the Ontario Hypnosis Centre, and she knows Shirley MacLaine. She was featured in a CBC documentary along with several of her clients, including Birgitta MacLeod, a fifty-three-year-old art gallery owner from Port Perry, Ontario. MacLeod's session with Cannon confirmed for her that she has had past lives. Under Cannon's spell, she says she re-experienced lives as a Druid in ancient Britain where she died with many children around her, as a West African woman who was killed in a massacre by a neighbouring tribe, and as an aristocratic French woman who died in childbirth. She was also a male farmer in a small town in Germany in the early 1800s who died of a heart condition. A CBC crew that flew with MacLeod to Germany verified the accuracy of some of her memories, including the names of the farmer's relatives, which were found in the marriage and baptismal records of a local Lutheran Church. MacLeod was "overwhelmed by a feeling of homesickness" when she visited the town. The experience was "profoundly spiritual," she says, enough to convince her that the soul is indeed eternal. "I believe our souls wear our bodies like clothing. When we don't need the clothes anymore, we discard them and get new clothing."

Her tale sounds like a fantastic confabulation, and yet the idea that we have past lives is more common than you might think. More than a billion people, mostly Hindus and Buddhists, believe their souls travel through many lifetimes. About one in four Americans believes in reincarnation, and, surprisingly, 22 percent of Christians do too, according to Pew Research. Some even equate the resurrection of Christ with reincarnation. Déjà vu, vivid dreams and the feeling of instant connection with someone are all used to bolster the argument that we have lived before.

Two prominent scientists have lent legitimacy to the idea of past lives. Dr. Ian Stevenson, a Canadian-born psychiatrist who worked at the University of Virginia School of Medicine for fifty years until his death in 2007, became internationally known for his research into reincarnation. He believed the etiology of many mental health issues could be traced to unresolved issues in past lives. He also examined the idea that gender identity dysphoria could be related to a person having belonged to a different gender group in a past life. Dr. Brian Weiss, an Oprah-endorsed physician and author who heads the department of psychiatry at Miami's Mount Sinai Medical Center, has sold millions of books with titles such as *Same Soul, Many Bodies* and *Many Lives, Many Masters.* The Yale-educated psychiatrist is known for observations such as, "You might look into the eyes of an infant, born mere minutes ago, to find that she is a thousand years old" and "We are all angels temporarily hiding as humans."

I book an appointment with Georgina Cannon two months in advance, since she is in popular demand. I consider the visit a lark that might result in an amusing anecdote or two. But the closer I get to my appointment, the more I start wondering: Who might I have been in another lifetime?

Turns out I was pretty boring.

Cannon doesn't dangle a pocket watch on a chain in front of my face. Instead, she speaks in gentle tones and slowly counts to twenty. I do get very sleepy. She allows me to tape the session on my phone while I relax in a recliner in her Toronto office. A recording of waves, whooshing and fading, lulls me, not into a trance but certainly into a relaxed frame of mind. The idea is that once total relaxation is achieved, the conscious mind takes a back seat to the subconscious and loosens up enough to go on a past-life journey.

Cannon instructs me to imagine a long corridor with lots of doors on either side, all slightly ajar, each one leading to a different time or place. I'm to pick one. Once I enter it, she informs me I'm now surrounded by a blue mist—"the mist of life between lifetimes"—and tells me to follow a bright white light that will take me through time and space, going "back, back, back, back" until I descend on planet earth.

"Look down. What's on your feet?" she asks.

"They're bare," I respond.

"Are you inside or outside?"

"Outside."

"What are you doing?"

"Just sort of wandering." I have to say something, but I feel like I'm making stuff up.

Then Cannon begins with the prompts. "Let's move to where you live in that lifetime."

I see a village with a big communal fire; everyone is gathered around. There are lots of women, I tell her.

"Let's move to an important event in that lifetime," she suggests. "One, two, three." And she snaps her fingers.

Ever the people pleaser, I keep going with my story. "I'm having a baby. I'm in a simple hut. I'm with some other women. There are bowls on a shelf."

"Let's move to another event in that lifetime," she says.

I'm uncomfortable. This feels fraudulent. "I don't know if this is just my imagination or what," I say.

"Just go with it," she urges.

I tell her I'm getting married. To someone important in the village. I need to do this to be safe. When she asks me how this woman dies, I say she dies after helping another woman give birth. "She knows her time is done, and she goes peacefully."

"What do you think gave this woman the most joy?"

"Babies. Children. Being among other women."

"What wisdom would she give you for your current life, do you think?"

"Focus on your children. Be with your tribe. Have a purpose."

"Now, thank her very much for that," says Cannon.

I do. It's unnerving how willing I am to follow her orders. I know I'm not hypnotized. I try again to convey this to Cannon. "I don't know . . . I think I'm making things up."

She doesn't seem to care. "Don't worry about that now," she says.

We go back to the blue mist. I choose another door. This one opens to a verdant garden of oversized plants and majestic trees. In the swing of things now, I tell Cannon I see a girl of ten or twelve running through the lush grass until she comes to her grandmother's cottage, where she is greeted with tea and cake.

"What do you do in this cottage?"

"I live with my grandmother. We sew fancy dresses for the women in the town."

I tell Cannon that I see the girl growing up and getting married. At her wedding, the guests dance around a maypole. A few years later the woman dies in childbirth.

Cannon asks me if I'm ready to experience another lifetime, but I've had enough. "Okay, let's bring you back then," she says and counts backward from ten to one.

I try a third time to tell her about my doubts. "I'm still not sure if I'm seeing all this or just making it up."

She brushes this off. "If you were making it up, you would have come up with something much more dramatic," she says.

I'm not so sure. I'm not that grandiose. I shop second-hand. I drive a beat-up car. I don't think I'd imagine myself as a princess or priestess.

"What do you make of it all?" I ask Cannon.

She throws it back to me: "What do *you* make of it? It's your life."

"It seems to be about birth and children and other women," I say. "Maybe about living simply. Seeing the beauty in the world. The men were sort of peripheral."

"Those are good lessons," she responds.

Cannon tells me that 80 percent of her clients have some sort of past-life experience under her guidance, and 60 percent walk away with a life-changing insight. In my case, I don't think the hypnosis took. Although images did pop into my head, I felt I was encouraged to tell a story. And I felt deceptive, stringing her along with my spiel. Maybe the tales I related were significant in some way, but I don't believe they came from previous lives. Hypnosis is related to areas of the brain associated with executive control and attention. Studies show responses vary widely, with about 25 percent of people incapable of being hypnotized. I tried it once before, in my twenties, to quit smoking. It didn't work then, either.

I'm sure Cannon, like the other practitioners I saw, believes in what she does. She's devoted her life to this work. Perhaps, in my eagerness to explore the mystic realms of healing touch, tarot and past lives, I've been gullible. Many would consider these "healers" charlatans. You'd think spirit guides or past lives would be compelling enough to appear all on their own, without having to fork over money to experience them. Maybe I'm too gentle on these practitioners, but my intuition tells me they are generally sincere.

Before I leave, I ask Cannon about her own past lives. She says in one she was a midwife who was killed by a drunken would-be father after his baby died in childbirth. "He was angry that his son died and picked up a big rock and smashed my head in." She claims learning about this life helped her heal from agonizing migraines. "After that session, I waited for my next migraine. It never came." Not only did her headaches disappear, Cannon says, but so did her fear of death. "I'm not scared of dying," she says, "because I know we just go into another room."

WHILE THE IDEA OF LIVING FOREVER MIGHT SOUND EXHAUSTING, maybe it makes death easier to accept. So, too, might the idea that we can reach our loved ones beyond the grave. That's the premise of Lily

Dale, North America's oldest spiritualist community, located an hour outside Buffalo on Cassadaga Lake in western New York. People have been coming here since 1879 to talk to the dead. Almost thirty years after my father's death, I go there myself to see if I can make some sort of contact with him. The place hosts about twenty thousand spiritual tourists annually. Each pays a $15 fee to enter the colony, which counts sixty registered psychics among its year-round population of three hundred.

Spiritualism, whose practitioners believe we never die and that communication between mortals and spirits is possible, had millions of followers in the mid- to late 1800s. Thousands came for meetings at Lily Dale, including celebrities such as Sir Arthur Conan Doyle and Harry Houdini. Spiritualists were at the forefront of social movements such as prison and welfare reform, women's rights and the abolition of slavery. When Susan B. Anthony, the grande dame of the suffragettes, visited Lily Dale, legend has it that a medium told her the spirit of her dead aunt was trying to communicate with her. Anthony was not impressed. "I didn't like her when she was alive, and I don't want to hear from her now," she's reported to have said. "Why don't you bring someone interesting like Elizabeth Cady Stanton?"

At Lily Dale, mediumship is believed to be a learnable skill. The town also offers more than one hundred educational workshops and lectures every season on topics ranging from numerology and reiki to crystal healing, telepathic communication with pets, quantum touch and astral travel.

Except for cars and electricity, not much has changed here over the past century. Some two hundred Victorian gingerbread cottages line narrow streets originally designed for horses and carriages. The hotel doesn't have air conditioning or an elevator. Some say Lily Dale is a shadow of its former self. Paint is peeling on many of the cottages; porches droop. People's gardens, though colourful, are unkempt. The village has a kitschy sensibility—you can't walk far without spotting a garden gnome or hearing a wind chime. Almost everyone who visits or lives here is female. Most are middle-aged or older. I spot only two dozen men among the couple of hundred people during my three-day stay.

I've booked appointments with three mediums, but I am dispirited after my first two sessions. The first doesn't have much to say that seems relevant to my life. The second tells me lots of nice things about myself—I emanate "beautiful colours," which reveal I'm a person who lives in her "heart space," and I "deserve to be treated like gold." But she gets a bunch of stuff wrong: she says I have three kids, not two; that I've lost a pet recently (our dog died four years ago); and that there's an Andy or an Andrew who is significant in my life (I know no such person). But then she mentions a "Jeff or a Jeffrey," and I'm taken aback. Suddenly everything she has to say—my grandfather is watching out for me, there's an exciting new project coming up—carries more weight. At the end of the session, she hands me back my $75 cheque, saying her policy is not to charge journalists. When I look at the cheque—which had been on the table beside her throughout our session—I see Jeff's name next to mine in the top left-hand corner.

But then I meet with Elaine Thomas, Lily Dale's longest continuously serving medium, who's been featured on the Oprah Network's *Beyond Belief* and in the HBO movie *No One Dies in Lily Dale*. Thomas quickly gains my confidence, because she gets a lot right. She talks about an upheaval in my life when I was nine (that's when my mother married my stepfather), describes my Oma as having "a backbone made not of steel, but of titanium" (true) and points to challenges in my relationship with my mother. She correctly observes that my biological father is dead and says he suffered from mental health issues all his life ("his chemistry was never right"), which made him unpredictable and unstable. Thomas says my father has a message for me. I brace myself and hang on her every word.

"He wants you to know that he simply didn't have the emotional equipment to be the kind of father you needed, and if he had stayed, things would have been worse—that you were better off without him," she says. "He wants you to know how much he loves you. He just didn't know how to show it. And he says he's proud of you, because in spite of everything you remained whole. He's telling me he knows he did one thing right in his life because you are on the planet."

I grab a handful of tissues from the box on the table and bury my face in them.

Some accuse mediums like Thomas of exploiting people who have suffered loss. They say those hopeful about making contact with dead parents, children and pets are deluded for thinking they can connect with the spirit world. But of course we want to believe we never die. That's why heaven was invented. Thomas had uncanny knowledge of many personal details of my life. I'm not sure what to make of that, but what harm is caused if people like her provide a bit of comfort?

By the time I leave Lily Dale the place will have touched me in unexpected ways. I still don't believe I'm surrounded by spirit guides or that my father actually sent me a message from beyond the grave. But I'd be lying if I didn't admit I found some consolation there. Like belief in any religion, Lily Dale requires a leap of faith.

Photo on next page: With Tim, the brother I never knew I had.

October

Stopping for Death

Because I could not stop for Death —
He kindly stopped for me —
The Carriage held but just Ourselves —
And Immortality.
—*Emily Dickinson*

IN A FEW WEEKS' TIME, DEATH WILL COME KNOCKING AT MY DOOR. It will take the form of goblins, ghosts and ghouls, along with small, hooded creatures carrying dollar-store plastic scythes up my front steps. I will open the door, laugh in its face and hand it some candy. I won't be scared at all, because it's nothing like the real thing.

Halloween celebrates death. Skeletons become set decoration, hanging from trees and propped up on front porches, looking like the last guests to leave the party. The trick-or-treat season lands in autumn when fading leaves perform a final pirouette, twirling to earth to decompose into mulch. Just as we will one day.

At fifty-six, I'm in the autumn of my life. According to Death-clock.com, an online calculator that predicts the date of your demise, my expected death date will be April 9, 2047. I will be eighty-four years old. At the time of this writing, I have 10,777 days, 20 hours, 27 minutes and 54 seconds left on earth, barring a sudden accident or an early diagnosis.

The boomer generation is creating a death boom. Five thousand of us die every day in the US. Most of us want to die at home, in our sleep or surrounded by loved ones, but about 75 percent of us will die in a hospital or long-term care setting, often hooked up to feeding tubes and ventilators, tended to by strangers. We are watching our aging parents die this way, and we don't like it one bit. Just as our demographic had an outsized influence on the civil and equal rights movements, we're now at the forefront of a death acceptance movement that's transforming the topic of dying from taboo to a normal part of life. We're seeing the rise of Death Cafes, green cemeteries, home burials and legislation for medically assisted dying. Death is our last great spiritual experience. We want it to be meaningful, and we want as much control over it as possible.

The first funeral I ever attended was for Mr. Blokhuis, an elderly friend of my grandparents who lived in the upstairs apartment of their home. He gave me my first job when I was eleven, cleaning his apartment on Saturday mornings for $5, and he died when I was thirteen. Halfway through his funeral I ran from the church in tears, stunned by the realization that everyone I loved was going to die. I still cry ferociously at every funeral I attend. It's embarrassing, especially when the deceased is your colleague's stepmother whom you never even met.

The hardest funeral was my biological father's. He died at forty-four of a heart attack while operating a backhoe on a construction job in Olds, Alberta. I didn't particularly want to go, but my mother called to say I should. "It's for closure," she insisted. My brother Henry and I sat strategically in the middle of Smithville Canadian Reformed Church, the two of us alone in a row behind my father's large extended family (he had seven surviving siblings), most of whom I hadn't seen in a dozen years or more. The church was packed behind us, filled with curious onlookers, none of them friends of my father. They were sniffing around the long-ago scandal of his wayward life. He had left this church and our family two decades earlier, but departures like my father's were so rare in this closed community that he still had a reputation among these people.

This church was where my teenage parents said their vows in 1961. A year later they stood at the baptismal font while a minister sprinkled water on my face, "a seal and trustworthy testimony" that I would have "an eternal covenant with God." This is where, as a young girl, I would rest my head against my mother's shoulder and wait for the moment (after the hymn singing, before the start of the sermon) when the rolls of *zoute* drops and King peppermints would emerge from purses and pockets to be noisily unwrapped and passed around, offering a reprieve during the interminable ninety-minute service. The minister back then, Reverend Kingma, was a dramatic man, so full of emotion on the pulpit that he would pull a large white handkerchief, seemingly endless as a clown's chain of hankies, from the breast pocket of his black suit and use it to wipe the tears he shed while admonishing the congregants for their sinful nature. When my mother told this minister that she was going to marry my stepfather—six years after my biological father had deserted her—Reverend Kingma told her she would go to hell if she remarried. He quoted Mark 10:12: "Any woman who divorces her husband and marries another, she commits adultery." My mother, twenty-seven years old at the time with two young children, was expected to wait for my father's return or live alone for the rest of her life. She married my stepfather, but told me she felt guilty for years for disobeying the church.

Much later I would learn of the bizarre wrangling around the planning of my father's funeral. The church told my father's family that the service should be at the local funeral home. The family said my father was a child of God and deserved a decent ending in the place where he had been baptized and married. There followed a drawn-out negotiation over the exact placement of my father's casket. The church said it should be put in the lobby at the entrance of the church, far from the altar, as a public reminder of my father's sinful straying. The family insisted it be at the front of the church, the same as any other funeral. Eventually, a compromise was reached; the casket was placed at the front of the church but off to the side, in front of the elders' bench. That seemed appropriate, since my father had felt judged by this church most of his life.

I was twenty-four, my brother twenty-one. I could not contain my sorrow and sobbed pitifully. My brother was stoic, but I knew he was hurting, too. I had always imagined I would see my father again one day, but now that window of possibility was shut as firmly as his casket. There wasn't any closure. I still had no idea who Mr. You Know Who really was.

All my life I had wanted to understand my father. My Oma said he was a charmer who could talk to anyone about anything—probably talk them into anything as well. I have a handful of snapshots of us together. In a couple of them he is beaming at me and I am bright-eyed under his gaze. For years, I fantasized that he would show up one day to shower me with gifts and offer a perfectly reasonable explanation for his years-long absence. He may have been a medium-height redhead, but I pictured him as Gregory Peck in *To Kill a Mockingbird*: tall, dark-haired, worldly and wise. I wanted to be like Scout, the apple of daddy's eye.

Clues to this mystery man would not surface until many years later, when I was almost fifty. I visited his brother's widow in a small town in South Carolina, and she unexpectedly unearthed a treasure: a sheaf of papers from a box in a spare bedroom. It was a handwritten document, twenty-one pages long, written by her late husband a year after my father died. Titled "A Christmas Story," it recounted my father's last Christmas, when my uncle flew him from Alberta to Ontario for the holidays and my father ended up staying for several months. The letter was filled with details: how my father had arrived in Toronto wearing a long overcoat and rubber boots, how he had a scruffy beard and no luggage except a bag containing some records—one of old Dutch hymns, another featuring Kris Kristofferson's greatest hits (including "Sunday Morning Coming Down," practically an anthem for my father's life). "He was a broken individual who lived under a cloud of damnation and fear," wrote my uncle. It was in this story that I first learned my father had been diagnosed with manic depression and often refused to take his prescription for lithium because of his embarrassment about having a mental illness. "He suffered from another illness too—that being the illness of rejection." My uncle's story also revealed a six-week trip my mother had taken with me when I was about a year old. "There were problems [in the marriage] almost immediately. I can't relate to you what happened," my uncle wrote. "The elders of the church became involved and decided that these two young people should have some time apart. They purchased a ticket for Henk's wife to the old country, Holland. Perhaps distance would make the heart grow fonder. The pain and sorrow of this action would follow my brother for the rest of his life."

The story went on to recount how my uncle had taken my father to visit several of his siblings and his mother and father, my grandparents, from whom he'd been estranged for two decades. "'I'm afraid to see them,'" my uncle quoted my father as saying. Reading these words,

I felt for him; I understood that kind of fear. The visit with his parents was tense. My uncle read everyone the story of the prodigal son from the book of Luke, but says in his account, "I saw that when a father or mother . . . rejects a son or daughter, no prayers to God will bring healing. God never wants us to let go of our children." The family visit ended on a hopeful note, however, with my uncle sensing the beginning of "a healing of spirit and body" in my father.

My uncle paid for my father to see a Christian psychologist, who later wrote my uncle a letter with his assessment: "Henk has a problem with the Canadian Reformed Church . . . His pain keeps his focus on what has transpired in the past. My advice to your brother is to let it go." But my father was not able to let it go. Despite the fact that my uncle found him a job and an apartment, my father would disappear again, chased away by his own demons. He hadn't paid his rent. His apartment was found strewn with dirty dishes, whisky bottles and rotten food. Eventually my uncle discovered my father wandering in downtown Hamilton and took him to a Salvation Army shelter. My uncle never saw him again.

On that same trip to South Carolina, I visited my aunt's son, a cousin in his forties I'd never met before. He surprised me, too, by producing a brown leather bag that contained my father's last possessions, passed down from the uncle who had tried to help him. I went through it, handling each item as tenderly as a forensic examiner, amazed—and saddened—by this evidence of my father's final days: a bottle of prescription sleeping pills, a tin of Export A tobacco, a motel room key, a receipt for $150 from the YMCA, a Canadian government benefit cheque for $348.00, salt and pepper shakers (the salt almost empty), a copy of an EKG chart, a cellophane-clad package of rum-flavoured wine-tipped Old Port cigarillos, three packs of matches, a metal shaver, a bar of Ivory soap and a slip of paper with his handwriting, indicating small amounts of money he owed people, including $4.95 to "Ron the waiter for 5 beers." I was struck, too, by what wasn't there—no letters, cards or photos. The bag unlocked some of the mystery of my father's life. He had so little. He had no home. His heart was about to give out—not just from the tobacco and booze and salt but also from his lonely life.

My mother used to say my father "ran away." In my child's mind I saw him wrestling himself into his coat as he took off on foot down the gravel driveway of our rented yellow clapboard house, away from our small town and out of our lives forever. He never stopped running—from province to province, job to job, woman to woman, leaving debts and despair in his wake. I think he was in despair himself, too. Perhaps he thought he'd find freedom by leaving his family and the church, but it seemed he was in a prison instead. He did not want to be found. Once, my mother told me, he had left his clothes in a truck at the lake so people would think he'd drowned. But after a while, no one bothered to search for him.

From South Carolina I travelled to Georgia, because I'd recently discovered there was something else—or, more accurately, someone else—my father had left behind: another son.

His name is Tim Van Egmond. He is six years younger than me. When one of his sons was experiencing some health issues, Tim got in touch with one of my father's siblings in Canada to determine whether there was a genetic component. When word filtered down to me, I sent Tim an email, and within minutes he called me, sounding excited. "A sister? I can't believe I have a sister!" On the first morning of our visit in Georgia we spent hours talking in his kitchen over coffee. I learned that our father had met Tim's mother about five years after leaving my mother and that he had left her, too, when she was six months pregnant with Tim. They never heard from him again. I had hoped Tim would be able to enlighten me about my father's life, but instead I was the one filling in some of the blanks: our father's mental illness, his life of restless wandering and the religious indoctrination that contributed to his guilt and shame.

Tim's two boys were the same ages as my daughters, and we talked about the joys and challenges of parenting. "I could never in a million years imagine leaving my children," he said. We caught up on the past forty-odd years. Tim had spent two years pitching for the Boston Red Sox before an injury forced him to retire from the game. He drove me around his neighbourhood, and when we passed a baseball diamond where he used to play, he told me how his single mom had signed him up with a local league, how he got a full baseball scholarship to Jacksonville State University, and how he shied away from the fame that came with playing in the big leagues. "Once Roger Clemens and I spent two weeks together, recuperating from injuries," he said. "We'd go out for lunch, and there would be a huge lineup of people waiting for him to finish so they could get his autograph. I knew that life wasn't for me." We swam in his pool and explored his five-hundred-acre property. He welcomed me into his man cave where he kept a boat, barbecue and riding lawn mower. I spotted a cabinet with his hunting gear, and when I revealed that I'd never even held a gun, Tim's youngest son was dumbfounded. Shooting guns is as Southern as eating fried chicken. "Why don't I give it a go?" I suggested, trying to be a good sport. Tim pulled a couple of guns from the cabinet, and we walked to the edge of the large pond on his property. As he threw a clay disc high into the air, his arm stretched so far back that his knuckles practically grazed the ground. It gave me a glimpse of the pitcher he once was. Despite my many attempts to hit the mark, I never did, but I had fun trying.

Tim and I spent less than seventy-two hours together, but an easy familiarity developed. Perhaps it was our common loss that united us. Perhaps we saw proof in each other that despite a legacy of parental desertion you can still be a loving and present parent yourself. From the wreckage of our father's failed relationships, it seemed something of value had been excavated. When I got home and unzipped my luggage, a card had been slipped inside, a note from Tim. "I'm so glad you reached out to me," he wrote. Meeting Tim helped me understand that my father's leaving had nothing to do with me. I knew this on an intellectual level. A three-year-old child can't be held responsible for her parent's desertion. But now I knew it on a gut level. Here was someone else who had been left behind. It wasn't Tim's fault, and it wasn't mine. Understanding this helped me finally lay my father to rest.

I'VE BEEN TO A COUPLE OF DOZEN FUNERALS IN THE YEARS SINCE MY father died. Most of these people, except for my Aunt Lonny who died of cancer in her late fifties, were elderly. Death always lies in wait, and in middle age its presence begins to loom. "We each live in the shadow of a personal apocalypse," the philosopher Stephen Cave says.

The Bible asks, "What is your life? For you are a mist that appears for a little time and then vanishes" (James 4:14). Shakespeare said much the same thing in *Macbeth*: "Life's but a walking shadow, a poor player that struts and frets his hour upon the stage and is heard no more."

The mist vanishes, the shadow fades—and then what? The French writer Michel de Montaigne wrote: "To begin depriving death of its greatest advantage over us let us deprive death of its strangeness, let us frequent it, let us get used to it." I decide to visit the country of death—albeit temporarily—to see if I can prepare for my own eventual one-way trip. Maybe staring death in the face will help soften its features. Maybe I can see about wiping that smirk from the Grim Reaper's face.

I start by reading the obituaries every morning in the paper, absorbing those that have a bit of feeling to go along with the facts. (One favourite, the obit of "HICKS, Sybil Marie," includes this line: "I finally have the smoking hot body I have always wanted . . . having been cremated.") I read popular death memoirs—*When Breath Becomes Air* by Paul Kalanithi, *Being Mortal* by Atul Gawande, *Option B* by Sheryl Sandberg and Adam Grant, *The Last Lecture* by Randy Pausch and *The*

Year of Magical Thinking by Joan Didion. I sign up as a member of the Order of the Good Death, founded by mortician and funeral industry rabble-rouser Caitlin Doughty. Her YouTube series *Ask a Mortician* covers topics from decomposition to necrophilia and has had almost sixty million views. "Death itself is natural," says Doughty, "but the death anxiety of modern culture is not." I download a ninety-nine-cent app called WeCroak that sends me reminders five times a day that I'm going to die. The app is inspired by a Bhutanese saying that "to be a truly happy person, one must contemplate death five times daily." The reminders come at random times, at any moment of the day, just like death.

For a few weeks I have a writing getaway while housesitting for friends who own a home on the edge of a large municipal cemetery. On my daily walks I greet the tombstones like old friends—"Hello there, John Milne" (a Conservative senator who died in 1922 and has the tallest monument in the graveyard), "Hello there, George Hamilton Mills" (mayor of my hometown in 1858). The graves of women, children and soldiers all become familiar. I can see the cemetery from almost every window in the house, and late at night the headlights of passing cars cast a fleeting glow, illuminating the markers that stand forever stoic. Some of them date back more than 150 years. I imagine clusters of mourners, sagging in grief over heaped piles of fresh dirt, dressed in petticoats and pillbox hats, driven here in carriages and Packards. Different eras but suffering in the same way—nothing to do but stand and weep. I rarely pass a soul on my walks, except an occasional dog walker. I never see anyone at a grave. We forget the dead. We'll be forgotten too. Walking through a graveyard puts everything in perspective.

Some people think talking about death is morbid. But of all the conversations in our lifetimes, few are as imperative as the one about our ending. Too often we avoid updating our wills (half of Canadians don't even have one), and most of us have never talked to our loved ones about do-not-resuscitate orders, what we want done with our remains or what kind of funeral we would like to have.

This is beginning to change. The move to lift the lid on death is being driven by trailblazers who want to break the monopoly the $20 billion funeral home industry has on matters related to death and dying.

Fifty-five million people die every year. In North America, here's what typically happens: We die in the ICU. Our body is wheeled to a basement morgue and then whisked into a mortuary car that pulls up at a back entrance. At the funeral home, our body is embalmed, a gruesome process that drains our blood, punctures our internal organs, and injects us with about three gallons of formaldehyde, methanol, and other solvents that slow the decomposition process. Small plastic caps are inserted around our eyes to avoid a sunken look and prevent our eyelids from inopportunely popping open and frightening mourners. Our mouth is wired shut, our lips stitched together with thread, and our nose and other orifices are packed with cotton to prevent leakage into the casket. Our thumbs are discreetly bound together before our hands are folded delicately over our stomach. Wax is used to cover up bruising, makeup freshens the face and hairstyling creates a photo-worthy posture of repose. All along the way, our body is handled not by loved ones but by strangers. A sled-like device engineers the gliding of our body into a casket (often priced at several thousands of dollars, the cost of which is considered a reflection of how loved we were). This is driven in a hearse to a cemetery, where it's placed in a cement vault in a hole in the ground that's concealed by a faux grass drape. After the mourners disperse, our grave is filled in and smoothed out, ensuring the plot is level enough for groundskeepers to mow and manicure. A fiery ending by way of cremation is another option, of course, but is it really better to burn out than to fade away? A crematorium's furnace needs to be cranked up to 760–1,150 degrees Celsius for seventy-five minutes to burn a single body and will spew a toxic mixture of vaporized mercury, dioxins and greenhouse gases into the environment.

Just as we have delegated the mechanics of deathcare to the funeral industry, so too have we left the spiritual aspects of death to the institution of religion, which often denies death's finality by promising everlasting life, for better or worse. "Perhaps the most pressing concern of human existence is that of mortality . . . and being 'saved' is a reprieve from confronting one's mortality," writes Marlene Winell in *Leaving the Fold*. "Fundamentalism suggests an even worse outcome than physical death—judgment and punishment in the afterlife, a kind of continuous death. Given this alternative, the offer of salvation is extremely appealing."

SBNR people don't believe in hell, but they are curious about death. That's one of the reasons Death Cafes have become so popular. These intimate gatherings, where strangers talk openly about death over tea and cake, are allowing people to confront the idea of their end and to consider matters both practical and philosophical, away from the influence of religion. "People want to engage with the topic of death in meaningful ways, and they don't see church as the place where that conversation is going to happen, because they think the church is going to impose its views on them," says Rev. Nancy Talbot, a minister at Mount Seymour United in North Vancouver. To address this, she arranged for an outside facilitator to organize a Death Cafe in the lobby of her church a couple of years ago. Twenty-five people showed up, and now Death Cafes are a regular outreach effort. They are "absolutely spiritual" because they allow participants to "foster authentic connections with each other," says Talbot.

Death Cafes began in North America in 2011. They're modelled after the Café Mortel created in 2004 by the Swiss sociologist and writer Bernard Crettaz, who, after the death of his wife, wanted to break the "tyrannical secrecy" around death. Now, there are about seven thousand Death Cafes in sixty-five countries. Anyone can organize one as long as they follow the basic directives: non-profit, non-denominational and with no specific agenda other than starting a conversation about death.

Death Over Dinner is another initiative. Participants are encouraged to gather friends and family to break bread and talk about what constitutes a good death—and a good life. Death Over Dinner was founded five years ago by entrepreneur Michael Hebb, and since then 200,000 dinners have been hosted in thirty countries. "The way we die in Western society is broken," Hebb said in an interview with the *Guardian*. "I had a hunch that open conversation about our end-of-life wishes could be the most impactful thing we could do to heal that system and to heal the way we die. We are death-illiterate, and when we don't discuss death, we are not empowered to make decisions."

The organization's website offers useful resources for hosting these dinners, including an invite to send to guests ("This could be the strangest dinner invitation I've ever sent, but read on—I think we are in for a memorable experience"), conversation prompts and readings for guests to mull over in advance of the meal. These include "Charlotte's Last Day," a chapter from E.B. White's beloved novel *Charlotte's Web*, in which Charlotte faces her death and tries to console Wilbur, as well as the raw and poignant self-written obituary of Jane Lotter, who died of cancer at sixty after taking advantage of Washington state's compassionate Death with Dignity Act. It reads in part: "I was given the gift of life, and now I have to give it back. This is hard. But I was a lucky woman, who led a lucky existence, and for this I am grateful."

I ask Rochelle Martin, a Hamilton nurse and death doula, to facilitate a Death Over Dinner for a gathering of women friends at my house. Martin is known for helping to start One Washcloth, a hospital-based project that invites family members to tenderly attend to the body of a loved one by wiping their face and hands with a washcloth. This creates a positive, tangible connection to the person who has died and helps bridge the gap between life and death. People have told Martin how this gesture has profoundly affected them in their hour of grief: "We cared for him, after the accident." "I was there. I loved her to the end." "I washed his beautiful face, for the last time."

As a death doula, Martin teaches people how to become comfortable with death. And as an emergency room nurse, she's had a lot more experience with death than any of the guests around my dining room table. Our dinner has a Last Supper feel: twelve of us are gathered together and the menu includes fish, loaves of bread and plenty of wine. There's lots of laughter, despite the seriousness of the topic, and a certain lightheartedness too—I've ordered a cake in the shape of a tombstone from a local bakery and placed a plastic skull at each place setting with the guest's name written in Magic Marker on the forehead. Six tealights glow in the black candelabra that serves as the centrepiece. In Eucharistic fashion, we eat and we remember. Martin facilitates the discussion, encouraging us to go around the table and share a significant death we've experienced.

My friend Ruth fights back tears when she remembers how she felt pressured to observe the strict visiting-hour schedule of her father's nursing home—she and other family members were asked to leave just a few hours before he died alone. Karen shares the haunting experience of visiting a relative in a ward where everyone was brain dead—their bodies hummed along while their minds were long gone. Nancy says she is thankful she was in the room when her father, who had been a difficult man when she was growing up but had softened in old age, took his last breath. Another friend shared her frustration at having been appointed executor of a relative's estate, only to find that a second executor had also been appointed and given much different instructions.

Jill's story is touching. When her seventy-seven-year-old father, a United Church minister, died at home, she helped wash his hands, feet and face after his death. "It felt like the stories I'd heard of Mary Magdalene washing the feet of Christ with her tears," she says. Just before he died, her father shared his vision of seeing his recently departed wife in the room. His breathing slowed, and he looked up to the ceiling. "It seemed to take some effort for him to pull himself away from where he was focused. He looked at me and said, 'It's beautiful.' Those were his last words; his last sermon, perhaps."

A good death—even a beautiful one—is possible.

But we have to plan for it. Rochelle Martin says there is much to consider. How do we hope to die? What do we want done with our body? Who will speak at our memorial? How much money do we want to spend? Where will our funeral be held? Who will be in charge? Who will speak for us? What music will be played? Have we conveyed our last wishes to anyone? If not, what are we waiting for? Most of the women around the table are in our fifties. Few of us have contemplated these things until now.

Buddhists used to stare at images of decaying corpses, and Trappist monks would wear scapulars with skulls and crossbones as a reminder of the inevitability of death. Thinking about dying enhances our appreciation of life. It keeps us alert to the transitory nature of our existence. Studies show that people who regularly contemplate their mortality actually have a less depressed mood (yes, downloading WeCroak could make you happier). In his book *59 Seconds*, Richard Wiseman writes that considering what might be said about us after we're dead can help us prioritize things in the here and now. "Asking people to spend just a minute imagining a close friend standing up at their funeral and reflecting on their personal and professional legacy helps them to identify their long-term goals and assess the degree to which they are progressing toward making those goals a reality."

Talking about death can also bring us closer to one another. "People experience a real sense of spirituality in having these conversations because this is a topic that touches us deeply, and it's one we haven't been able to explore together," says Martin of the death dinners she's facilitated.

My friends linger at the table long after the tombstone cake is served. It's almost midnight, but we are reluctant to part company. Much has been shared that had not been spoken out loud before. The candles flicker and fade. Who among us will be first to go? Who will be the last? We have a better sense now of how we might help each other when the time comes. There are long hugs at the door as we say good night.

INSTEAD OF OUTSOURCING OUR DEATHCARE, MARTIN ENCOURAGES people to take greater control of it themselves. She sets a fine example. She's only forty-three, but she's already purchased and stored the dry ice packs she'll need to keep her dead body chilled during the funeral she's planned to have for herself in her own home. There's a $125 card-board casket ready for assembly in her basement. She's measured it to ensure it will fit nicely in her Audi minivan. She's also told her three teenage children she would like them to help dig the hole at her pre-purchased plot in Union Cemetery, a green burial site in Cobourg, Ontario. "The digging has to feel like hard work, because then it will be meaningful for them," she says.

She's left no stone unturned.

I've made a will, but no other preparations for my own death. Time to change that.

I start with shopping for a coffin, looking for less expensive options. Turns out Costco sells a "serenity cherry" model for $1,799 and even promises expedited shipping (although who wants to chance a last-minute snafu with the courier?). At Hamilton's Affordable Burial & Cremation, Josh, one of the sales clerks, shows me the dozen or so models on display, including a $350 particle board box most often used for unclaimed bodies and a perfectly respectable eco-friendly casket made of honeycomb cardboard with a plush white interior. It starts at $895; the price increases if your body exceeds the three-hundred-pound weight restriction. The shop also has an "end-of-the-line" sale on miniature urns ($69) and cremation jewellery, including a keychain with the thumbprint of the deceased ($190) and a silver ring with a heart-shaped locket that holds a pinch of "cremains" ($230). A dark willow wicker casket catches my eye. It looks as cheery and cosy as an oversized picnic basket. Lifting the lid, I half expect it to be lined in red gingham. Josh says I can put it on hold with a $585 prepayment, but I'm hoping I'm still a few decades away from needing it. I take a picture instead. My oldest daughter squirms when I show it to her. "Seriously, Ruby, this is what I'd like," I tell her. "Okay, okay," she says, impatient to move on from any talk of death. I mention that she could toss in a gingham tablecloth. "That would be kind of cute," she concedes.

Next, I talk my husband into a day trip to Niagara Falls to check out Section 16 of the new 736-plot Willow's Rest green burial site at Fairview Cemetery, one of North America's largest and most beautiful burial grounds. One Thomas Whittaker, age fifty-six, was the first person to be buried here on July 20, 1883. Ever since, the cemetery has embraced innovation in burial ground trends, with a tissue donor memorial recognizing those who sacrificed their bodies to science and a remembrance garden where loose ashes from human remains are buried.

Mark Richardson, the city manager of cemetery services, gives us a tour of what's essentially a two-acre wildflower meadow framed by weeping willows, their branches sweeping the earth. Green burials aim to return a body to the earth as naturally as possible with the least amount of environmental impact. To that end, certain rules apply: no headstones, embalming or cremation, and only biodegradable caskets or shrouds are permitted. "Why try to reduce the impact on the environment by composting and recycling your entire life only to spoil all those efforts at the end?" Richardson asks. He makes a good point. Most graveyards project a serene landscape, but underground there's a churning stew of noxious embalming chemicals (more than 800,000 gallons of embalming fluid are buried every year in the US) as well as tons of non-biodegradable cement vaults and varnished coffins.

This simple woodland lot seems a fitting final resting place. My husband and I stand side by side in the middle of it. Century-old trees and well-tended garden beds add to the tranquil setting. It's quiet here, but if you listen carefully, you can hear the far-off sound of traffic, people coming and going, busy with their lives until they aren't anymore.

I wonder—is this where we will end up?

"Whaddaya think?" I ask my husband.

"Sure, doesn't really matter to me," he says.

As usual, he'd be content anywhere.

We've been together so long. Will we last into eternity, side by side, under a thick blanket of earth? Will we be one of those couples—when one dies, the other passes within mere weeks, broken-hearted? Some days neither of us is sure anymore whether we want to stay committed until death do us part. Some days our marriage feels like a habit—routine, yet hard to break. Lately we've each admitted that we sometimes think about a new beginning, a different kind of life, maybe even with someone new. It feels agonizing, contemplating the possible end of our marriage. It's a much harder thing than what we're doing now, contemplating where our bodies will be laid to rest. It would be convenient for the children if they had only one gravesite to visit. It occurs to me now: How will they find us if there's no headstone? "The office keeps a detailed map," says Richardson. "And they can always use GPS co-ordinates."

There's an ever-expanding array of creative options for green burials, from mushroom burial suits (the spores devour human tissue) to alkaline hydrolysis, also known as aquamation, in which the body is placed in a stainless-steel vessel with a special solution that dissolves it within twenty hours. You can also choose to be buried at sea and arrange to be wrapped in a shroud, hand-sewn by New England sail makers, before being dumped overboard.

Green burial really isn't so odd. It's how many observant Jews, Muslims and Quakers have always buried their dead—without embalming and in a simple casket or wrapped in a shroud. It's how many of the dead used to be buried: in a pine box on their own land. Embalming methods were first used during the Civil War to preserve the corpses of soldiers so they could be shipped home for burial.

Funerals too were once a simple practice. Until the mid-1800s, families cared for their deceased on their own, often with the help of women in the community who would assist with the "laying of the dead" by washing, dressing and displaying the body. A local carpenter would be hired to construct a coffin. Visitation was held in the front parlour, followed by a procession to the family graveyard or church cemetery.

Today, home funerals are making a comeback, according to the US National Home Funeral Alliance, created in 2010 to help people care for their dead by offering practical guidance on things like keeping the body cool and reporting communicable diseases to local health authorities. With home funerals, families can sit vigil over a few days, and avoid the exorbitant costs associated with traditional funerals (they average about $10,000), as well as the spiritually disaffected services run by a funeral home employee or a member of clergy who may not even have known the deceased.

The documentary *In the Parlor* chronicles the experiences of three families who opt for home funerals. Each is an exercise in intimacy and tenderness, marked by rituals such as allowing visitors to draw on the casket of a young man who has died and draping a silk scarf bearing the handprints of her siblings over the casket of an older woman. "Death is part of life," one of the mourners says in the film. "Death is as natural as being born. Interesting how so many people want to hide from that."

I tell my kids I'd like a home funeral, too; that I hope they'll hoist that wicker casket with me in it onto the dining room table, where we've shared thousands of meals. I hope they'll be comfortable enough to come and sit by my side—to hold my hand the way I held theirs when they first learned to cross the street; to not be afraid to touch the lips that planted thousands of kisses upon them. I hope there will also be a service at my Unitarian Church; that my friends who are still standing will sing some songs and have some nice things to say about me. I hope there will be a boozy catered lunch somewhere afterwards, and that everyone will summon an Uber to get them home safely. I hope they'll say to one another, "Well, wasn't that great?" My nearest and dearest will ride out to the green cemetery to weep as they bury me deep. Then I hope they'll wipe their tears, go home and carry on with their lives.

Oh, death, where is thy sting? Yes, it's gonna hurt. But perhaps, if we plan it right, it doesn't have to be quite so painful.

I'm inspired, yet again, by Mary Oliver, who considered her own mortality with a spirit of anticipation. In her poem "When Death Comes," she wrote about being full of curiosity about death, that "cottage of darkness," and how she was determined to live in amazement, taking the world into her arms. We spend our lives acting as if we are never going to enter the cottage of darkness. "Do any human beings ever realize life while they live it—every, every minute?" asks Thornton Wilder in *Our Town*.

What happens when we die? Everything's a theory, right? I'm with the Unitarian minister Forrest Church, who wrote in *Love and Death*, a book he completed while he was living with terminal cancer, about his skepticism regarding the stereotypical images of heaven: "Many of them really are quite silly, an eternity of harps, halos and hymnals, the heavenly hosts fluffed up on clouds singing hosannas forever. Whatever happens after we die, I hope it isn't this. So defined, heaven might best be described as punishment for good behavior." I also share his disbelief in hell: "However bad I may have been at times, the God I believe in is too good to sentence me (or any of God's creatures) to eternal damnation. I am confident that when we die, we will all experience peace."

That's what I'm hoping for, too.

THERE'S NOTHING LIKE PONDERING YOUR OWN DEATH TO MAKE YOU realize that every little thing is a miracle—waking up in the morning, finding fresh strawberries in the fridge, listening to your dog snore contently beside you on the couch while you tap away on your computer keyboard.

But it's often not until the end of our days that we gain clarity about what's really important; and then it's too late. Bronnie Ware, an Australian palliative care nurse, recorded the top five regrets of the dying in her book of the same name. "The regrets touch upon being more genuine, not working so hard, expressing one's true feelings, staying in touch with friends and finding more joy in life," she writes.

The dying, Ware found, often have a lot of regrets.

The same is true for the living. One of mine is that I never had the chance to make peace with my biological father. I passed up the opportunity to do that with my stepfather, too.

When my brother Henry called earlier this year to tell me my stepfather had been diagnosed with cancer and things didn't look good, I immediately thought of my mother. She was only seventy-three, too young to be a widow. I'd been estranged from my parents at that point for almost ten years. Was I expected to visit now that he was sick? My mind was full of justifications for why I shouldn't have to: it seemed hypocritical when we hadn't gotten on for years, he probably didn't even want to see me, we'd never been close, it would just be awkward. But in truth I was afraid my stepfather would plead with me on his sickbed to return to religion, to come back to the fold.

This fear was legitimate. A decade earlier, as my mother's younger sister, my Aunt Lonny, lay dying in hospital, I'd paid her a final visit. It was the first time I'd ever had to say goodbye to someone in that situation. I Googled "What to say to a dying person" and found good advice: ask the person how they are feeling physically. Ask them how they are doing emotionally. Tell them something you've always appreciated about them. I followed this advice to the letter. My aunt told me her pain was well controlled. She said she knew she wouldn't be leaving the hospital and talked about going to heaven. I'd always appreciated her sense of humour, I said. My aunt was a merry prankster. As a joke she once passed around a plate of candy at a party that included squares of chocolate Ex-Lax. I loved her for the levity she brought to our extended family gatherings. After I told her this, she handed me a book, *Hope for Each Day* by Billy Graham. And she had something to tell me. She'd learned from my mother that I was going to the Unitarian Church, and she said I'd hurt my mother deeply by choosing this path. She urged me to turn toward the Lord and assured me it was not too late to be saved. "Don't be a fool, Anne," were her last words to me. I made it to the hospital hallway before dissolving in tears. When I got home and opened the book she'd given me, there was an inscription: "Our prayer is that this devotional may be an inspiration to you. That you may know the only true God that will lead you and your two wonderful little girls to eternal life. We love you, Anne."

I couldn't bear a repeat of that kind of scene. Self-preservation kicked in and overrode my feelings of guilt. I didn't visit my stepfather.

People often think the worst about stepfathers. They assume awful things if you say you didn't have a good relationship with yours. My stepfather could be impatient and blunt, but that was as bad as it got. He took pride in "telling it like it is." Once, in my early twenties, stuck in a job I didn't much like, I told him about a half-baked plan to open an antique shop with retrofitted furniture. "That turkey ain't never gonna fly," he said. I didn't know whether to laugh or cry. Politics got him riled up to an unbelievable degree. My emerging liberal views made him angry, and he'd often yell, "Are you nuts?" if I disagreed with him over some point or another. In our worst argument ever—about some political issue now long forgotten—I pleaded with him to see my point of view.

"But Dad . . ." I sputtered.

He lost his temper. "Don't you ever call me that again," he said.

"Klaas!" my mother scolded him.

Furious and hurt, I gave him the silent treatment for a few days. Eventually I started calling him "Dad" again. What else was I going to do?

I was nine when my mother married him. Too old to hug him without it being awkward, but young enough to want a father figure. I figured he didn't like me, that I was just part of the package that came with marrying my mother. And of course I was. He was good to my mother but had difficulty showing any sort of tenderness to me. Perhaps this was compounded by the fact that he had lost his own mother when he was only three and wasn't close to his stepmother. A few weeks after they married, I ran to my Oma's house to report, "He's mean!" "He's your father now," my Oma said. "You have to accept him." He and my mother would have two biological children together, and he was able to be affectionate with them. I couldn't blame him for this. Could I?

My stepfather did some nice things. He got us a dog, Kingsley. He taught me to catch a baseball and a football. He brought old-school country music into our home, introducing me to the likes of Hank Williams, Patsy Cline, Marty Stuart and Dolly Parton, music I love to this day. He had a record of a long song with a wild drumbeat called "Wipe Out." Henry and I would dance to it until we were sweaty, then ask my stepfather to play it again. We'd dance again and collapse, laughing, on the green brocade couch in our living room.

A couple times my stepfather rescued me. Once, and only once, I asked my parents if I could borrow some money. I was twenty-one, earning a pittance as a community newspaper reporter, and an expensive car repair had left me short on the rent. My mother, angry at me for leaving the church, said they couldn't help out. I got in my car, crying, to drive home, but my stepfather came out of the house, took a wad of cash from his pocket, peeled off some bills and handed them to me through the car window. I think he was the one who finally talked my mother into coming to my wedding. Looking back, I saw that maybe he was more of a peacemaker than I'd realized.

Instead of visiting my stepfather when he was sick, I wrote him a letter, letting him know I was hoping for the best possible outcome. Aware this might be my last communication with him, I included what I'd appreciated about him—that he was a good provider, and that it couldn't have been easy for him when he married my mother and had to support two stepchildren as well. I thanked him for standing up for me to that mean Mr. Torenvliet who whacked me across the head in Grade 7. And I thanked him too for the joy he expressed when I was pregnant with my first child. I could still remember his words, corny but affecting: "Now you will really have the full experience of being a woman."

I sent this letter in place of a face-to-face goodbye. Did that make me a cowardly stepdaughter? Or someone who was setting appropriate boundaries? I wasn't sure. We think impending death will change everything, that it will magically fix relationships that have been fraught for years. Sometimes it does. But when relationships have suffered, it can be hard to know if we should aim for a last-minute fix or just leave things be.

A few weeks after I sent my letter, my mother sent me a card: "Dad got your letter. You are welcome to visit anytime." Not exactly a request, I assured myself. I still didn't visit, though I felt like a coward. When he died a few months later, and I called my mom to offer my condolences, it was our first conversation in years. I told her I'd like to go to the funeral.

"Well, that's up to you," she said, her voice frozen.

I arrived early at the church, and my stepfather's siblings and their partners—an aunt and uncles I hadn't seen in years—greeted me warmly. One whispered in my ear, "You're so brave." I found this unnerving—was there a reason I needed to be brave? What had been said about me? My Uncle Dick, my stepfather's older brother, always so cheerful and friendly, gave me a hug. "Please don't be a stranger," he said. I shook hands and shared hugs with at least a dozen cousins. When the family gathered in a side room before filing into the church, I went to my mother. She turned her cheek to me and I kissed it.

The minister preached a sermon on Psalm 23, "The Lord Is My Shepherd." I thought about how I'd sung the hymn based on this psalm forty-five years ago at my parents' wedding. "No matter how far the sheep have wandered, they can always come home to the Lord," said the minister.

Was he looking at me?

I was surrounded by dozens of church-going relatives—so much family, and yet we were like strangers to each other. Religion separated us. It made my heart hurt, but I didn't know what to do about it. I didn't think they could accept me just as I was. They'd want me to adapt my views. I'd have to sublimate myself in order to fit in, and I couldn't do that.

I lingered at the reception, drinking coffee and eating raisin buns stuffed with gouda cheese. My mother and I avoided each other until there were only a few people left.

I touched her arm. "How are you, Mom?"

She was eager to talk about my stepfather and told me the story of his final day. How my brother Derek was with him when he died. How his last word was "home." This brought her great comfort. "He died with a smile on his face," she said. "He knew he was going to see his mother again. He knew he was going to be with his Lord and saviour.

"He was a good husband," she added. Then, "And a good father."

I nodded.

"When we got married, he promised he'd never lay a hand on you or Henry."

Was that what made him a good father? The fact that he hadn't hit me? That seemed to set the bar low. I didn't say anything.

My brother Henry, always a joker, cut in to relieve the tension. "Well, there was that time he kicked me in the butt with the point of his cowboy boot. But I'm sure I deserved it."

The three of us laughed. Life seemed full of small miracles.

Before I left, the minister, whom I'd never met before, pulled me aside. My stomach clutched in anticipation of an awkward conversation, a possible come-back-to-the-fold attempt.

What he said was, "Please look out for your mother."

In the natural order of things, my mother's death would be next. I didn't want to have more regrets. Was there a way to make things right between us? I didn't know, but I realized I was willing to give it another try.

Photo on next page: My mother and me in 1981. I'm eighteen, she's thirty-six.

November

The Ultimate
Spiritual Practice

"Gratitude is the wine for the soul. Go on. Get drunk."
—*Rumi*

FACING DEATH, MY STEPFATHER WAS ABLE TO BE THANKFUL. JUST
weeks before he died, he had stopped to admire a small wildflower
poking through a cement walk. "Look—how beautiful," he told my sister, Laura, pointing it out with his cane. A few months earlier, before

his surgery for a new heart valve, my mother had asked my stepfather if he was scared. He said he wasn't. "It's a win-win," he told her. "If I die, I go to heaven; if I live, I get to be with you a while longer."

You don't have to believe in a final payoff to face death with a spirit of gratitude. Oliver Sacks, the neuroscientist who called himself an "aggressive atheist" and described religious extremism as "the most dangerous thing on the planet" dismissed the idea of an afterlife. At eighty-one, shortly after receiving his terminal cancer diagnosis, he stated simply, "My luck has run out." In his book *Gratitude*, a slim volume of essays he compiled as he was dying, he wrote that the prospect of death allowed him to view his remarkable life in a new way, "as from a great altitude." "I cannot pretend I am without fear," he writes. "But my predominant feeling is one of gratitude. I have loved and been loved. I have been given much and I have given something in return. Above all, I have been a sentient being, a thinking animal on this beautiful planet, and that in itself has been an enormous privilege and adventure."

His final essay concludes: "And now, weak, short of breath, my once-firm muscles melted away by cancer, I find my thoughts, increasingly, not on the supernatural or spiritual but on what is meant by living a good and worthwhile life—achieving a sense of peace within oneself."

If there's an art to dying, surely that is it. Isn't a sense of peace what we all long for? No two men could be more different than my stepfather and Oliver Sacks, yet both achieved mastery over their deaths by being grateful at the end.

Philosophers, poets and prophets have long identified gratitude as key to a meaningful life. "A thankful heart is not only the greatest virtue, but the parent of all other virtues," said the Roman statesman Cicero. I've spent a great deal of my life ignoring this wise advice. Often, I've been discontent. The dissolution of my relationship with my family is a wound I've compulsively picked at. It has made my foundation seem fragile, and I have often felt I can't ground myself properly, especially if other dissatisfactions are heaped on the pile. I'd like to change that, and I'm hopeful that learning to be more grateful will give me a more positive perspective.

Certainly the research shows that being thankful improves virtually all areas of life. It decreases depression, envy and materialism, improves sleep, exercise and diet, boosts productivity, and vastly improves the experiences of marriage, parenthood and friendship. One study indicates that an attitude of gratitude can add nine years to our lives, another that being grateful boosts our happiness levels by 10 percent, the equivalent of doubling our salary. A regular gratitude practice can even affect the neural pathways of the brain associated with social bonding and stress relief. It's not happiness that makes us grateful, it's gratefulness that makes us happy, says the Benedictine monk David Steindl-Rast.

If gratitude is so good for us, why don't we express it more? It should come easily to those of us raised in an abundant Western culture. But that culture is based on consumerism and competition, which makes it seem as though we never have enough or are enough. There's the problem, too, of adaptive behaviour—once we have what we need, we start taking things for granted. Some influential thinkers, such as the evolutionary biologist Richard Dawkins, argue that our ungratefulness is inborn, a type of original sin, although the famous atheist would probably never use that term. This group believes human behaviour is driven by survival instincts motivated by self-interest; that even when we do good it's only to boost our status. The seventeenth-century French writer François de La Rochefoucauld said much the same thing: "Gratitude in the generality of men is only a strong and secret desire of receiving greater favours."

In religion, gratitude is often expressed through prayer. More than half of Americans say they pray every day, according to Pew Research. So do a sizable minority of people who aren't religious.

I was taught to pray as a toddler, the rush of rehearsed words spilling out in one breath before every meal: "Godblessthisfoodand-drinkforjesussakeamen." In grade school I could recite the Lord's Prayer back to front. At bedtime, there was the macabre though strangely comforting "Now I Lay Me Down to Sleep." My stepfather said the same prayer before every single meal ("Heavenly Father, we come to you before this meal to ask for your blessing on this food . . ."). When we ate out in restaurants, I'd squirm in embarrassment as my parents silently prayed over their plates. I prayed in church and at school. Prayer was as everyday as brushing your teeth and considered regular hygiene for the soul.

Sometimes people used their ideas about prayer as a form of judgement. Once, my mother was scolded for keeping her eyes open during prayer when two elders came to our house during a "home visit," our church's annual checkup on a family's religious status. There were times, too, when family members, including my mother, would tell me they were praying for me because they felt I'd lost my way. Did they really think they had the power to invoke God on my behalf?

During my teens, my prayers were always of the selfish variety. I did not pray for other people, only for myself—that a certain boy would like me or that I wouldn't be pregnant (these were the most fervent prayers of all). When my faith in God faltered, my prayers fell off, too. I would still bow my head if the occasion called for it, but I no longer believed anyone was listening. I became uncomfortable with prayers spoken aloud. They seemed so pious. Since most prayers were private, desperate pleas, weren't they best suited to silence? Even the Bible is wary of public prayer: "When you pray, go into your room and shut the door and pray to your Father who is in secret" (Matthew 6:6).

The last time I prayed hard, really hard, was twenty years ago. I was eight months pregnant, hooked up to a machine in the hospital following premature labour pains. A nurse ran an ultrasound wand over my protruding belly, stared at a video monitor and tried to detect a heartbeat. There wasn't one. Several minutes passed. Round and round the nurse went with her wand, rubbing my belly as if it were an oil lamp, trying to coax the magic genie that was my baby to appear on the screen. Her brow furrowed and she left the room to get a doctor. My husband stood at the foot of my bed. We looked at each other wordlessly, our hearts seized with panic. When the doctor who took over still couldn't find a heartbeat, I started my earnest silent praying, my bargaining, begging and beseeching. I didn't even believe in the kind of prayer that expects a supernatural deity to intervene personally to save one baby while millions of others die of starvation. But this did not stop me from crying out for mercy in my hour of need. It was a spare-tire supplication, a last resort. When all hope seems lost, praying means you're at least doing something.

After searching in vain for another couple of minutes, the doctor cocked his head, picked up the cord attached to the ultrasound machine and dangled it in front of our eyes. It hadn't been plugged in. Our baby was alive, though not because of divine intervention. This made me think about what Mark Twain must have meant when he said, "Under the circumstances, swearing seems more apt than prayer."

Some might have called this incident a miracle. We called her Ruby.

Now, though, since prayer is at the forefront of a spiritual life, I dig out the mala beads I bought with the intention of repeating a nightly mantra. One of these is the Mani Mantra ("Om Mani Padme Hum") practiced daily by Tibetan Buddhists. (It sounds like "ohm man-ee pad-mae hoom" and, translated literally, means "Hail to the jewel in the lotus.") According to Buddhist tradition, the 108 beads represent the 108 defilements of the mind, which include lust, obstinacy, haughtiness, gambling and dipsomania (basically, boozing).

I'm hoping the soothing repetition of these mantras will put me in a peaceful, loving frame of mind before sleep, but the rote recitation just bores me. The beads last less than a week before I drape them on my bedpost, where they do decorative duty rather than serving any spiritual purpose. They didn't feel right in my hands. I couldn't shake the feeling that I was trying out another culture's sacred practice in a trite experiment. I decide to concentrate on being more grateful instead.

"Thank you is the best prayer that anyone could say," wrote the novelist Alice Walker. There's a whole group of gratitude gurus with books urging us to cultivate this underestimated emotion: *The Gratitude Diaries* by journalist Janice Kaplan, *Grateful* by historian Diana Butler Bass, *365 Thank Yous* by John Kralik and *Thanks a Thousand* by A.J. Jacobs, to name a few.

None of these has come close to the success of the gratitude blockbuster *Simple Abundance: A Daybook of Comfort and Joy*, written more than twenty years ago by Sarah Ban Breathnach, a freelance writer who was living paycheque to paycheque until her book hit the *New York Times* bestseller list, thanks to an endorsement from Oprah. Once Breathnach got rich from the book, she had difficulty adhering to her own philosophy; she hired nine assistants, flew on the Concorde, amassed a collection of Manolo Blahniks and, after a newspaper called her the "Isaac Newton of the simplicity movement," scooped up the mathematician's nine-hundred-year-old stone cottage in England. Her third husband mismanaged her money, and she frittered away her fortune. "I lost my heart, I lost my home, I lost my bearings, and I lost my way," Breathnach said in an interview with ABC News. She also lost credibility with her readers.

Perhaps gratitude takes more than positive thinking. My friend Meghan is fond of saying that "discipline brings joy," whether that means committing to a daily walk, giving up wine during the week or finding a few things to be thankful for every day. To me that sounds right. Gratitude is within our grasp, but it's a spiritual muscle that needs to be strengthened.

For some, gratitude comes naturally. Abraham Maslow, whose hierarchy of needs attempts to explain human motivation, said: "The most fortunate are those who have a wonderful capacity to appreciate again and again and again, freshly and naively, the basic goods of life, with awe, pleasure, wonder, and even ecstasy." The rest of us have to work at it. Parents start drumming those two little words, "thank you," into their kids from the time they learn to walk, because children are notoriously ungrateful. Shakespeare understood this. "Ingratitude! Thou marble-hearted fiend, More hideous when thou show'st thee in a child, Than the sea-monster!" he wrote in *King Lear*.

The single most powerful practice recommended by the experts is writing down what it is we are thankful for. It doesn't matter whether we use an old-fashioned diary, slips of paper in a jar, Facebook posts or a gratitude app on our phone. Translating our thoughts into concrete language is what makes the exercise meaningful.

Keeping a gratitude journal can help us stay positive through challenging times. My friend Shirley, a retired schoolteacher who was diagnosed with scleroderma, a chronic autoimmune disease, more than thirty years ago, says the daily habit of noting special moments, no matter how small they seem, has made a big difference in her outlook. She recalls a particular day when she was in great mental and physical anguish: "All I could think to write down was that I had seen some lovely white trilliums on the side of the road on my drive home from work." No matter how deep her pain, there was always comfort to be found in identifying "one true thing."

Canadian journalist Ann Dowsett Johnston, author of the bestselling memoir *Drink*, was newly out of rehab and struggling with the prospect of a life of sobriety when she made a pact with a friend: every morning they would email each other a list of at least five things they were grateful for. They made two rules: be as specific as possible and no repetitions during any one week. It wasn't enough to be thankful for a pretty sunset: they had to explain exactly why the sinking orange orb caused a feeling of gratitude. Dowsett Johnston didn't miss a single day. Even when her father died, she broke up with a long-term love and she dealt with depression, the five-minute daily exercise offered her a profound sense of contentment. "It's brought a lot of radiance to my world, a real luminosity and a sense of peace and comfort," she says. "Many of us who are practising gratitude are spiritual, yet we aren't finding ourselves at home in a traditional house of worship. This gratitude process of mine is like a prayer each morning—it's a ritual, a connection of intimacy with my friend, and it causes me to look deeply at my life. It provides me with many of the things people get from going to church."

Time and again this year I've failed at maintaining my new spiritual practices. My home altar was a bust. I haven't spent as much time in nature as I wanted to. I've missed days at a time meditating with Andy on Headspace. I haven't carved out enough time for solitude. And I'm still drinking too much wine. However, taking a couple of minutes to open the free Happy Tapper Gratitude app on my phone and type five things I'm thankful for is something I've been able to stick with since January. A few fabulous things have made the lists ("Dozens of fireflies lit up the trail on my walk tonight!" "Lucy got accepted to film school!" "Got invited on a press trip to a dude ranch in Colorado!") but most are simple, even banal ("The breeze coming in through my bedroom window," "My kids made dinner," "Stayed in bed most of the morning reading a good book"). A gratitude practice can give you a stockpile of satisfying memories, a collection of life's small positive moments, most of which we'd forget if we didn't write them down. Documenting things means we can feel gratitude for these experiences long after they occurred.

University of California psychologist Robert Emmons, the world's foremost scientific expert on gratitude, says a gratitude practice has to be a long-term commitment if you hope to get the maximum benefit—keeping a gratitude list for only days or weeks won't result in lasting change. His basic advice? Stop. Notice. Write it down. It's like money in the bank—a sure-fire get-rich scheme.

⤳

FINDING THINGS TO BE GRATEFUL FOR IS EASY WHEN YOU HAVE YOUR health, enough money to pay the bills and friends and family who make life meaningful. But the gratitude evangelizing so prevalent in popular culture can make people who are in desperate pain feel worse because they can't count their blessings.

"It's not that the urge toward gratefulness is wrong. Rather, it's that the popularly expressed approach needs to consider the vast number of people who have unjustly or chronically suffered," writes Mitch Horowitz in an article for the *Washington Post*. The gratitude movement, he argues, falters when "its leading voices purposefully and somewhat cheaply recoil from the ethical and intellectual heavy lifting of addressing the lives of people in deep or implacable distress." Yes, it's good to be grateful, but sometimes we "must acknowledge that there's no way to spin profound personal loss. Life may never be whole again," says Horowitz.

If our lives are generally content, doesn't the act of jotting thanks for our good fortune seem superficial, even self-congratulatory, given the reality of unimaginable suffering around the globe? Six million people die every year from starvation, twenty-five million refugees have had to flee to other countries and nearly half the world—more than three billion people—live in poverty, on less than $2.50 a day. Statistics like these are overwhelming. Being more appreciative does not eliminate despair. But sometimes gratitude can help lessen suffering, especially if we use it as a motivating force to make a positive contribution, whether that's sponsoring a child, tutoring a newcomer, giving to charities that are working to right the inequities in the world—or reaching out to those in our own circles and communities who are in need. Horowitz argues the onus is especially on the privileged to regularly express gratitude, lest we "enter a narcissistic bubble of self-concern and petty complaint."

In his book *Thanks! How Practising Gratitude Can Make You Happier*, Robert Emmons offers examples of how some people are able to transcend desperate circumstances through gratitude, pointing to the survivors of Hurricane Katrina who lost their homes but were thankful just to be alive. "Processing a life experience through a grateful lens does not mean denying negativity," he writes. "It is not a form of superficial happiology. Instead, it means realizing the power you have to transform an obstacle into an opportunity. It means reframing a loss into a potential gain, recasting negativity into positive channels for gratitude."

He wonders if gratitude can become part of a person's psychological immune system, in the same the way optimism and religiousness work to alleviate suffering. "Without minimizing the severity of traumatic events, can reminding oneself to be grateful or to maintain a grateful attitude be an effective way of coping with a particularly stressful life circumstance?"

Few things are as stressful as being homeless. I wondered what people without any kind of permanent home could find to be thankful about. To find out, I head to the Salvation Army shelter for transient men in downtown Hamilton, close to where I live. The shelter is right across from the library. I pass it often, and my heart always tugs a little when I see the ragged crew milling around outside. My own father spent some time here in the months before he died. I screw up the courage to approach a few of these men, tell them I'm doing research on gratitude and hand over a prepaid coffee card in exchange for a few minutes of their time.

Steve, sixty-one, tells me he developed an addiction to opioids after experiencing severe back pain. He had to leave his apartment a few weeks earlier because it was infested with bedbugs. "Is there anything you feel grateful for?" I ask. "I'm grateful I'm here instead of on the street," he says. When he gets his monthly $740 disability cheque, he takes $20 to 541 Eatery & Exchange, a volunteer-run local restaurant and charity, where patrons can purchase buttons that are used in turn by people who don't have the money to order food from the menu. "I try to pay it forward whenever I can," says Steve.

Craig, forty-two, has been at the shelter for two months. He's initially wary about speaking with me, but then asks if we can sit together on a nearby bench. His mental health issues quickly become obvious in the way he frenetically looks over his shoulder and mutters so fast that I can barely catch his words. When I ask him if he feels grateful for anything, he answers bluntly, "Not at the moment," then reconsiders. "Actually, I'm thankful for the hot lunch I had today. They serve it to you here on a tray along with a salad and a bun—it's like being in a restaurant."

George, a fifty-nine-year-old former factory worker, says that he's "thankful just to be alive and to have a place to be out of the cold." Anthony, fifty-five, is grateful to finally be on a short list for afford-able housing. "You don't realize how much you miss having your own place until you don't have it anymore," he says. Matthew, who looks at least a couple of decades older than his forty-six years, is sitting on a curb on the side of the road. With only a couple of teeth left in his mouth, he's difficult to understand, but I do hear the words "coffee" and "tobacco." When I thank him for his time, he starts singing "Puff the Magic Dragon" with all the enthusiasm of a school boy. I stand there awkwardly until he's done. Passersby are gawking. It's a surreal moment on a street not far from my own.

My father was in his early forties when he checked in to the Salvation Army. Did he look as weathered and worn as these men, I wonder? I don't have any photos of him from that time. Was he holding on to some bit of hope that his luck would turn? Was there anything he was thankful for?

My father's life was a world apart from mine. So was my step-father's. Neither of them finished high school. They did hard, physical work all their lives, carrying metal lunch buckets and wearing hard-hats on construction sites. They grew up in an era when men did not show soft emotions. They were both raised in homes where there was a deficit of expressed love, at least the doting kind.

A couple of weeks after my stepfather's funeral I call my mom to ask if I can take her to lunch.

"It's up to you," she says.

"Do you want to or not, Mom?" I ask.

"It's up to you," she says again.

"Mom, I'm not going to force it if you don't want to."

The floodgates open.

"I feel sorry for Ruby and Lucy that they never knew their grand-father," she says. "All those Christmas cards and birthday cards, and I never got a reply from them."

She's right. The girls didn't reply, and I never made them. I sent cards on our behalf—for my mom's birthday, Mother's Day and Christmas. That had been the extent of our relationship for years.

She mentions my brother's former wife. "Even she cared enough to come see Dad in the hospital."

It was wrong of me. I see that now. I should have had more courage. I don't say anything.

"You didn't have to turn your back on us," she says. "You never cared enough to come when I was going through a hard time. I loved you," she says. Past tense.

I tell myself I won't cry. But when it comes to my mother, all I want to do is cry. I'm that girl again, the one trying to avoid the side-walk cracks.

Now she is crying too. "I'm sorry," she says. "I'm having a bad day."

I've never heard my mother apologize before.

"I know Dad could be rough. He wasn't brought up with any love."

"It's okay, Mom," I say. I tell her I'm sorry I hurt her. And him. There's a pause while we both try to manage our tears.

"So how about I come next Thursday?" I say. I can barely get the words out.

"Okay," she says.

"Okay."

The following week, on a grey November day, I make the hour-long drive to see my mother, passing all the familiar landmarks. There's Chapel Hill Memorial Gardens, the cemetery where my biological father was buried almost thirty-five years ago. Then Smithville (population 5,400), home of John Calvin Christian School, where I was cast out by the girl tribe in Grade 7, and the Smithville Canadian Reformed Church, where my parents were married. The house where my father grew up is just a dozen houses away from the church. Twenty minutes down the road and I'm in Fenwick (population 1,500), where my grandparents owned a large home. There's the old Green Lantern, now called the Grill on Canboro, where I flipped burgers and served pie for four years after school, learning to earn and save money. Just up the street is Mrs. Leopard's old house, where the back screen door slammed shut the morning my father left for work and never came back. Around the corner is Ridderikoff's butcher shop, which kept my Oma's fridge stocked with sliced horsemeat and where my stepfather would buy ham hocks to make pea soup on Saturday nights so my mother wouldn't have to cook on Sundays. There's the local schoolyard where my parents caught me smoking with a couple of girlfriends when I was fourteen. They grounded me for two weeks—not because I smoked, my mother (a smoker herself back then) explained, but because I lied about it. There's the backsplit my stepfather built for us a year after he married my mother. He lined the long driveway with a dozen elm trees and dug out a pond where my brother and I would play hockey on winter nights with the neighbourhood kids. Finally, I pull up to the seniors' building where my parents bought a condo a few months before my stepfather died.

It's been a decade since my mother and I have been alone in a room together. She invites me to sit in the living room, pours coffee and then pours out her heart about my stepfather. He's all she wants to talk about. As she does, a different picture emerges from the one that's been fixed in my mind all these years.

She tells me about the months of tending to him while he was sick. How he would lie in their bedroom with the door open and how they both took comfort in knowing the other was in the next room. How she cooked his favourite foods, homemade pudding, liver and onions and

Dutch meatball soup, even though he didn't have much of an appetite. "I would have been happy to care for him for a long time," she says. She tells me about the night he couldn't walk anymore, when she had to call the ambulance. How she picked out his final outfit, laying his collection of forty ties on their bed and selecting the red one with a white cross. "I miss his presence so much," she says. She cries, and I reach out my hand to hers.

My mother and stepfather had twenty years alone together after their last child moved out. They took a few trips—one to Cuba, where they handed out Bibles to villagers. They went on a cruise with my brother Henry. They spent the majority of each day together—drives in the country, getting groceries, going out for dinner, visiting friends, going to church, shopping at their favourite stores in Niagara-on-the-Lake.

"He was so good to me," says my mother. "He even had a pet name for me."

"Really? What was it?" I ask.

"Once when I said, 'I'm an old lady now,' Dad said, 'Well, you're m'lady.'"

He kept calling her that—M'lady.

"I've never told anyone that before," she says, and I'm pleased at this shared intimacy.

Every Christmas my stepfather bought my mother an expensive piece of jewellery. He'd have it wrapped in a box and bow and would tuck it near the top of the Christmas tree.

"This sounds silly, but I bought myself a watch last week and asked the jeweller to wrap it. I'm going to put it under the tree to open on Christmas morning."

"It's not silly," I say. "It's a nice way to remember what Dad used to do for you."

On the drive home I consider my parents' marriage. And my own. How different they are. Jeff and I are supportive of one another, but we lead independent lives and have different interests. Our children unite us, but soon they will be gone. Then what? I can't remember the last time just the two of us went for a drive or out for dinner. Children rarely consider the romantic nature of their parents' relationship. I know I didn't with my mother and stepfather. But now I understand how close they were.

The next day I write my mom a letter. I tell her I love her, that I am sorry for any hurt I caused her or my stepfather. I tell her I have a new appreciation for how strong their marriage was. I mention getting together again, but I don't hear anything back. Maybe, I think, this visit is all the closure we're going to have. I'm not sure. As has so often been the case with my mother, I don't know whether to keep trying or let it go.

My friend Donna inspires one final gratitude practice this month. Every Wednesday she sends a handwritten card or letter of appreciation to someone. Sometimes she stamps and sends it, sometimes she pops it right into their mailbox. I've been on the receiving end of her correspondence and I know how good it feels. I steal her idea, and, in the weeks leading up to Giving Tuesday (the first Tuesday after American Thanksgiving), I set a goal of thanking someone every day for twenty-one days by delivering a $10 Tim Horton's gift card and an appreciative note. This turns into an almost selfish exercise because I get a feel-good boost with every card I give away. It's surprisingly easy to find someone to thank, whether it's the people across the street for maintaining a beautiful garden, my daughter's boyfriend for raking the leaves, neighbours who had us over for drinks, the woman who grooms our dog or the art teacher who is encouraging my youngest daughter's creative pursuits. The guy at the corner store—where I buy milk when I run out—looks at me funny when I hand him the card, but the next time I'm in the store he's all smiles. One morning when I'm lying in bed thinking about whom to thank, I hear the garbage truck beeping on the street outside. I run out in my robe to catch it, handing out cards to two surprised city workers.

In all the decades other people have done the dirty job of hauling away my trash, never once have I thought to thank them.

I think about what Robert Emmons, the gratitude researcher, has written—that true thankfulness is about acknowledging our profound dependence on other people. The words of the Unitarian minister George E. Odell once again come to mind: "All our lives we are in need and others are in need of us." We can never go it alone. We are dependent on parents and partners, children, friends, workmates and the wider community. Gratitude isn't just about recognizing the nice things that happen in our lives, it's about appreciating the people who have shaped us, who are there for us, who have helped us. Gratitude binds us together.

When I look at my life through a gratitude lens, it challenges the way I've viewed adverse events. If my father had not left my mother when I was young, I might have grown up in a dysfunctional, alcoholic home instead of a stable, financially secure environment that allowed me to get a decent education. If my mother hadn't defied the church to marry my stepfather, she might have had a lonely life. If I hadn't upset my parents by leaving the church, I might never have learned to stand up for myself. My mother and I lost a lot of years because of the division that religion created. This hurt us both.

I want to stop wishing that the past was different, stop yearning for what might have been. Consciously cultivating gratitude, I find, gives me a stronger foothold in the present. Emmons describes gratitude as being like "a firewall of protection" against the anger, resentment and bitterness that can harm relationships.

I think about how thankful I am that my mother grounded me in love when I was young. That's the missing piece for so many who suffer—those who land in jail or who struggle with addiction. Some people live their whole lives struggling with the gaping absence of early love. It's almost impossible to backfill it if you've missed out on it initially.

An early Christmas card arrives in the mail. It's from my mother. In the corner of the card she's printed a short note: "It would be nice to see you over the holidays."

I pick up the phone to call her.

Photo on next page: Marked for life with a new tattoo.

December

Letting Go

"All changes, even the most longed for, have their melancholy;
for what we leave behind us is a part of ourselves; we
must die to one life before we can enter another."
—*Anatole France*

IT WASN'T UNTIL I HAD A HOME AND FAMILY OF MY OWN THAT I
really understood how much effort my mother had put into Christmas.
She's one of those women who had a special set of Christmas china
that she used one night a year. In addition to doing all the gift shopping
for us four kids, plus her parents, in-laws and assorted relatives, my

mother would spend most of Christmas Day in the kitchen, whipping up mashed potatoes, gravy, stuffing, a big turkey, Brussels sprouts, carrots and peas and her famous seven-layer salad. Christmas baking involved a month of Saturdays making dozens of cookies and squares, including my favourite: candied cherry nut bars. The house would be beautifully decorated—an entire lit-up miniature village displayed on the fireplace mantel, a real tree with dozens of elegant, decades-old ornaments in the den and a smaller one, her "cardinal tree," decorated with clip-on bird ornaments, perched on a ledge in the front window. Flowers filled the place—massive poinsettias, berry-studded English holly, red and white carnations with baby's breath and star-shaped, fragrant stephanotis. It was perfect. Who could blame her if she sometimes seemed on edge by the time we all sat down to heap our Christmas plates with the feast she'd prepared?

After a month focused on gratitude, I'm thankful for the coming season. But gift-giving and merrymaking are behind me. For years I resented the oppressiveness of Christmas. By the middle of December, my crankiness always started to grow with my to-do list: shopping, baking, decorating, entertaining, wrapping, travelling to see out-of-town family, attending cookie exchanges, parties and neighbourhood open houses, last-minute teachers' gifts, running to the corner store on December 24 when we ran out of Scotch tape. I didn't recall applying for the position of head elf, but it seemed the only criteria in the job description was being a woman. (My particular holiday tradition is Christmas; if yours is something else, likely it too comes with a long to-do list.)

Sure, there were elements of the holiday I enjoyed, like seeing the delight on my kids' faces when they opened their presents on Christmas morning. But mostly the whole thing was . . . exhausting. Heaven and nature did not sing. Joy to the world? More like joy to the mall. Ho-ho-ho, off we went. I usually got to "rest" after the holidays, when I inevitably came down with the flu after having waved a wand all month to make the magic happen.

Many women complain about Christmas. I sure did. Yet we will go to ridiculous lengths to make it Pinterest-perfect for everyone but ourselves. No matter how deep our particular family dysfunction, we strive to create scenes of cosy contentment, wrapped up in red velvet bows and lush evergreen garlands. We pipe icing onto gingerbread houses and spend entire Saturday afternoons in search of the gift that will prove to others just how much we love them. Many of our mothers did this before us, and many of us are training our daughters to do the same. It's gender-driven, self-inflicted suffering, and we have no one but ourselves to blame. Christmas celebrates the birth of a martyr, but it has become our cross to bear.

My idea of the perfect Christmas holiday is simple. It looks like this: stay home, keep out of the mall, spend more time on the couch reading than in the kitchen cooking, hang out with the kids, invite friends over to play games. Spend as little money as possible. Did I mention napping? All of this seemed an impossible dream. Then came the epiphany a few years back: there was only one thing preventing this dream from becoming a reality and that was me.

The Christmas cards were the first to go. Initially, I felt guilty. What would my sisters-in-law think if they didn't get a personal postage-stamped holiday greeting? It would reflect poorly on me, not on my husband. Jeff has never mailed a Christmas card in all his sixty-three years. It wouldn't occur to him. I decided to take my chances, and after the first year, ignoring the cards was easy.

Once I'd lowered my expectations for the holidays, I lowered them some more. I ditched the turkey. I quit buying presents for everyone but the kids, who now get a crisp $100 bill, some chocolate and a few small items in their stockings. When I suggested to Jeff that we stop giving each other presents, he looked relieved to be done with the last-minute Christmas Eve scramble. I put my daughters in charge of decorating the tree, a task they took on willingly; they enjoy reminiscing over their childhood keepsakes, from the crumbling playdough preschool creations to the Tinker Bell and Tigger ornaments from their Disney phase. On Christmas Eve we'll stop in at a friend's annual open house, then head to a short candlelight service at our Unitarian Church. Back at home we'll watch *How the Grinch Stole Christmas* (the Jim Carrey version, which we've watched every year since it came out in 2000). Before bed, my husband, Scotch in hand, will write a letter to the girls from the Grinch, as he's done every year since they were little. He'll outline their milestones over the past year and let them know how proud the Grinch is of them. On Christmas morning the girls will go to the mailbox, retrieve these letters and read them aloud as we share a simple breakfast of champagne and orange juice, French toast, baby potatoes and berries. Stockings are opened and homemade cards are read before we head out for a walk in the woods with birdseed in our pockets to feed the chickadees. In the afternoon, I nap and read. Later, we'll sometimes go to a movie with friends or order Chinese takeout. I don't bake, cook, shop, wrap or decorate. I usually say "no, thank you" to a few lovely holiday invitations. This is the hardest part—I'm a people pleaser and hate to let anyone down. But in order for Christmas to be sane, simple and enjoyable, saying no is necessary. When I go to bed that night, I feel content instead of exhausted—and everyone else seems happy too. I fall asleep with sugar plums dancing in my head because the next day is Boxing Day and I will stay in my pyjamas for the duration.

My mother sounds pleased when I call and invite her to Sunday dinner a couple of weeks before Christmas. I feel hopeful when she arrives at the door bearing a plate of candied cherry nut bars. She's here with my brother Henry, his wife and two of their grown sons. My girls are here too. I pour cups of eggnog with extra rum in a bid to loosen the tension. The visit begins awkwardly. "I wish you'd come to Grandpa's funeral" is one of the first things my mother says to my oldest daughter, whom she hasn't set eyes on in years. Ruby apologizes, and my mother seems to take this in stride. She looks at Ruby and says, "You're so beautiful." And just like that, the awkwardness evaporates.

When we sit down for dinner, my mother asks if she can pray. She offers thanks, at times haltingly, for the food, for us all being together, for the celebration of Jesus' birth.

"I'm not very good at it yet," she says when she finishes. My stepfather always said the prayers.

There are new ears listening, and she is eager to talk about him—the details of his death and their long, happy marriage. "I loved him more on the day he died than the day I married him," she tells my girls, just as she told me on our last visit. She tells us how brave he was at the end, how he never complained despite his pain and discomfort, and how she took pleasure in doing the simplest things for him. I can see it's good for my mother to talk about him. She's in a grief group too, she says. "There's a woman who hasn't decorated for Christmas in the three years since her husband died. I've had the house decorated for weeks. Dad loved it when I decorated!"

She's almost giddy now, sharing all this. "Maybe I'm talking too much," she says. "Go ahead, Mom," I say, refilling her wine glass. It's good to see her so animated.

"He put his arms around me in bed every night," she says, and her longing hangs in the air, making me think of my own. I'm stifling tears. "Don't cry, Anne," she says, touching my hand.

But it's hard not to cry, especially because of what she says next. "Sometimes when I was sad because of what happened with you and me, Dad would say he thought it was his fault. He thought you never accepted the fact that he married me. Maybe that was part of the problem."

Maybe it was. All these years I thought my stepfather didn't like me. It never occurred to me he would think I didn't like him. Or that my opinion would matter to him.

It's been years since I sat around the table with my family like this. Sure, it's dysfunctional, disjointed, disconnected, whatever you want to call it. Show me a family that isn't one of those things at times. But right now, it feels as though some sort of repair is being made.

After dinner, the young people head off to watch a movie, and it's just my mother, my brother and me and our spouses. My mother is still in the mood to talk. There are things I've been afraid to ask her. Now's my chance.

"Mom, do you mind if I ask you some stuff about the past?"

"Ask me anything," she says. Her forthrightness surprises me.

I tell her I'm curious about the mysterious trip to Holland she took when I was a year old. In the story my uncle wrote, he said my father was angry at the church for years because it had sent my mother and me away.

A different story emerges this evening. My mother tells me a relative came to her a couple of years after she was married to tell her that my father was having an affair.

"I was devastated. I went to talk to my parents. They said maybe I should go away for a while." My mother took me to Holland with her for six weeks, ostensibly to teach my father a lesson. When she got back, he decided the three of us should start over in British Columbia. They bought a house and he got a job in construction. My brother Henry was born during this time. But then my father started staying out late at night, drinking. Once, my mother told me, we all went to a motel for a weekend getaway. My father told her he was going out to get cigarettes and then didn't come back. "I went out in the morning with Henry in the buggy and you by the hand to go looking for him. Of course, I couldn't find him." When she made her way back to the motel, hours later, she opened the door and there he was on the bed, out cold.

They moved back to Ontario and not long after, my father gave her a kiss on the cheek, left for work, lunch bucket in hand, and disappeared. "He just didn't come home," says my mom. "He didn't even take anything with him." But he had planned his departure carefully, stealing thousands of dollars from his brother's business, taking his brother's truck, driving it to the airport and leaving it there while he flew to the United States. My mother didn't hear from him for a year.

"I don't know where he went or what he did. He was in jail once—for what, I don't know. I was hateful toward him for a long time. Later on, I felt sorry for him. He missed out on a lot," she says, looking at Henry and then at me. In the decade or so before he died, my father used to call her once a year, she tells us. "He would ask how the two of you were doing, but other than that, he really wasn't that interested."

This last part stings.

"It must have been awful for you to be left on your own," I say.

"In some ways it was a relief. I was always worrying about him: Is he going to come home? Is he drinking? Once he was gone, the worrying was over. I had two kids, and the two of you became my life."

My father, she concludes, was always searching. "He must have gone to ten different churches. He was always trying to find peace. He was always so restless."

Restless. Searching. That's familiar. Maybe I am more my father's daughter than I want to admit.

"Even though he couldn't find what he was looking for, he was always a believer," she goes on to say. "Later in life he asked me for forgiveness. He felt the Lord had forgiven him. I believe he went to heaven."

For so long I've viewed my mother through the lens of a rejected daughter. Now, when I consider the reality of her early life, I see how challenging it was. She was forced to quit school in Grade 8, to help out on the family farm and get a job in a local nursing home, because her family needed the extra money. Money was tight for many of the Dutch families that immigrated to Canada in the 1950s. My father had to hand over his entire paycheque to his parents, which was one of the reasons he wanted to get out of the house and marry my mother. That and the fact that his father hit him. I'd also heard from other relatives that my Oma pressured my parents to get married because they'd been intimate. There was no birth control pill available then—and even if there had been, my parents' religion forbade it. How different might their marriage have been if they'd had a few years of togetherness before the responsibilities of children? I've had choices my mother never had. When I wanted to quit high school in Grade 10 because I'd gotten a job at the Green Lantern, my mother refused to let that happen. When my heart was broken at seventeen after catching my boyfriend kissing someone else at a party, she gave me some good advice, gleaned from hard experience: "Don't be sad, get mad." I got to go to college. I married at twenty-three, which was young enough, but still six years older than she had been. Unbeknownst to her, I was on birth control at nineteen.

How little she had when my father left us, and yet how well she managed. She had to be so strong. Now, after losing my stepfather, my mother is more vulnerable than I've ever seen her. Our roles are reversing. Listening to her as she talks, my heart cracks, then opens with a cautious blooming.

Later that night, after everyone leaves, Jeff and I take the dog for a walk around the block. A light snow is falling, and the neighbours' homes are decked out in pretty Christmas lights. We walk without saying anything for a while. It's been a surprising evening. Jeff breaks the silence. "Does this mean you're going to start going home for regular visits?"

He sounds wary. Can I blame him? I think back to all the tense Sunday dinners in the early years of our marriage, when he would be a witness to the tears that followed. Visits when I would feel their disappointment in me. Religion created a divide I didn't know how to bridge.

Jeff doesn't want me to go back to that. I don't want to go back to that, either.

"I'll visit on my own," I tell him. "It might be different now."

There's a chance it will be. I am fifty-six. My mother is seventy-four. We are running out of time to set things right. I feel hopeful after this visit. Lighter, too.

AS THE YEAR COMES TO A CLOSE, IT'S TIME TO TACKLE A FINAL TASK on my spiritual to-do list: simplifying. I want to expand my newfound sense of lightness into other areas of my life, specifically my home. If I could downscale Christmas, then surely greater domestic tranquility is possible if I can also downscale my possessions. As always, Mary Oliver is an inspiration. "I have a notion that if you are going to be spiritually curious, you better not get cluttered up with too many material things," she writes.

The average North American home contains 300,000 items, more than triple what a home fifty years ago held. I count 136 ornaments on our Christmas tree, thirty-one dresses in my closet, and fifty-odd containers of lotions and potions in my bathroom cabinet. I'm guilty of being cluttered up with too many things.

There's long been a band of dissenters—from the Quakers ("'Tis the gift to be simple") to Thoreau ("Our life is frittered away by detail . . . simplify, simplify!") to the reformed Grinch (who questioned whether Christmas comes from a store)—urging us to reconsider conspicuous consumption. To have less and live more. Now, a whole new crop of minimalists have entered the mainstream. This includes the popular podcast *The Minimalists*, the international Buy Nothing Day protest against consumerism and books such as *The Gentle Art of Swedish Death Cleaning*, which recommends that each of us undertake a process of decluttering, known as *döstädning*, so that others won't have to tidy up for us after we're gone.

But no one reigns more supreme in the organizing universe than Marie Kondo, the diminutive, eminently capable Japanese Mary Poppins. Her KonMari method, outlined in her bestseller *The Life-Changing Magic of Tidying Up*, has put millions of women (and a few type-A men) into major organizing mode. She's become a cultural phenomenon—her multinational empire includes a follow-up book called *Spark Joy*, a hit Netflix show and a merry crew of KonMari-certified consultants—by tapping into our desire to be released from the tyranny of our stuff. What makes Kondo different from other organizational gurus is her spiritual approach. In her world, it's a holy enterprise to undertake a household purge. She suggests starting with a prayer-like attitude by arising early to begin the sacred task of paring down your possessions, lighting a votive to sanctify the space, examining your heart to determine which items truly "spark joy" and elevating the mundane task of folding into a sacramental act by parsing your underwear into tight rectangles that can be stacked upright in a drawer, neat as a row of tacos. To ease the pangs of parting, she advises offering a nod of gratitude to your old concert T-shirts and ratty bras, thanking them for their valiant service. This ritualistic farewell is in keeping with Kondo's practice of Shintoism, the traditional religion of Japan, which promotes the idea that *kami*—or divine essence—exists in inanimate objects, even in your saggy underwear. That's why she taps books to "wake them up," folds clothes in an exacting way so they can "rest more comfortably" and recommends a formal goodbye to the goods you give away.

And the point is to give away *a lot* of your goods. Kondo claims her method helps clients reduce their possessions to a third or even a quarter of what they started with, the equivalent of seventy trash bags for a family of three. She offers the seductive promise that her method will bring transformation. She even makes the fantastic claim that slimming down your possessions will also slim your tummy. Whittled-down closets *and* waistlines? No wonder her books have sold more than eleven million copies.

I'm ready to be counted among Kondo's legions of Konverts. Although I consider myself fairly organized—I rearrange my closet seasonally and get a thrill shopping for storage solutions at IKEA—my clothes are suffocating from a lack of breathing room, my bookshelf contains paperbacks I haven't opened in decades, and I feel dispirited every time I venture into the basement or garage. Home organization is women's work, at least in my house, and I've gotten myself into a Sisyphean rut trying to manage our mountains of stuff. I resent this task, yet once again I have mostly myself to blame, since I'm responsible for bringing the majority of it into our house in the first place. I recently met a woman in her seventies who told me about how she packed every single one of her belongings (including snow tires) into her *car* and moved from Calgary, Alberta, to retire on the east coast of Vancouver Island. Talking to her, I felt the same pang of envy I get when I read about people who are somehow able to live in tiny houses.

I devour Kondo's book in one day. According to her, major tidying only has to be done once in a lifetime. I'm in a merciless mood when I propel myself out of bed the next morning. Usually I hum and haw about what to keep and what to toss, but her simple question—"Does it spark joy?"—helps me make decisions quickly. As the KonMari method advises, I start with my clothes, heaping them in piles on my bed and floor. I swear I can hear my closet exhale in relief.

After stacking my clothes by category, I get to work, holding up each item and listening to the quiet voice within. The answers come quickly. The ripped red T-shirt I've been wearing to bed for the past year? Goodbye. Loose stretchy tops that are forgiving around the middle but make me feel frumpy? Nope. The six sparkly holiday tops I own? I rarely go to fancy parties. I keep just two. The pretty pale pink bodysuit with the uncomfortable snaps at the crotch? Out it goes. The emerald-green satin blouse? I might not wear it often, but I love it. It stays. Commemorative T-shirts? There are only two I can't part with— one from the Women's March on Washington and the one emblazoned with the words "We Believe the Women" from the Bill Cosby protest. An hour in, I am tossing items left and right over my shoulders, giddy with my newfound nonattachment.

Four hours later, I've said goodbye to 131 items, about 40 percent of my wardrobe, and filled six trash bags to donate to a local second-hand store. When I put the remaining items back in my vacuumed closet and dusted drawers, they look beautifully pared down and organized.

I can't resist taking photos and posting them on Facebook. Simple is the new status symbol.

A couple of days later I tackle my books. The trick here, says Kondo, is not to get emotional. Don't open anything. If you haven't read a book yet, you probably never will. Those books you think you'll read again? You won't. Kondo says thirty is an ideal number of books to keep. I have about 250. Once again, I pile everything onto the floor and then begin the businesslike sorting, chucking out my copy of Strunk & White's *The Elements of Style* from journalism school; the memoir *Now*, signed by Lauren Bacall herself when I met her at a reading in Boston; Hillary Rodham Clinton's 512-page autobiography, *What Happened*, which I knew I'd never get around to reading. I hesitate when it comes to books that have been inscribed to me by authors and friends, then decide to tear out the inscription pages and put some of those books in the discard pile. When I get rid of half a dozen parenting manuals, I feel empathy for the anxious mom I once was. I so wanted to get everything right.

My husband carts a handful of my discards to his bookcase in the study. "Why would you want to get rid of these?" he asks. He's hung on to books from his university days. He's still upset about parting with his record collection when we had a garage sale a few years back. I try not to look on him pityingly, smug in my new "less is more" enlightenment.

There's no theme to the books I keep except that they are meaningful to me: a sappy book of Rod McKuen poetry from when I was thirteen, the *Complete Works of William Shakespeare* my mother gave me when I was fifteen, some fiction by my favourite trio of Canadian writers (Margaret Laurence, Margaret Atwood and Alice Munro), Dorothy Parker's *Laments for the Living*, Eve Ensler's *The Vagina Monologues*, two collections of essays by Gloria Steinem, *The Official Visitor's Guide to New York* and a hiking guide called *Exploring the Dundas Valley* written by a friend. After an hour, I'm down to twenty-seven books. They take up two compact rows on a small bookcase in my bedroom.

The children's books are more challenging. There are about eighty, including a dozen from my own childhood. The latter are Bible story books, my name printed inside each in my kindergarten scrawl. I can't part with them. I call Ruby over to help me go through the books I used to read to her and her sister. "I loved this one," she says, holding up *Baby Beluga*, a board book featuring Raffi's popular song. We sing a few bars together. We select about twenty other favourites, including *The Paper Bag Princess*, *Miss Rumphius*, *The Mitten*, *Bye Bye Baby* and *Goodnight Moon*.

Tucked in among the kids' books I find a copy of *The Girlfriends' Guide to Pregnancy*, a daily diary I kept while I was pregnant with Ruby. I read some of the entries aloud to her: "November 28, 1996—Pregnant! Dazed and euphoric." "December 7, 1996—Worrying about possible miscarriage." "March 10, 1997—Jeff feels the baby kick for the first time." "June 30, 1997—Ruby is born and everything has a new hue of wonderful." My twenty-year-old daughter and I both have tears in our eyes. I put the book back on the shelf.

Kondo's directive when it comes to papers is pretty much "discard everything," and so I do—copies of the newspaper where I got my first job, magazines where I worked, dozens of folders of notes for articles, bank statements, old bills, newspaper clippings, theatre and concert programs—it comes to another five bags for recycling. The *komono* (miscellany) category fills another two bags. I clear out junk drawers, get rid of mysterious electrical cords and go through the bathroom cabinet and the kitchen cupboards. I descend with dread into the netherworld of the basement and the garage with the intention to heed Kondo's advice to discard those things that no longer serve their purpose so that I can truly value the things that are important. Again, I'm practically flinging things over my shoulders: roller blades, ice skates, inflatable toboggans, a camping cot, picnic baskets, a bucket of water guns, extension cords, a broken humidifier, flashlights that don't work, lawn furniture, luggage, two guitar cases and a large bag of grass seed.

I go through the bins of Christmas, Halloween and Easter decorations and pare those down by a third. When I'm done, I feel exhilarated. I also need to nap.

Kondo recommends tackling sentimental items last, after you've had time to hone your decluttering abilities. There are some bins of keepsakes in the basement I haven't opened for years. They are a treasure trove from my past life—love letters from that boy I met when he was visiting from Holland when I was sixteen, tiny school head shots of classmates going back to grade school, decades of birthday cards, materials from a women's retreat I once led, all my high school report cards. (Did I really get 36 percent in Grade 10 math?) Kondo says we fear that if we throw away special things, we'll lose the memories attached to them. But "to put your things in order means to put your past in order, too," she writes. I let a lot of stuff go. But not everything—not the poems my husband wrote for me in the early years of our marriage, not the eulogy I composed for my Oma's funeral. I find the typewritten letter, dated September 15, 1985, sent from the minister of the Canadian Reformed Church after I withdrew my membership, chastising me for my "act of disloyalty to God the Father and His Son." Why have I felt compelled to keep it all these years? Evidence, I suppose, of the church's condemnation. It goes back in the box. There's another letter, a painful one, that I'd forgotten about, written to me by my sister almost ten years ago, after the final estrangement with my mother. "What kind of a person does not call their own mother in over a year? Certainly not a caring one," she writes. "I guess it wasn't that hard for you to forget about us." I flush with shame as I read her words. I nurtured my own hurt, but did I fully consider the hurt I caused others? This letter, too, is evidence— of my culpability. It goes back in the box.

I've kept almost everything my children ever made for me—the Mother's Day card, for example, from Lucy when she was five. On a rudimentary drawing of a queen, she printed the words "crown," "wand"

and "slippers" with arrows pointing to these various parts of the picture. At the top she printed "Mom." I discover a stash of more than fifty notes on small squares of paper. My girls believed in fairies when they were young, and for years I'd leave messages in tiny handwriting beside their beds when they were sleeping, and they'd write back. I put a few pieces of artwork in the garbage and then retrieve them. It feels like I'm throwing away part of their childhood. Or maybe my motherhood. In the end I buy two large, clear containers with lids and fill them with their childhood keepsakes. One day my daughters can decide what they want to keep.

Finally, the photos. Like most mothers, I am the documentarian of our family's life. There are boxes filled with old albums, framed photos on every shelf in the house and almost ten thousand digital images on my phone and computer. I begin by hauling the albums up from the basement and stripping the images from their sticky backings. I throw out about four hundred photos, along with all the old albums themselves. I make a pile of images for each of the girls and put these in separate photo boxes. I always loved going through my mother's albums, the white-rimmed Kodachrome images placed carefully under cellophane. I want my girls to have the same experience. My plan is to put together an album for each of them for next Christmas. I promise myself that before then I'll also start deleting and organizing the photos on my computer. Going forward, I resolve I'll try to stay in the moment when something special is happening, rather than compulsively documenting it.

The things we own are a reflection of who we are. Going through everything, I can't help but process the past and consider the stages I've gone through: the girl who left her church, the eager newspaper reporter, the young wife, the estranged daughter, the mother of two, and now the middle-aged woman with a neck she doesn't recognize and a future that seems less certain than she expected. As I sort and discard, pause and ponder, the questions Stevie Nicks poses about sailing through the changing ocean tides and handling the seasons of my life in her song "Landslide" keep looping through my head.

I don't love everything about Marie Kondo. Some of her decluttering directives are baffling. She doesn't acknowledge that some possessions, like the snow shovel, say, or the lawnmower, are never going to spark joy. Nor does she address the reality that our relentless acquisition of goods is choking not just our homes but, more seriously, the planet. Never once does she admit that the real "magic" in achieving a life of simplicity lies in buying less stuff. Still, when your home is clean and uncluttered, Kondo writes, you have no choice but to consider your inner state. "From the moment you start tidying you will be compelled to reset your life." She's right. A huge reset, I realize, is taking shape for me.

THE INTERNAL WORKINGS OF A MARRIAGE ARE HIDDEN, LIKE THE mysterious wiring of a clock. Once the mechanism wears out, it can't keep time the way it used to. My marriage had worn out for all the usual reasons, along with some that were singular to us. I finally found the courage to face this difficult fact. While it had taken only days to get my house in order, my marriage had been unravelling for years. Wrenching as it was to admit, our union, which had once been electric, no longer sparked joy. Not for me, not for my husband.

We told the kids together. We said the right things: "Don't let anyone tell you thirty-two years is a failure." "We can't be a couple anymore, but we will always be a family." Jeff and I held hands as we broke the news. Our daughters cried, and so did we. When it was over we stood in a circle and hugged each other. Jeff and I kissed the tops of our daughters' heads. Next to giving birth, it was the most painful and most tender moment of my life. The hardest thing can be done if it's done with love.

Jeff and I both made mistakes. We didn't always put each other first, the way we should have. But what unquestionably endures is our shared love for the two people we brought into the world. Jeff is a great dad. I think he will make a good ex-husband. I plan to do my best to be a good ex-wife. Our children need us to be the shore they can always keep in sight.

"WE MUST DIE TO ONE LIFE BEFORE WE CAN ENTER ANOTHER," Anatole France wrote. My rebirth was aided by my experiences over the past year and the unique collection of people I met—people I would never have encountered if I hadn't embarked on this spiritual adventure. It all helped me to understand that an ending had to happen, and that I could face a new beginning with more fortitude and less fear. None of us escapes loss. Cultivating our spiritual lives can steady us when we face it. Sometimes this can even transform our despair into determination.

I've spent most of the last twelve months with my head in the clouds, sometimes literally. I'm not sure I'm ready to come back down to earth. That's partly because my spiritual to-do list remains unfinished. There are a bunch of things I'd still like to try: ecstatic dance for one, gong therapy for another. I'd like to see if I can still my tongue long enough to make it through a seven-day Vipassana silent meditation retreat. A croning ceremony, an affirming rite of passage for women over fifty, is also on the list. I'd like to wear ribbons in my hair, frolic through a field of wildflowers and ceremoniously toss my Spanx to the wind.

Now that my year-long experiment has come to an end, people ask if I feel more spiritual. Sometimes they even look at me suspiciously, as if I might be sizing up their aura. I certainly haven't figured out all of the answers to living a spiritual life. I don't spend my days floating from one supremely life-enriching task to the next. I expect I'm much like you, living a life that is messy and complicated and far from perfect.

But the year did result in some changes, big and small, that brought more joy and meaning to my life. I did manage to slow down. By dramatically reducing my screen time, I got back a whole lot of hours, enough to read more than two dozen books in the past twelve months. I've also reduced my wine consumption by about half, reserving it mostly for the weekends. I'm more comfortable with solitude than I've ever been. Content with my own company, I'm not as quick to fill up my social schedule. I still try to meditate for ten minutes every day. I experience more moments of appreciation, sometimes even amazement. I literally got my house in order, and I'm much more thankful. There's more singing in my life, too. My friend Donna and I started a monthly Soup and Song—we gather with friends and everyone brings a song to sing together. It's a beautiful bonding experience, lifting our voices in unison, even as we tackle raucous numbers like "Bohemian Rhapsody" and "Paradise by the Dashboard Light." I also try to go to every local protest I can for the causes I believe in. I always walk away with the same confusing mixture of helplessness and determination, but I think it's important to show up.

"There are years that ask questions and years that answer," wrote Zora Neale Hurston. For me, this year offered answers about how to live more attentively and authentically in the world. It made me consider what it means to be a good daughter, a good wife, a good mother, a good person. It meant forgiveness, not just of others but of myself. I was raised to believe that salvation comes from an external source, but now I believe it can come from within.

I WANT THE EXPERIENCES OF THE PAST TWELVE MONTHS TO LEAVE a lasting impression. "Wear your heart on your skin," advised Sylvia

Plath. So I do. I get a tattoo. It's external evidence of an inner shift. I opt for a simple black-and-white barn swallow, perched at the top of my right shoulder, fashioned in the old-school Sailor Jerry style. Swallows return to the same location every year to mate and nest, pulled along by their own internal compasses. It's believed they protect sailors from storms and shipwrecks and guide them safely home. If a sailor dies at sea, the bird will carry his soul to heaven.

I'm no seafarer, and I'm not sure where my soul will go when I die. I was raised to believe that there are only two options. But I prefer the idea of my soul being carried aloft, guided by an unseen force that sets me in the right direction. Who knows what the final destination will be—when it will rest its wings? Perhaps the flight itself is the whole point. Perhaps the joy is in the journey.

Acknowledgements

WRITING THIS BOOK HAS BEEN A LABOUR OF LOVE. IT TOOK NINE months, the typical period of gestation. The seed was planted in 2014 when Jocelyn Bell, my editor at the *United Church Observer* (since renamed *Broadview*), proposed that I write a monthly column called "Spiritual But Secular" to report on the practices of the rapidly growing spiritual-but-not-religious demographic. Almost fifty columns later, I was ready to experiment with some of those practices myself and the magazine commissioned me to write a blog, *My Year of Living Spiritually*, which eventually led to the book you are holding in your hands. Thank you, Jocelyn, for your editorial vision and for creating a magazine any writer would be proud to contribute to. Thanks to the rest of the *Broadview* team—David Wilson, Kevin Spurgaitis, Kristy Woudstra, Caley Moore and Elena Gritzan—for their dedication to top-notch journalism and for polishing up my prose.

Thanks to my generous friend Miranda Hill, who saw the potential for a book in my blog and recommended me to her agent. Thank you, Amy Tompkins at the Transatlantic Agency, for representing me and selling my book. To the folks at Douglas & McIntyre, you've been a dream to collaborate with. Anna Comfort O'Keeffe, thank you for taking a chance on a first-time author with a book on spirituality. My heartfelt gratitude goes to editor extraordinaire Barbara Pulling, who knew what to leave in and what to take out (specifically, 20,000 words!) and who made the editing process far less painful than I anticipated. Rebecca Pruitt MacKenney, thank you for your good cheer and excellent organizational skills throughout the publishing process. Thanks also to copy editor Caroline Skelton and proofreader Arlene Prunkl for their wonderfully keen eyes and to Terri Rothman for her valuable assistance in securing permissions. Thank you again, Anna, along with Carleton Wilson, for the beautiful cover design. For a book to be successful it needs an audience. Thank you to publicist Corina Eberle for your efforts in helping me find mine.

Many people and organizations had a role in informing the experiences I write about in this book. They include: Dr. Marlene Winell, Siobhan Chandler, Rev. Harry Oussoren, Dr. Gail Bigelow, Circle Studios, Holly Hill Hobby Farm, The Spiritual Emporium, Willow Den, Happy Soul, Saje Natural Wellness, We Are Not Saints AA, Kimberly Carroll, Zee Float, Ben Porchuk, Choir! Choir! Choir!, The Tuesday Choir, Singin' Women, Jocelyn Rasmussen, Suzanne Maziarz and the Comfort Choir, Growing the Voices, Susan McBride, Tracey Erin Smith of SoulO Theatre, Wild Ginger, Debbie Anderson, Debra Harding, Dortmund Mattioli, Malia Ronderos, Giselle Urech, Leslie Urquhart, Georgina Cannon, Elaine Thomas, the men at the Salvation Army, Mark Richardson, Anne Van Egmond and Tim Van Egmond.

Dear friends and writing colleagues provided early valuable feedback on the manuscript as well as ongoing support. They include Denise Davy, Ruth Hanley, Meghan Davis, Jen Dawson, Kate Cayley, Colleen Friesen, Valerie Neilsen and Karen Trollope Kumar. Thank you to Doreen Knol, Regan Russell and Mark Powell, who provided comfortable and quiet spaces to write. I am fortunate to have other friends who have also been wonderful companions on my life's journey: Melanie Cummings and Paul Mitchison, Christine Naughler and Norm Nelson, Bruce Lea, Dan Nolan, John and Kelly Sherwin, Nancy Webb, Karen Welds, Rosalind Stefanac, Vicki Wood, Elizabeth Garel, Camilla Cornell, Shirley Haslam, Christina Paradela, Elysée Nouvet, Audrey Johnman, Jennifer Kaye and Les Sasaki, Diane and Bob Shamchuk, Alison Diamond, Kathy Garneau and Hugh McLeod, Colette Kendall,

Shirla Schellenberg, Cheryl Paterson and Monica Bennett. Special thanks to Donna Caprice for her enduring friendship and inspiring love of life.

To the folks at First Unitarian Church in Hamilton, Ontario, I am thankful to be among your tribe. And to the community of people who have been part of the 6-Minute Memoir "speed storytelling for a cause" project—either on the stage or in the audience—thank you for sharing your passion for truth-telling.

Gratitude goes to my family of origin for our shared history and the lessons learned. Special thanks to my mother, Aafke Bokma, for reading this book and providing valuable new information. Thank you to Jeff Mahoney for being my first reader and my co-creator in parenthood. Finally, to the wonderful young women I am lucky to have in my life: Dori, I'm thankful you are part of the family. And Ruby and Lucy, thank you for opening my heart and filling my soul.

Resources

For those who are looking for support as they consider leaving their religion:

Journey Free: https://journeyfree.org/
Freedom from Religion Foundation: https://ffrf.org/
Recovering from Religion: https://www.recoveringfromreligion.org
Ex-Christian.net: https://new.exchristian.net/
Ex-Jehovah's Witnesses support: https:www.facebook.com/Ex-Jehovahs-Witnesses-Support-118780261481037/
Footsteps (for those in the ultra-Orthodox Jewish community): https://www.footstepsorg.org/
Recovery from Mormonism: www.exmormon.org
Unfundamentalist: http://unfundamentalists.com

For those seeking community:

Canadian Unitarian Council: https://cuc.ca/
Unitarian Universalist Association (US): https://www.uua.org/
Unitarian Universalist Humanist Association: http://huumanists.org/
The Center for Inquiry: http://centreforinquiry.ca/ (Canada) and https://centerforinquiry.org/ (US)
Humanist Canada: https://www.humanistcanada.ca/
American Humanist Association: https://americanhumanist.org/
Secular AA: https://secularaa.org/

Grief Beyond Belief: http://griefbeyondbelief.org/

The Clergy Project (for clergy who no longer believe in God): http://clergyproject.org/

Suggested Reading

These books have been helpful to me on my spiritual journey. Perhaps you will find something of value in them too.

A Religion of One's Own: A Guide to Creating a Personal Spirituality in a Secular World (2014) by Thomas Moore

Choosing Our Religion: The Spiritual Lives of America's Nones (2016) by Elizabeth Drescher

Faith Unraveled: How a Girl Who Knew All the Answers Learned to Ask Questions (2014) by Rachel Held Evans

Good Without God: What a Billion Nonreligious People Do Believe (2010) by Greg Epstein

Grace Without God: The Search for Meaning, Purpose, and Belonging in a Secular Age (2017) by Katherine Ozment

Traveling Mercies: Some Thoughts on Faith (1999) by Anne Lamott

Leaving Church: A Memoir of Faith (2012) by Barbara Brown Taylor

Leaving the Fold (2013) by Marlene Winell

Leaving the Saints: How I Lost the Mormons and Found My Faith (2006) by Martha Beck

Leaving Your Religion: A Practical Guide to Becoming Non-Religious (2013) by James Mulholland

Losing My Religion: How I Lost My Faith Reporting on Religion in America—and Found Unexpected Peace (2009) by William Lobdell

Relax, It's Just God: How and Why to Talk to Your Kids About Religion When You're Not Religious (2015) by Wendy Thomas Russell

Spiritual, but Not Religious: Understanding Unchurched America (2001) by Robert C. Fuller

Stalking God: An Unorthodox Search for Something to Believe In (2018) by Anjali Kumar

The Nones Are Alright: A New Generation of Believers, Seekers, and Those in Between (2015) by Kaya Oakes

The Power of Meaning: Crafting a Life that Matters (2017) by Emily Esfahani Smith

Unorthodox: The Scandalous Rejection of My Hasidic Roots (2012) by Deborah Feldman

Waking Up: A Guide to Spirituality Without Religion (2014) by Sam Harris

With or Without God: Why the Way We Live Is More Important than What We Believe (2009) by Gretta Vesper

Works Cited

Epigraph

Wendell Berry, *The Unforseen Wilderness: Kentucky's Red River Gorge* (Emeryville: Shoemaker Hoard, 2006), 43.

Introduction

Marlene Winell, *Leaving the Fold: A Guide for Former Fundamentalists and Others Leaving Their Religion* (Berkeley: Apocryphile Press, 2007).

January

Annie Dillard, *The Writing Life* (New York: Harper & Row, 1989), 32.
Sam Harris, *Waking Up: A Guide to Spirituality Without Religion* (New York: Simon & Schuster, 2014), 3.
Erica Jong, *Fear of Flying* (New York: Penguin Books, 1973), 127–28.

February

Thomas Moore, interviewed by Oprah Winfrey: http://www.supersoul .tv/tag/thomas-moore. Used with permission.
Rachelle Mee-Chapman, *Relig-ish: Soulful Living in a Spiritual-But-Not-Religious World* (St. Louis: Chalice Press, 2016).

March

Courtney E. Martin, "To See One Another Broken," *On Being* (blog), August 7, 2015, https://onbeing.org/blog/to-see-one-another-broken/. Used with permission.

Caroline Knapp, *Drinking: A Love Story* (New York: Bantam Dell, 1996), 70–71.

Tom Flynn, "Religious Humanism (Or Something) Gone Wild," *Advocatus Diaboli* (blog), Center for Inquiry, February 14, 2013, https://centerforinquiry.org/blog/religious_humanism_or_something_gone_wild/, accessed June 20, 2019.

A. Verghese, E. Brady, C.C. Kapur, and R.I. Horwitz, "The Bedside Evaluation: Ritual and Reason," *Annals of Internal Medicine* 155 (2011), 550–53. Used with permission.

April

May Sarton, *Mrs. Stevens Hears the Mermaids Singing: A Novel* (New York: W.W. Norton, 1965), 183.

Excerpt from *Birds Art Life* by Kyo Maclear, Copyright © 2017 Kyo Maclear. Reprinted by permission of Anchor Canada/Doubleday Canada, a division of Penguin Random House Canada Limited. All rights reserved. With permission of the author.

Sam Harris, *Waking Up: A Guide to Spirituality Without Religion* (New York: Simon & Schuster, 2014), 13.

Excerpt from Mary Oliver, *Upstream: Selected Essays by Mary Oliver* (New York: Penguin Press, 2016). Copyright © 2016 by Mary Oliver. Used with permission.

May

Robert Louis Stevenson, Charles Curis Bigelow and Temple Scott, eds., *The Works of Robert Louis Stevenson, Vol. IX: Essays and Reviews* (1906), 133.
Jack Cooke, *The Tree Climber's Guide: Adventures in the Urban Canopy* (London: HarperCollins Publishers, 2016).

June

Muriel Barbery, *The Elegance of the Hedgehog*, translated by Alison Anderson (Paris: Europa Editions, 2008), 185.

July

Terence McKenna as quoted by The Beckley Foundation on its Facebook page: https://www.facebook.com/TheBeckleyFoundation/posts/1150746624969194, accessed June 20, 2019.
Adrienne Rich, *Of Woman Born: Motherhood as Experience and Institution* (New York: W.W. Norton, 1976).
Michael Pollan, "The Trip Treatment," *New Yorker*, February 2, 2015, https://www.newyorker.com/magazine/2015/02/09/trip-treatment, accessed June 20, 2019.
Bill Wilson, *Pass It On: The Story of Bill Wilson and How the A.A. Message Reached the World* (New York: Alcoholics Anonymous World Services, 1984), 370–71.
Aldous Huxley, *The Doors of Perception* (New York: Harper Perennial, 1954), 17, 30.
Moksha by Aldous Huxley, edited by Michael Horowitz and Cynthia Palmer. Published by Inner Traditions International and Bear & Company, © 1999. All rights reserved. http://www.Innertraditions.com Reprinted with permission of publisher.

August

E.O. Wilson, *Consilience: The Unity of Knowledge* (New York: Alfred A. Knopf, 1998), 6.

Excerpt from *Cat's Eye* by Margaret Atwood, Copyright © 1988 O.W. Toad Ltd. Used by permission of Emblem/McClelland & Stewart, a division of Penguin Random House Canada Limited; Doubleday, an imprint of the Knopf Doubleday Publishing Group, a division of Penguin Random House LLC; and Bloomsbury Publishing Plc. All rights reserved.

© Johann Hari, 2018, *Lost Connections: Uncovering the Real Causes of Depression—and the Unexpected Solutions*, Bloomsbury Publishing Plc., 103, 161, 181.

Contact, a 1997 film directed by Robert Zemeckis, written by James V. Hart and Michael Goldenberg, based on the novel by Carl Sagan. Production companies: Warner Bros. and South Side Amusement Company.

"Form for the Excommunication of Non-Communicant Members," Canadian & American Reformed Churches (website), https://canrc .org/forms/form-for-the-excommunication-of-non-communi-cant-members, accessed June 11, 2019.

"Unitarian Universalist Humour," Bert Christensen's Cyberspace Home, https://bertc.com/subtwo/uu_humour.htm, accessed June 11, 2019.

Dave Webster, *Dispirited: How Contemporary Spirituality Makes Us Stupid, Selfish and Unhappy* (Winchester: Zero Books, 2011), 1.

His Holiness the Dalai Lama and Franz Alt, *An Appeal to the World: The Way to Peace in a Time of Division* (New York: William Morrow, 2017), 8.

Rachel Fershleiser, and Larry Smith, eds., *Not Quite What I Was Planning: Six-word Memoirs by Writers Famous and Obscure* (New York: HarperCollins, 2008), back cover and 162–63.

Rachel Fershleiser, and Larry Smith, eds., *It All Changed in an Instant: More Six-Word Memoirs by Writers Famous & Obscure* (New York: HarperCollins, 2010), 44.

September

Arthur Conan Doyle, *The Wanderings of a Spiritualist* (Berkley: Ronin Pub., Inc., 1988), 17.

Bill Hayes, *Insomniac City: New York, Oliver, and Me* (New York: Bloomsbury, 2017), 130.

Brian L. Weiss, *Miracles Happen: The Transformational Healing Power of Past-Life Memories* (New York: HarperOne, 2012). Used with permission.

October

R.W. Franklin, ed., *The Poems of Emily Dickinson: Reading Edition* (Cambridge: Belknap Press, 1999), 219.

Marlene Winell, *Leaving the Fold: A Guide for Former Fundamentalists and Others Leaving Their Religion* (Berkeley: Apocryphile Press, 2007), 48.

Stephen Moss, "'Remember you will die'—and 11 other tips for a better death," *Guardian*, October 30, 2018, https://www.theguardian.com/lifeandstyle/2018/oct/30/remember-you-will-die-tips-for-better-death-michael-hebb, accessed June 11, 2019. Used with permission of Michael Hebb.

Jane Catherine Lotter obituary, *Seattle Times*, July 28, 2013.

Thornton Wilder, *Our Town: A Play in Three Acts* (New York: HarperCollins Perennial Classics, 2003), 108.

Mary Oliver, "When Death Comes," *New and Selected Poems, Volume 1* (Boston: Beacon Press, 1992), 10.

Love & Death by Forrest Church. Copyright © 2008 by Forrest Church. Reprinted with permission from Beacon Press, Boston, Massachusetts.

Bronnie Ware, *The Top Five Regrets of the Dying* (Hay House, 2012), https://bronnieware.com/blog/regrets-of-the-dying/.

November

"Alice Walker Calls God 'Mama,'" Beliefnet.com (website), https://www .beliefnet.com/wellness/2007/02/alice-walker-calls-god-mama. aspx?p=2, accessed June 21, 2019.

Mitch Horowitz, "The benefits—and limits—of today's gratitude movement," *Washington Post*, December 16, 2018, https://www. washingtonpost.com/entertainment/books/the-benefits--and-limits--of-todays-gratitude-movement/2018/11/21/876e57f4-ec32-11e8-baac-2a674e91502b_story.html?utm_term=.f82b2239a207, accessed June 11, 2019. Used with permission.

Robert Emmons, *Thanks! How the New Science of Gratitude Can Make You Happier* (Boston: Houghton Mifflin Company, 2007), 35.

December

Anatole France, *The Crime of Sylvestre Bonnard* (New York: Dodd, Mead, 1918). Translated from the French, *Le Crime de Sylvestre Bonnard*, first published in 1881.